James Hepburn i
scriptwriter who l
for *The Times* and other national newspapers.

The Black Flag

True Tales of Twentieth-Century Piracy

James Hepburn

HEADLINE

First published in 1994 by
HEADLINE BOOK PUBLISHING

First published in paperback in 1995 by
HEADLINE BOOK PUBLISHING

10 9 8 7 6 5 4 3 2 1

ISBN 0 7472 4439 1

Typeset by Avon Dataset Ltd., Bidford-on-Avon, B50 4JH

Printed and bound in Great Britain by
Cox & Wyman Ltd, Reading, Berks

HEADLINE BOOK PUBLISHING
A division of Hodder Headline PLC
338 Euston Road,
London NW1 3BH

Contents

Introduction

Like a lot of children, I was brought up on *Treasure Island* and the skull and crossbones. I was twenty-two years old before I learned that piracy had not died with Captain Kidd.

In 1982 I was in Central America with a vague idea of being a journalist. I had no contacts, no experience and no talent. Even so, I could perhaps have made some sort of a living. In 1982 more or less all bus routes in Central America led to war or revolution. The whole region was stuck in civil war. In Guatemala General Rios Montt was launching his scorched earth offensive against the mostly unarmed Indians of the highlands. A third of El Salvador was in guerrilla hands. Nicaragua was under continual attack from US-trained 'Contras'. Instead I chose to go to the one country where absolutely nothing was happening. I went to Belize.

Aside from its love affair with violence and oppression, Central America is a beautiful and seductive place. Living is cheap and the weather is warm. The region attracts Europeans and North Americans seeking escape from a murky past or a failed present. The hotels of San Jose and Tegucigalpa bulge with fat-bellied retired mid-west feed-salesmen searching for a teenage wife and a retirement of sun-soaked oblivion. In the virgin jungle south of Belmopan, I spent the Falklands

War with a Vietnam veteran living in a rusted wheel-less Volkswagen van. He worked from dawn to dusk slashing and burning the jungle. The jaguars had eaten his cats. His only company was a collection of tarantula spiders kept in jam-jars on the van's cracked dashboard.

In a hotel bar in Belize City I first heard about the new pirates. The bar was full of off-duty British soldiers and on-duty Belizean prostitutes. The girls were bored. The soldiers were Scottish. Sober, they were nice boys a long way from home. Drunk, they staggered, vomited, pawed the girls and fought about football. That night they were drunk and scenting the blood of an Englishman. I took refuge in the lobby with a quiet American couple. They looked like twins, indistinguishably wiry and wrinkled by the sun. They had the clear blameless blue eyes of an ordered life and an easy conscience. They were in their mid-sixties and their dream had come apart.

It was the sort of dream that many have, but few realise. They had sold up his haulage business in Chicago's northern suburbs and bought a yacht. They had no itinerary and enough savings to drift until they died. They had set off from Florida to sail south. In Fort Lauderdale they took on two clean-cut all-American teenagers to help with handling the yacht. The boys were looking for a little adventure before college. They sailed through the Yucatan Channel and down to the coast of Belize. While the old couple were ashore eating sea-food on a quiet cay off the Belizean shore, their nice crew disappeared with the boat. When I met them, the castaways were stuck in Belize waiting for news, traipsing forlorn from the consulate to the police station. No one held out much hope for recovery. They clung to one consolation – they were still alive.

Later, in Corazal Town, near the Mexican border, I met a man who used several names to obscure an unusual past. He suggested I call him Jeff.

Jeff was a charming and generous Canadian in his mid-fifties with a red face, a fringe of lank hair, thin legs and a fat stomach. His great achievement in life had been to introduce the automatic car park to England. In 1956 he set up his barriers on a bomb-site in Catford, south-east London. He made a lot of money and returned to Canada with his wife and young son. In 1972 he flew to Montreal on a business-trip. On his return he found that his wife had removed all of their savings from the joint account and disappeared with the boy. He never saw either of them again. Something in him broke. He sold up his house and travelled south. Eventually he ended up in Belize. For a while he ran a brothel in Corazal. He had a child by a Salvadorean woman young enough to be his granddaughter. For sixteen hours of every day he drank rum and pineapple juice and ate papaya for his ulcer. Apart from one thing, Jeff was perfectly happy. No one would play cribbage with him.

We played for three solid days in a rum and pineapple haze in the front room of Jeff's shack on the hill overlooking Corazal. Jeff knew a great deal about the Caribbean Coast of Central America. He had himself owned a yacht but in the mid-seventies came under pressure from dubious individuals to lend the boat for a 'business trip' to Florida. He was too old for that sort of enterprise and thought it wiser to sell the yacht. He was a little scornful when I told him about the forlorn American couple stuck boatless down in Belize City. He thought they had been lucky to meet such kind-hearted boys. Most new pirates hated to leave owners alive. Jeff had

3

a poetic turn of phrase. He pointed out of the window in the general direction of the muddy mangrove coast. 'This sea looks pretty,' he said, 'but the thing with shit in water is that it floats just below the surface.'

Eleven years later, when I began to research this book, I began to appreciate what Jeff had meant.

Piracy is one of those fossilised crimes – stuck in the seabed of history. The enduring image of the pirate was created in 1724 with the publication of *A General History of the Robberies and Murders of the most notorious Pyrates* by Daniel Defoe writing as 'Captain Charles Johnson'. It was this book, along with a late seventeenth-century work, *The Buccaneers of America* by Alexander Exquemelin, which set the 'Skull and Crossbones' in stone.

There had been pirates before. As early as the seventh century BC the Assyrian King Sennacherib led an expedition to clear pirate fleets from the Gulf of Hormuz. A pirate tribe, the Rus, who controlled the waterways and lakes of Central Europe from the Baltic to the Black Sea in the ninth century later gave its name to an empire. In the late fourteenth century, Stertebeker, an incorrigible German drunkard, set up a pirate confederacy which all but paralysed trade on the Baltic. When Stertebeker was finally captured in 1402, the mast of his flagship was found to be filled with a core of solid gold.

However it was Exquemelin and Defoe who gave to the trade its aura of dubious romance. They concentrated on the Caribbean and the scum of the sea who threatened the Spanish and Portuguese sea-routes from the New World to Europe.

The 'Buccaneers' took their name from the Indian word for a method of curing meat over a fire of green wood. In their purest form, in the second half of the seventeenth century, they were small groups of deserters or shipwrecked sailors washed up on deserted Caribbean islands. Contemporary accounts credit them with two main characteristics – accuracy with a musket and appalling bodily odour. They dressed in bloody untreated animal hides and smeared their bodies with animal fat as protection against mosquitoes. Their favourite food was still-warm marrow from the bones of freshly-slaughtered beasts.

In the early years of the eighteenth century, the Buccaneers briefly emerged as rulers of the independent state of New Providence with its capital at Nassau. They virtually halted legitimate movement in the Caribbean through to the 1720s.

The Buccaneers of the Spanish Main outdid in barbarism and sheer strangeness anything which could be invented in fiction. The worst of them was Francois Lolonois, a Frenchman with a psychopathic antipathy to Spaniards. It was said that his head had been turned when he was wounded in a Spanish raid and spent a day feigning death beneath a pile of corpses. His favourite method of torture was to tie a cord around a captive's head and twist it until the eyes popped out. Like several buccaneers, he dabbled in cannibalism. During a raid in the interior of Nicaragua he is said to have encouraged obedience from a group of prisoners by ripping open a Spaniard's chest and eating his heart. Captain Henry Morgan, who ended his days in stuffed respectability as Lieutenant-Governor of Jamaica, used a human shield of captured nuns as cover in an assault on the Spanish garrison at Portobello.

It is to this period that we owe the picture of the composite pirate – skull and crossbones flag, mad staring eyes, grog, pieces of eight and treasure-chests buried on deserted shores.

Robert Louis Stevenson completed the image with the parrot on Long John Silver's shoulder – 'maybe 200 years old, and if anybody's seen more wickedness it must be the devil himself.'

Until recently most assumed that piracy was dead. However, what was actually dead was the sort of piracy described by Defoe. Murder did not stop when Jack The Ripper ceased to prowl Whitechapel. Piracy did not die when Francois Lolonois's hate-filled corpse was torn to pieces by unfriendly Nicaraguan Indians and his limbs thrown one by one onto the embers of their fire.

Behind all the myths, piracy is no more than violent crime on board a vessel. While there is still sea, there will still be ships and while there are still ships there will be crime on board. There is no natural law that inhibits murder and mayhem beyond the line of the shore.

However, crime at sea *is* somehow different. The myth of the buccaneer obscures this difference with its paraphernalia of plank-walking and 'yo-ho-ho'. The real difference – what makes piracy more terrible and dramatic than the same crimes on land – is the isolation of the sea.

Each vessel that passes beyond sight of land becomes a country in itself. As with all countries, the laws are ultimately determined by power. If power falls into the hands of the mad or the bad, then there is nowhere for the helpless to run.

Over the past decade there has been a lot of newspaper coverage of the resurgence of piracy in the seas of Asia. However, it was not this that first attracted me to write this book. I was in a library on the Walworth Road reading back copies of *The Times*, taken at random from the past century. I was on a typically futile freelance quest – looking through the Personal columns with the idea of selling the paper an article on its own lonely hearts. At the foot of a page in the edition for 15 April 1903, I noticed a small Reuters report from New York: 'Mr Duckworth of Liverpool police now at Biloxi, Mississippi, investigating alleged murders and mutiny on British barque *Veronica* – sailed from Ship Island, near Biloxi on 11 February 1902.' I followed the scanty coverage of the *Veronica* case through the trial in May 1903 to 2 June and the execution of Gustav Rau, the psychopathic German deck-hand, and Willem Smith, his Dutch accomplice.

Understandably enough, *The Times* turned down the article on shady assignations, but the story of the *Veronica* stayed with me. It had a strange nightmarish quality – a drab ship with a drab cargo taken over without warning by a madman; a crew of eleven reduced to five over a week of strange and meaningless insanity a hundred miles from sight or smell of land.

Some of the stories in this book are well known, at least by name. The cases of the *Achille Lauro*, the *Rainbow Warrior* and the Vietnamese boat people are part of contemporary history. Others, such as the *Santa Maria* and the *Bluebelle* had their fifteen minutes of fame but are now largely forgotten. Each one, in its different way, shows the reactions of ordinary people to unexpected catastrophe.

At times of disaster, the human character shows up best or worst but always sharpest. Some people break, like Eban Abbott, Chief Engineer of the *Morro Castle*, sending his assistant down to the engine-room as the ship burned and casting off in a near-empty lifeboat, leaving passengers and crew to their fate.

Some emerge as heroes – the brylcreamed entertainments

officer on the *Morro Castle*, clutching the dying boy's head above the waves; the unnamed crewmen aboard the *Sunning* who died rather than betray the comprador; and eleven-year-old Terry-Jo Duperrault, her family slain, adrift for three days on a tiny float in the Caribbean. For all its obvious faults, the British Empire succeeded in breeding a strong inclination to bloody-mindedness. It is hard not to admire the officers of the *Sunning* playing jazz in the saloon while the ship headed towards the pirate base at Bias Bay or the endurance of the *Nanchang* hostages as they were dragged for months through the bamboo flatlands in the Manchurian summer. However, this conventional bravery pales when set against the almost inconceivable courage of Than-Hung, Ngoyen Phan Thuy and thousands more forgotten Vietnamese who survived the pirates of the Gulf of Thailand.

Most, naturally enough, emerge as neither heroes nor villains. They handle the crisis with varying degrees of *sang froid* and try to emerge alive. Their attackers are rarely monsters. George White Rogers, the man who sunk the *Morro Castle* was almost certainly mad. Gustav Rau may too have been a psychopath, but no one can know the whole truth of what took place aboard the *Veronica*. Henrique Galvao and General Delgado-Chalbaud, two men with dreams of conquering nations, were both certainly, at least by the end, responding to strange alien voices. However, generally the pirates themselves appear to be ordinary enough men and women driven a step too far by necessity or blurred ambition.

There was no malice in the starving Chinese peasants who seized the *Nanchang* officers in the Liao delta. It is harder to have sympathy with clean-cut, well-fed American boys who steal a boat from a friendly old couple to make a turn in the cocaine trade. However, as Jeff said, these represented the philanthropic end of the 'yachtjack' era of the seventies and early eighties. The crew of the *Kamilii* were given little chance, dropped off in mid-ocean with a leaky raft and no food or water. Many others were given no chance at all. At sea there are as many crimes and grades of evil as on land.

The normal convention in books on crime is to claim some social or moral purpose. Stories of serial rapists are sold on cover pictures of strangled models dressed in negligees. Inside we are told they are serious and caring studies of criminal psychology. I cannot make any such claims for this book. I wrote it because I am fascinated by strange events and by strange places. Acts of piracy tend to bring these two together. Probably the fascination is unhealthy. If so, I am sorry. I have no excuse. I was not, as far as I know, banged on the head as an infant.

James Hepburn
April 1994

1.

'Oh, Lor, Captain – I'm Shot'

On 11 October 1902 the three-masted barque *Veronica* left Ship Island at the mouth of the Mississippi River bound for Montevideo, Uruguay. She carried a crew of twelve and a cargo of timber. There was nothing strange about the ship or her journey. The *Veronica* was one of many thousands of small, forgotten trading-craft which have clung through the centuries to some sort of commercial existence. She offered a small rate of return to her Liverpool owners and poor rates of pay to a shifting crew of misfits and down-and-outs from every continent; the scum of the seafaring world. In the normal course of events she would have ended her career unnoticed in an Atlantic storm or rotting in the mud of a tidal estuary. However, for the *Veronica*, there was something more sinister in store.

Seventy-eight days after the *Veronica* left the North American coast, the British steamer *Brunswick* put in for water at Cajueira Island in the estuary of the Parnaiba River on the sweltering north-eastern coast of Brazil.

Cajueira Island was little more than a deep-water bay – a group of huts and a fresh-water spring a few miles from the equator. As the *Brunswick* dropped anchor in the bay, a boat cast off from the island's jetty with five men on board. The men were hauled up onto the deck of the *Brunswick*. They were the sole survivors of the crew of the *Veronica*.

The men were dressed in rags, their heads protected from the equatorial sun by strips of woollen stocking. One had a horribly bloodshot right eye with an ugly scar trailing up his forehead.

Two of the men – Moses Thomas, a negro from Norfolk, Virginia and Gustav Rau, a former seaman in the German Imperial Navy – claimed to be officers. They were led down to the captain's cabin. George Browne, the *Brunswick*'s captain, listened as Rau recounted his story – a tale of disaster and privation in an unseaworthy ship. Thomas stayed silent, adding no details, staring at his feet.

From Rau's account, the voyage of the *Veronica* was cursed from the start. In the Florida Straits, passing from the Gulf of Mexico into the Atlantic, Gustav Johansen, a Swedish deck-hand, died of yellow fever. The winds were strong against them on the long haul south past the West Indies and the coast of Venezuela. On 23 November, Mcleod, the Chief Officer, fell from the main top-sail onto the deck. He was dead on impact. Thomas, as Second Officer, took Mcleod's place and Rau was made up to Second Officer.

On 20 December, without warning or explanation, the ship caught fire. The flames spread quickly along the rotten planking, catching the timber piled on the deck. The crew ran to their allotted boats and cast off. They had no time to collect their belongings. During the night that followed, Rau, Thomas and their companions lost contact with the captain and four remaining crew in the other boat. With a small barrel of water and eleven ship's biscuits they steered by the stars for the coast of Brazil. Five days later, starving and destitute, they reached Cajueira Island.

The *Brunswick* was headed for Europe. Captain Browne agreed to give the shipwrecks passage as far as Lisbon.

The story might have ended there. No trace was ever found of the *Veronica* or her lost crewmen. No other vessel had sighted her since leaving Ship Island. No one alive except for Rau, Thomas and their three companions aboard the *Brunswick* knew what had taken place during those seventy-eight days.

While the *Brunswick* crossed the Atlantic, Moses Thomas kept apart from his fellow-survivors. This was not so strange. Racism was as common at sea as on land. Three of the others were German – Rau, Otto Monson and Ludwig Flohr – and the sailor with the battered head was a Dutchman – Willem Smith. The Europeans slept in the forecastle with the *Brunswick* deck-hands while Moses Thomas bunked with another American negro in the galley.

On 12 January, the ship put into Madeira for water and then set out on the last leg to Portugal. Soon out of Madeira, William Watson, Chief Officer of the *Brunswick*, drew Rau to one side on the deck. 'What's the matter with your cook?' he asked, 'he's been up to the Captain blubbering and crying about his mother.' Rau shrugged. 'He's always like that,' he said, 'crying about something.'

Moses Thomas had approached Watson the day they sighted Tenerife and asked for an interview alone with Captain Browne. The first time he had met the Captain, Thomas had stayed motionless and silent. Now he was trembling and sweating with fear.

The story Thomas told Captain Browne is laid down in

Thomas's own awkward words in the statement he dictated at Liverpool police station on 9 April 1903. Most of the detail was later corroborated by Ludwig Flohr. It is a story from a world gone mad.

Thomas was then twenty-four years old. For ten years he had earned his living on the sea. At the beginning of October 1902 Thomas and Willem Smith were paid off from a voyage on the coastal trader, the *G.A. Bartlett,* in the port of Mobile, Alabama. They drifted down to Biloxi and together they signed on as hands on the *Veronica.* The *Veronica* was a three-masted sailing barque of 1,100 tons, registered in Liverpool, working the coasts of Central and South America. She carried three officers and eight crew. Flohr and Monson were already aboard, along with the captain and first mate. They sailed out to Ship Island in the mouth of the Mississippi to take on board the remainder of the crew and their cargo of timber.

Ship Island at that time was a staging-post for the dregs of the ocean. A vessel like the *Veronica* could not afford to be selective about her crew. The final ship's company was an odd collection. Alexander Shaw, the Scots captain, was nearly deaf. The Chief Mate Alexander Mcleod, a native of Prince Edward Island in the Gulf of St Lawrence, was a powerful figure who effectively ran the ship. The Second Mate, Fred Abrahamson, was a boarding-house keeper from Ship Island. The boarding-houses acted as recruiting agencies for short-handed vessels and received a commission on each man enlisted. Abrahamson was on the run from the authorities on suspicion of shanghaiing a Scandinavian seaman. Apart from the Germans, the Dutchman and the American, the crew consisted of an Irishman, an Indian and two Swedes. Two of the company, Rau and Smith, were sailing under assumed names. The Indian, Alexander Bravo, had never before been aboard a ship. He had been recruited by Abrahamson and had spent his working life as a coachman in Scranton, Mississippi.

According to Thomas's account, the first month of the voyage passed without incident. Thomas kept to the galley and chose not to notice, or not to remember, the growing tensions on board. Flohr, in close contact with his fellow-Germans, saw a different picture.

From the start, according to Flohr, there were problems between Rau, Smith, Monson and the officers. Even before the *Veronica* sailed, Rau talked of desertion. When Flohr threatened to tell the Captain, Rau whispered in his ear: 'if you did I would kill you . . . you would not go quick. I would put something in your mouth or tie you fast somewhere and place a revolver against your head.' They constantly muttered against the First and Second Mates. One time Smith ignored an order from Mcleod and was punched to the ground. He swore revenge.

From the end of October to the middle of November the *Veronica* battled against severe weather, with winds from the south so fierce that they broke the main top sailyard and the spankerboom. On 13 November the wind dropped, to be followed by dead calm. As they neared the equator the sun beat down on the still decks and tempers shortened. To compensate for the delay, rations were cut. As the food became fouler, Rau's resentment and paranoia grew.

Rau was the main voice of discontent. There are strong racial undertones in the events aboard the *Veronica*. Rau deeply resented being under the command of British officers.

He was proud of his training in the German Imperial Navy. In the little world of a three-masted barque in mid-Atlantic he set out to mirror the aspirations of the Kaiser for German naval power.

The turn of the century was a time of fundamental change in Germany – the time when Admiral Turpitz and Kaiser Wilhelm II laid the foundations for their ambitions to dominate the world. The Kaiser believed that Germany had been held back from her mission to colonise the heathen by the domination of the British Fleet. Admiral Turpitz proposed a programme of naval construction that would rival Britain and challenge her control of the sea routes of the world. In the late 1890s he created a frenzy of popular enthusiasm for this plan, built on a deep sense of grievance at British superiority. In 1899 Germany watched with admiration and frustration as their cultural brothers, the Boers, took on the British Empire. They gave moral support, but could offer no practical help since the British dominated the 6,000 miles of sea that separated Europe from Africa. The frustration exploded in January 1900 when three German mail steamers were stopped and searched by British cruisers off the African coast. In the passionate nationalistic atmosphere that followed, there was hardly a dissenting voice when Turpitz's full programme was passed by the Reichstag.

This was the atmosphere that hung over the events aboard the *Veronica*. Rau, as an ordinary seaman, would have caught a pale reflection of the struggles of the Great Powers. Like all members of the Imperial Navy he would have been impressed with two things: the decay of the British Empire and the Destiny of the German People.

There is another aspect to Rau's dogma, an aspect that

might explain why he was no longer on the roll of the Imperial Fleet and why he was enlisted under an assumed name under a hated flag. Somewhere he had picked up echoes of the anarchist and communist rhetoric that was seeping underground through Central and Eastern Europe at the end of the nineteenth century.

On 5 December, Rau and Monson approached Flohr, the other German, on the forecastle deck. They told him that they had overheard the officers discussing how they planned to throw Monson and Flohr overboard. Rau said that their only hope was to act first and kill Shaw, Mcleod and Abrahamson. Flohr was horrified. 'I cannot see a pig killed,' he protested, 'and how should I see a man killed?' 'I thought you were a German,' Rau replied, 'don't you care for your life? And what do you think I came on board for? Do you think we have brought along revolvers and cartridges for nothing?'

Ludwig Flohr was a strange creature, only nineteen years old. He had been at sea for two years, but in many ways was still a boy. He kept apart from his fellow-countrymen. He felt he was socially superior to his shipmates. He had an uncle who was an architect in Minden and he used this as a pathetic barometer of his elevated status. When he continued to protest, Rau lost patience. 'All such people as those in the cabin,' he told Flohr, 'all such people and your uncle too should be killed. You will go the same way too if you don't help us. What do you say? Yes or no?' In the end, Flohr's answer had to be 'yes'. He was a child far from home among desperate men. He had no choice.

Rau planned to take the ship on the night of 8 December. The *Veronica*'s crew was divided into two watches. The Chief

Officer's watch was from midnight to four in the morning. It comprised Gustav Johansen, one of the Swedes; Paddy Doran, the Irishman; Smith and Flohr. From four until eight, the Second Mate was in charge of Rau, Monson, Alexander Bravo and Julius Parsson, the other Swede.

Flohr was told to wake Rau and Monson in the middle of the first watch. With Smith's help, they would slit Doran's and Johansen's throats. They would then go aft, armed with belaying-pins, the bars used to fasten the rigging onto the sails. They would murder the Chief Officer, the Captain, the Second Mate and the cook.

Shortly after 2 a.m., Moses Thomas was woken by the sound of two shots. He heard someone run through the dining-room towards the captain's cabin and a shout of 'Oh Lor, Captain, I'm shot.' A fist banged against the door of Thomas's cabin and he heard Rau's voice from the passage outside: 'I've killed the Chief Officer, the Captain and the boatswain. There's no one left now but the cook. Come out now, you son of a bitch, come out.' In fact, the Captain and the boatswain were still alive. Things had not gone precisely to plan. Flohr had woken Monson and Rau at 2 a.m. Doran was on look-out at the forecastle and Johansen was at the wheel. Rau led Flohr to the forecastle and told him: 'Stick your knife into Paddy's throat.' But Flohr hung back. Doran was leaning on the rail. Rau came up beside him and asked if he could still see the North Star. They were on the equator. When they crossed to the Southern Hemisphere, the North Star would disappear from the sky. Doran bent to look under the fore-sail and Rau hit him twice on the head with a heavy iron belaying-pin. Doran fell onto the deck, bleeding and unconscious, and Smith helped Flohr stuff his body into the port locker beneath the forecastle head.

Mcleod, the Chief Officer, appeared at the entrance to the forecastle. He sensed that something was wrong. 'Where's Paddy?' he said, 'where is the man from the look-out?' Flohr and Smith stood dumb and frozen. 'He must be around here somewhere,' said Rau from the darkness behind Mcleod. As Mcleod turned, Rau swung his belaying-pin, missing Mcleod, but striking Smith full in the face. Smith fell to the deck. Mcleod flinched backwards and Rau hit him twice on the top of the head. Mcleod fell unconscious. Smith, heavily concussed, staggered to his feet and helped Rau throw Mcleod's body over the rail into the sea.

Rau had two pistols stuck in his belt. He gave one to Smith and they went aft, leaving Flohr to guard Doran. Abrahamson had been woken by the noise of the struggle. He was crossing the deck as Rau and Smith emerged from the forecastle stairway. They shot at him, hitting him in the neck and the stomach. He ran back for the officers' quarters, screaming that he had been hit.

Gustav Johansen was still at the wheel. Flohr had failed his first test. He had flinched from slitting Doran's throat. Rau wanted some proof of his commitment. He gave Flohr an iron belaying-pin and ordered him to kill Johansen and throw his body overboard.

According to Flohr's account, he switched the iron belaying-pin for a wooden one. He went up onto the bridge and gave Johansen a half-hearted swipe. Johansen ran screaming for the front of the ship. Flohr followed him at a safe distance. He found Johansen begging for mercy, backed up against the wall of the forecastle, Rau pointing a revolver at his chest. Johansen swore he would tell nobody of what had taken place. Rau pushed him into the forecastle where Monson was guarding Bravo and Parsson, and told Flohr to take the wheel.

From the wheel Ludwig Flohr saw what was the most extraordinary sight of all those he witnessed aboard the *Veronica*. Down on the aft deck in the moonlight, his back to the wheel-house, alone in his deaf world, unaware of the disaster that had overtaken his vessel, stood Captain Alexander Shaw. As Flohr watched, Rau and Smith approached by the gangway on the port side. Sensing their presence, the Captain turned. Smith threw a belaying-pin at his chest and Shaw fell forward. As he fell, Rau shot him twice. The wounded man half levered himself to his feet and then collapsed down the stairway that led to his cabin. Watched by Rau and Smith he crawled into the cabin and bolted the door.

Back outside the forecastle door, Flohr found Monson standing by a spreading pool of blood. Monson was younger than Flohr, barely eighteen. He was completely under Rau's spell. There was fever in his teenage eyes. 'Julius tried to come out through the window,' he said, 'and I struck him once. He was quite dead and I threw him overboard.' He held out to Flohr a long iron belaying-pin, wet in the moonlight. 'Look at this,' said Monson, grinning, 'it's a damned good belaying-pin.'

In the accounts of Flohr and Thomas, all the events of that night are shrouded in senseless nightmare; into each gruesome scene walks the squat figure of Gustav Rau. Doran, shut in the locker beneath the forecastle, had recovered consciousness. He emerged now from the locker, like the ghost of Hamlet's father, his head streaming blood, swaying on his feet, trembling with fear and confusion. Rau was there in the doorway to meet him.

Rau had set out with the general idea of killing everyone but his racial brothers. He proved somewhat flexible with Johansen, Bravo and later with Thomas, but he held a particular grudge against the Irishman. Throughout the voyage they had squabbled incessantly as to who was the better seaman. Doran had mocked the professionalism of the German Imperial Navy. Rau wanted revenge. Doran's first words on emerging from the locker were 'Give me a glass of water, please.' 'All right,' said Rau, 'I'll give you a good drink . . . Harry, give me that belaying-pin.' Flohr gave him the pin. Rau struck Doran once on the head. Doran fell dead. Johansen helped Flohr throw his body overboard.

It was now nearly daylight. Three were dead and the Captain and Second Mate wounded in the navigation room aft. Rau was thirsty.

Thomas had barricaded himself in his cabin. He had listened in terror to the confused sounds of struggle on the deck outside. At daybreak, he emerged, fell down on his knees in front of Rau and begged for mercy. Rau, with his keen sense of humour, pointed his revolver at Thomas's head and let the hammer drop on an empty chamber. He told Thomas to make coffee. From then on Thomas provided the refreshments as Rau's tea-party turned progressively more insane.

Rau had no plan beyond murder. He boarded up the cabin where Shaw and Abrahamson had taken refuge. The surviving crew steered the ship south in the sluggish equatorial breeze. Thomas cooked. Rau brooded over his new command. Two days passed.

On the morning of the third day, Rau decided he needed a compass and a chart from the captain's cabin. He forced open the cabin skylight and pointed his revolver down into the darkness. Flohr beside him was struck by the foetid stench. As his eyes accustomed to the gloom, he made out the Captain laid on his bunk, a blood-soaked handkerchief wrapped round his neck, his shirt soaked in blood from a wound in his midriff. The Second Mate's neck was caked with dried blood. The Captain raised himself on his elbow. 'What for do you want to shoot me?' he said, 'I thought everything was going on well. If there's anything wrong you only have to tell me and I'll fix everything right. Spare my life. I have a wife and children and would like to see them once more. For God's sake, give me a drink of water, and I'll give you my gold watch. I'll bring you into any port you want.'

Captain Shaw would have known that his plea was useless. The mutineers had gone too far to allow him to live. He was unarmed. Rau could have finished it then, but that wasn't his way. He gave his prisoners a little water in exchange for the compass and charts and resealed the skylight.

In the early afternoon, Rau directed the deaths of Shaw and Abrahamson. He stood with Smith and Monson, all three armed with revolvers, on the poop and ordered the Second Mate out of the cabin and up the steps to the deck. Abrahamson stood and tried to focus, blinded by the sun after the darkness. He looked up at the three revolvers. Weakened and dazed as he was, he set off at a faltering run for the bows of the ship. Smith fired, hitting him on the shoulder. Knocked sideways by the force of the bullet, he seemed to continue running through the deck-rail into the air.

Rau ordered Johansen to turn the vessel about. As they

passed by Abrahamson, struggling in the water, all three fired until the body disappeared beneath the surface of the sea.

Two hours later, Rau sent Alexander Bravo with an axe down the companion-way to the cabin door. Bravo, more terrified than his captain, pushed Shaw up the steps to the deck. Half way, the Captain's legs buckled. Rau gave Flohr Monson's pistol and told him to kill the Captain or himself be shot. Flohr fired and missed three times. Shaw stood, shielding his face with his hands, and staggered up to the deck. Rau pushed Flohr aside, put his revolver to the Captain's head and pulled the trigger. Smith and Bravo helped him throw the corpse overboard.

That day Rau officially took command of the *Veronica*. He dressed himself in the Captain's clothes and put the boatswain's whistle in his breast pocket.

They continued to steer south. Rau was terrified of meeting another vessel. He constantly demanded proof of loyalty from the crew. Thomas was forced to swear on his knees that he would never betray them.

Slowly a plan began to form in Rau's diseased brain. He invented the story that he later told the captain of the *Brunswick* – ill-winds, yellow fever, the First Mate's fatal fall and the spontaneous fire. Twice a day he blew the boatswain's whistle, lined the crew up on the deck, stood on the poop with his revolver and made the crew repeat the details of his invention.

Johansen and Bravo had poor memories. Rau decided that they were a liability.

At 8 p.m., three days after the murder of Captain Shaw, Moses Thomas, at work on the pumps, heard a shot. He looked up and saw Johansen running towards him. The Swede's shirt was stained with blood. Smith was behind him, a revolver in his hand. Johansen put his arms around Thomas. 'I'm shot,' he said. By now the grotesque was normal. Rau came up smiling and held Smith back. He ordered Thomas to bandage Johansen's wound, acting as though the attack had been an accident.

The following day at noon, Smith came up behind Johansen in the galley. He put his revolver against Johansen's head and fired. Smith strung a piece of hoop-iron around the body and threw the Swede over the rail. Now there were six.

Flohr had still done nothing to prove his loyalty. There remained the problem of Bravo, the confused Indian coachman from Scranton, Mississippi. Two days after Johansen's death, Bravo was helping Smith on the rigging. He let go the spanker-boom and a hook swung free, striking Smith above the eye. Smith's head by now had taken a terrible pounding. He later claimed to have spent the whole time from the first night of the mutiny to arrival on the *Brunswick* in a concussed stupor.

Rau was furious at Bravo's ineptitude. At seven in the evening he gave Flohr his revolver and led him over to where Bravo and Thomas were hauling the mainbrace. Rau told Flohr to shoot. When Flohr hesitated, Rau smiled and winked. Flohr still could not pull the trigger. Rau smiled again, through clenched teeth. Flohr shot three times. He later claimed that he shot wide. Thomas remembered each bullet striking Bravo's body, the impact throwing him off the rigging into the water. Flohr claimed that Bravo fell from shock alone. Now there were five. It was time to leave the *Veronica*.

Rau fitted out a lifeboat and ordered Flohr and Thomas to chop wood, spread it across the saloon and pour paraffin over the deck. They let loose the other boat, set fire to the paraffin, and cast off. They watched from a distance as the *Veronica* sank in flames beneath the waves. They took nothing from the ship. They earned nothing from the murders. They left behind even their own possessions. Rau's fifteen-day orgy of killing and torture had lost them the little they had ever had.

After five days they sighted Cajueira Island. They threw overboard all their surplus stores. Rather oddly, Rau made them throw away their hats and replace them with lengths cut from his own woollen stockings.

On Christmas Day 1902 they landed and three days later threw themselves on the mercy of the *Brunswick*.

After hearing Thomas's account, George Browne, Master of the *Brunswick*, handed the five for questioning to the consulate in Lisbon. Flohr corroborated the bones of Thomas's story and they were sent on under guard to Liverpool. On 14 May Rau, Smith and Monson were tried for wilful murder and for piracy on the high seas at the Liverpool Spring Assizes.

The Liverpool Assize was not used to drama on the scale of the *Veronica* mutiny. The case was held before Mr Justice Lawrence. It was preceded by the trial of John Pilkington for stealing two gas meters. It was followed by that of William Brady for 'committing and perpetrating the abominable crime of buggery on John Fray in the village of Leigh'. The trial lasted three days. The jury were out for twelve minutes. All three were found guilty and sentenced to be hanged. Monson was recommended for mercy on account of his youth. His sentence was commuted to penal servitude for life. Rau and Smith were hanged at Walton Gaol on 2 June 1905.

There was no doubt in the minds of the jury that the cook's story was the truth. The picture of megalomaniac Hunnish brutality fitted closely with the British prejudices of the age. When, in October 1901, Joseph Chamberlain had declared that British 'concentration camps' in South Africa did not compare in barbarity and cruelty with German atrocities in the Franco-Prussian War and in China, he was cheered through the streets of London and Birmingham. There was a general feeling that, although the British Empire might occasionally go too far out of enthusiasm, the German character was essentially murderous and brutal. Rau was a miniature illustration of a mad, bad nation.

The jury gave no credence to an alternative version of events presented at the trial by Rau, Monson and Smith. However, ninety years on, there is a lot in their story that makes more sense than the pure nightmare vision of psychopathic blood-lust given by Flohr and Thomas.

By the account of the defendants, the voyage had been rotten from the start. Captain Shaw was a weak man who handed over all authority to Mcleod and Abrahamson. The First Mate was a huge, muscular bully who took any opportunity to brutalise the crew. Mcleod held Smith personally responsible for the Boer War. When Mcleod punched and kicked him, Smith complained to the Captain. The Captain did nothing except report the complaint back to Mcleod who beat Smith again and promised that neither he nor his German friends would ever reach Montevideo alive.

The ship seethed with sexual tension. Abrahamson was obsessed with the two teenagers. 'The Second Mate,' Rau testified, 'wanted to use Monson and Flohr like a woman . . . I seen him in the lazarette with Monson with his head in a sail and wanted to fuck him.' When Rau pushed him off, Abrahamson turned to Monson and said: 'You would do it alright if your chum wasn't aboard, but I fix it.'

Flohr was a lonely, strange and pathetic figure. He rejected the friendship of his compatriots and this left him with no protection. Doran tried to befriend him, but his motives were the same as Abrahamson's. The cook was held responsible for the disgusting food and hated by all the crew. Alexander Bravo was incapable of even the simplest seaman's task. Captain Shaw believed he was a curse on the ship. 'If we pitch that dog overboard,' he declared, 'the winds will turn in our favour.' The whole crew lived in terror of their lives.

According to their version, the crisis came when Moses Thomas discovered that the officers were planning to throw two of them overboard. It was Thomas himself who killed the First Mate in the early watch. In the struggle that followed, the Captain and Second Mate killed Doran, Parsson and Johansen. Woken by the noise, Rau, Smith and Monson emerged from their bunks to find the cook gone mad on deck, raving that he had stopped a plot to kill them all. They had a choice. If they sided with the officers, they would be next. Thomas was acting for all of them. They helped the cook drive the Captain and Second Mate to the captain's cabin. It was Thomas who insisted that Shaw and Abrahamson must die, and it was he who shot them. It was the cook who killed Bravo for his incompetence and it was he who ordered them to set fire to the ship.

On the voyage to Lisbon, the cook's nerve had failed. Fearing that the others would give him away, he conspired with Flohr to concoct a story against Smith, Rau and Monson.

It is impossible to believe all of this story. It is unlikely that Rau and Smith, both strong and experienced sailors, would meekly follow a negro cook. The main flaw in the tale is the idea that Thomas, when it seemed the original story had been believed, would risk everything by implicating his accomplices. And why should Flohr have gone along with the deception?

However, it is equally hard to believe that Rau, Smith and Monson should kill seven people with no provocation and no prospect of material gain.

Perhaps the most likely explanation is that events up until the mutiny happened more or less as related by Smith, Rau and Monson and from then on as described by Thomas and Flohr. Thomas was no ringleader and it was absurd of the accused to build their story on that basis. Almost certainly it was Rau, Smith and Monson who did the killing, but, at least at first, from fear and not from madness.

In the statements of the accused there is a strong flavour of sincerity – of genuine outrage at the cruel dilemma of powerless deck-hands adrift in the hands of brutal and sadistic officers with no court of appeal for two thousand miles. It is hard not to accept Monson's final appeal to the court as the words of a man who has been faced by a terrible decision: 'Gentlemen,' he said, 'we have not done anything wrong, for we fought for our lives. If the gentlemen who go to far distant lands, where one lives his life every day in insecurity, and who may read this story, they will be able to say if it is right or wrong.'

The prisoners received the sentence with composure, but whilst Rau and Smith walked steadily from the dock, Monson was seen to falter and press his hands nervously to his forehead. He paused with a slight effort and then he, too,

walked briskly below. Rau and Smith went to their deaths at
Walton Gaol still declaring their innocence.

There is a strange postscript to the story of the *Veronica*.
The 'message in a bottle' is now a seaside joke, but at that
time it was the final desperate means by which shipwrecked
sailors communicated with the outside world. Messages were
published in *Lloyd's List*. Most, of course, were lost on some
deserted shore. Others took many years to reach their
destination. On 2 April 1903, a sealed bottle was picked up
in the estuary of the Maltraeth River in Anglesey, North
Wales. Inside was a message written on paper in lead pencil.
No position was marked. There was no clue as to how long
the bottle had been drifting. The message read. 'Good-bye
all. Ship sinking. Captain. Veronica.' Captain Shaw might
have wished for such a natural end to his own *Veronica*.

2.

The Reckoning

On 17 October 1904, on a morning of rain and bitter cold, the Imperial Russian Second Fleet sailed into the Great Belt, the channel that threads through the Danish Islands from the Baltic to the North Sea. The ships' hulls were painted funereal black.

On the bridge of the flagship *Kniaz Suvoroff*, in an overstuffed armchair, sat Rear-Admiral Zinovi Petrovich Rohestvensky. Rohestvensky was a formidable figure – tall with the nose of a Roman emperor and deep black humourless eyes. This should have been the crowning moment of his life. At the age of fifty-five, he was leading a fleet of forty-two ships to rescue the honour of the Russian Empire.

Rohestvensky had enlisted in the navy at the age of seventeen. His career had been a strange mixture of good and bad luck. In 1877, at the age of twenty-one, he had made a name of sorts during the Russo-Turkish War. He had been a sub-lieutenant aboard the gunboat *Vesta* attacked by a Turkish squadron in the Black Sea. According to the Captain's account, the *Vesta* beat off the Turks against fearsome odds. The tiny ship became a symbol of Russian heroism. It only emerged after the war that the *Vesta* had actually turned tail at the first sign of the Turks. Rohestvensky gave testimony against his own captain. The Captain was disgraced and Rohestvensky promoted. He went on to reorganise the Bulgarian Navy and become the finest professional seaman in the Russian Fleet.

By 1902, however, Rohestvensky seemed to have reached the end of his career. He was captain in command of the gunnery practice squadron of the Baltic Fleet. His life was sliding towards thwarted retirement. The very highest ranks of the navy were reserved for those with connections in the imperial court. Talent mattered less than a title. Rohestvensky was dour and charmless. He had no patience with fools and among the fools he counted everyone who failed to share his passion for precision gunnery at sea. He had no connections at court and his attitude won him no friends. He seemed doomed to drift along the margins of power while the Russian Fleet remained in the hands of inane and witless aristocrats. His best hope was to end his days lamenting the unfairness of life in a Bath chair at an unfashionable German spa.

His deliverance came in 1902. Britain was then the only serious world power at sea. There was intense competition among European rulers to challenge this supremacy. In July, Kaiser Willem II visited his cousin Tsar Nicholas. As part of the entertainment, the Kaiser reviewed the Baltic Fleet. The highlight of the review was a gunnery demonstration by Rohestvensky's squadron. It was a spectacular success. Rohestvensky worked himself to such a frenzy of enthusiasm that he threw his binoculars overboard. The Tsar was able to impress his cousin. The Kaiser was heard to say that he wished he had such splendid admirals as Captain Rohestvensky in his own navy. At last Rohestvensky had imperial recognition. In October, he was promoted to Rear-Admiral, Chief of Naval

Staff and aide-de-camp to the Tsar.

Less than two years later, Russia was at war. Trouble with Japan had been brewing since the 1890s. Japan wanted a slice of empire on the Asian mainland. War with China in 1894 had given her Taiwan and treaty rights over Manchuria, the Liaotung Peninsula and the vital harbour of Port Arthur. Russia resented Japanese ambitions. After five hundred years of Western expansion into Asia, there was something sacrilegious in the idea of a growing Eastern empire. For the Japanese, Port Arthur was a national symbol. Her troops had taken the town from the Chinese over mounds of bodies in wave after wave of suicidal assaults. In 1897, pressure from the great powers forced Japan to hand the port over to Russia.

Japan turned a blank face to the humiliation and prepared for war. When the attack finally came, it took the same form as the attack on Pearl Harbour forty years later. It displayed a quite ungentlemanly contempt for European conventions of chivalry. On 8 February 1904, Admiral Togo, Commander of the Japanese Fleet, sent torpedo-boats into the harbour of Port Arthur. There had been no ultimatum; no declaration of war. The Russian batteries were unmanned. The torpedo-boats used Russian signals. They crippled two battleships and a cruiser of the First Pacific Fleet. The following day, Togo's battleships bombarded the harbour.

In the months that followed, disaster followed disaster for the Russians. The fleet remained blockaded in Port Arthur, constantly harried by Togo, ships picked off one by one by mines and Japanese guns. Japanese land forces invaded Korea and pushed back the Russian army through the merciless frozen winter. By the end of April they had reached the River Yalu on the Manchurian border.

Russian reinforcements poured into Manchuria along the Trans-Siberian railway to hold the Japanese advance. However, while the Japanese held control of her sea lanes to the Asian mainland, she continued to press the attack on Manchuria and block access to the Russian Pacific port of Vladivostock. The Tsar needed another navy in the Pacific.

The navy existed, but it was 18,000 miles away in the Baltic. In the port of Libau in Latvia, 100 ships were gathered in the spring of 1904, waiting delivery of four modern battleships – the *Kniaz Suvoroff*, the *Borodino*, the *Alexander III* and the *Oryol*.

On 20 June, the Tsar gave command of the Baltic Fleet to Rohestvensky, the man who had thought his hour would never come. Rohestvensky had three months to train and provision a fleet of forty-two ships. By the time the fleet was ready to sail in late September, Japanese forces had cut Port Arthur off from Manchuria, and Togo's navy still held the harbour entrance. Two more Russian battleships, several cruisers and two commanders-in-chief had been sent to the bottom of the bay.

The Tsar and the Tsarina inspected Rohestvensky's ships at Reval in Estonia. It was a glorious occasion dripping with the ancient pomp of Russian Orthodoxy. The Tsarina presented each vessel with a communion chalice made with her own hands and each with a chapel to hold the chalice. The Admiralty issued a standing order that the guns and the decks be sprinkled with holy water before each engagement. The Tsar boarded seven of the warships. On each one he made the same speech, calling on the seamen to 'take vengeance on the insolent Japanese who have troubled the peace of Holy Russia, and maintain the glory of the Russian

Navy'. In the streets of St Petersburg and Moscow there was a hysteria of jingoistic expectation.

The fleet left Reval on 11 October and put in at Libau to take on coal. Here they received a final message from the Tsar, ordering them to 'wipe the infidels from the face of the earth'. On paper, the Tsar's optimism was justified. The weaponry on the new battleships was far superior to anything possessed by the Japanese. Their twelve-inch guns could throw a shell weighing a third of a ton up to ten miles.

On 17 October, the forty-two ships cruised out of the Baltic. From the moment they left the protection of Russian waters, there were rumours of danger. The British were sympathetic to the Japanese. Royal Navy gunners and navigators had been loaned to Togo's fleet. The Russians believed that the British had rushed through a sale of destroyers to attack Rohestvensky as he sailed down the English coast. The consulates in Norway, Germany and Denmark reported Japanese naval activity in the Baltic, the Great Belt and the North Sea. Torpedo-boats had been sighted in the fjords on the Scandinavian coast. There were rumours of submarines, of armed merchantmen, of mad maverick vessels armed for suicide attacks.

As they passed through the Great Belt, there was fear and apprehension among the untested crews of the Russian Second Fleet. Watches were doubled. In the bitter damp cold, the men stood night and day by their guns. Rohestvensky issued orders that 'no vessel of any sort whatever must be allowed to get in amongst the fleet'. The Admiral delegated two ships to sweep the passage for mines, but the cable continually snapped and the attempt was abandoned.

Out of the Great Belt, south-west of the Skaw, the fleet

anchored to regroup. A message from St Petersburg announced that Rohestvensky had been promoted to Vice-Admiral. In the clear moonlit night of the 19th came further word of enemy preparations. Trawlers armed with torpedo-tubes were waiting in the fishing grounds of the North Sea. Unidentified boats were leaving secret bases off the coast of Norway. Two 'silvery shapes' were sighted in the air, moving from the south-west to the north-east. They could only be enemy reconnaissance balloons. There was a sudden red glow on the horizon to port.

The morning of 21 October barely dawned. In thick fog the fleet steamed into the North Sea. Vladimir Semenoff, a young officer aboard the *Suvoroff* described the fleet advancing through the fog – the ships 'trying to outdo one another in the loudness of the stentorian halloos, uttering shrieks of agony as if to announce some terrible misfortune'. The original plan had been to sail around the north of Scotland, but Rohestvensky decided to take the more direct route east of England to the Channel. He divided his command into six divisions, with himself and the *Suvoroff* in the last of the six. At midday, when the fog cleared, the *Suvoroff* and her division was alone in the North Sea with a clear horizon. Rohestvensky set course on a line seventy miles east of the British coast.

They were approaching the time of greatest danger. If the reports were accurate, at any time they could expect to sight Japanese torpedo-boats.

At 9 p.m. the *Suvoroff* received a message from the *Kamchatka*, a repair vessel in the Fifth Division. The *Kamchatka* reported that she was being 'chased by torpedo-boats', and then that she was 'firing on them'. The *Suvoroff* radioed for more information: 'How many boats and from which side?' 'About eight,' replied the *Kamchatka*, 'from all directions.' The *Kamchatka* requested the *Suvoroff* to signal her position by searchlight. Rohestvensky suspected a trick. 'If you have escaped the danger,' he replied, 'steer west. Indicate your position, then a further course will be given to you.' The radio went dead. What was happening ahead in the North Sea? The *Suvoroff* continued on her course, anxious and afraid, anticipating attack.

Vladimir Semenoff's account of the voyage of Rohestvensky's fleet is steeped in a mystic sense of doom. He called his book *Rasplata* which translates as 'The Reckoning'. From the moment the ships nosed out of the Baltic, he believed they were heading for destruction at the hands of a malign destiny. At 10 p.m. Semenoff retired to his cabin. On his writing-table he kept a photograph of the Russian naval hero, Admiral Maharoff. The photograph was mounted with a thin strip of red paper. A few drops of water had run down the bulkhead and seeped inside the frame onto the centre of the photograph. The water had been stained red from the cheap red paper 'and in running down onto the table formed a narrow red streak like blood across the Admiral's face and breast'. 'Many people laugh at omens,' concluded Semenoff, 'but I believe in them.' He may have had a point.

On the bridge of the *Suvoroff* at twenty minutes past midnight, the lookout sighted two green flares ahead to starboard. The flagship swung her searchlights in the direction of the flares. Rohestvensky was in his cabin. The duty officer gave the signal to 'Engage Enemy'. The searchlights quartered the surface of the sea and finally fixed on a group of small vessels half a mile ahead, bathing them in bright light. The *Suvoroff*'s guns swung onto the vessels and opened fire.

The *Borodino* followed the flagship's lead and started up with her heavy twelve-pounder. There was a crash from somewhere amidships and the crew prepared to abandon ship.

There was confusion aboard another of the Russian vessels, as later reported by the Steward to Edgar Wallace of the *Daily Mail*: 'All the sailors were lying on their faces and the officers were all under cover and were talking at the tops of their voices. Midshipman R— was waving a drawn sword crying out "The Japanese! The Japanese!"'

For five minutes they poured fire onto the small ships. Then, suddenly, powerful searchlights shone out from the west, sweeping the division's decks. The gunners aboard the *Suvoroff* were blinded. Gun-muzzles flashed from behind the searchlights and shells whined overhead and sent spumes of spray over the *Suvoroff*'s decks. In the darkness on the bridge of the flagship someone shouted: 'The real attack is from there! The Japanese cruiser fleet!' The *Suvoroff* swung her twelve-inch guns towards the searchlights and began a furious volley of random fire.

At twenty-five minutes past midnight, Semenoff had been woken by the sound of a bugle call. He rushed up to the after-bridge, nearly knocking down the junior torpedo-officer who was directing the beams of the rear searchlights.

'What is the meaning of this?' he shouted. 'What are they firing at?'

'Torpedo-boats! A torpedo attack!' replied the lieutenant, pointing to starboard. 'There! There!'

The searchlights were pointing ahead to starboard and the six-inch guns were pouring heavy fire into the pool of light.

Semenoff made for the fore-bridge. In the searchlight beams he saw, only a few cables off, a small steamer with a single mast and funnel, slowly moving away to starboard. A second steamer was steering on the opposite course, heading straight for the *Alexander III*, 'as if with the intention of ramming her'. The *Alexander III* was firing a hail of projectiles into the steamer. As Semenoff watched, the steamer sank. A third small boat slowly crossed the *Suvoroff*'s bows from port to starboard. The gun-layer of the port six-pound gun fired several rounds at her. Semenoff stopped to watch, still fuddled by sleep and shock. As the gun-layer reloaded, Admiral Rohestvensky himself appeared from the darkness, his eyes wild. He seized the gun-layer by the shoulder and shouted furiously into his face: 'How dare you? And without orders! Don't you see – fishermen!'

Rohestvensky's Sixth Division had found an unusual enemy. They had attacked the Hull trawler fleet. The searchlights arriving from the west belonged to the cruisers *Aurora* and *Donskoi* of the Admiral's own Fifth Division. The Russian navy had blundered, like a pantomime cow, into piracy.

The 'Gamecock' Fleet of sixty 100-ton single-screw trawlers had left Hull in clear weather on a calm sea on the morning of 19 October. On the evening of the 21st they reached the Dogger Bank, 220 miles east by north of Spurn Head. They were accompanied by the *Magpie*, a vessel especially designed for storing the fleet's catch.

According to international convention, the trawlers showed five lights to warn passing ships of their presence: the Duplex fishing signal at the mast-head, the white light below it, the red light on the port side, the green light on the starboard, and a white light on the stern. The sun set in a slight haze. In the dark each ship lit acetylene flares to illuminate the work on deck. Aboard the trawler *Ruff* the 'Smacksmaster', commander of the fishing fleet, gave the order to shoot the trawls. Aboard each ship, the crew of eight let down the huge nets. The vast 'leads' fell to scrape along the sea-bed and the ton-weight 'doors' held open the nets' mouths, funnelling them into cones a hundred foot long. The engines switched to full power to tow the trawls at a steady four knots through the shoals of cod, haddock, turbot and herring.

The sea was moderate, but on deck it was bitterly cold. At ten o'clock a brisk south-west breeze blew up, sending icy rain into the fishermen's faces.

Shortly after midnight, the crews sighted ships' lights to the north-east, steering directly towards them in naval 'loose-line ahead' formation. They assumed that the ships were the Channel Fleet and waited for them to change course in response to the trawlers' warning lights. But the warships came on.

The trawlers sent up two green flares as another sign of their presence. When the ships kept to their course, the 'Smacksmaster' gave the order to steam to windward to avoid collision.

The searchlights from the *Suvoroff* blinded the sailors on the trawler decks. When the guns opened fire most of the trawlers still assumed it was the Home Fleet engaging in night gunnery practice. Still worried only about the danger of collision, they cut their trawls and steamed at full power further to windward.

A group of trawlers – the *Crane*, the *Moulmein*, the *Gull*, the *Mino*, the *Alpha*, the *Snipe* and the carrier *Swift* – had been fishing slightly to one side of the main 'Gamecock' Fleet, directly in the path of the *Suvoroff*. It was on these that the Russians concentrated their searchlights and then directed their fire.

The Captain of the *Swift* later testified that the Russian searchlights shone directly onto the distinctive trawler markings on the side of his boat. It should have been impossible to mistake the *Swift* for a torpedo-boat. On board the *Snipe* the fishermen held up fish in the glare of the lights to show their peaceful intentions. 'I held a big plaice up,' recalled one fisherman, 'and my mate, Jim Tozier, showed a haddock.'

The *Crane* was at the centre of the Russian fire. She was steaming towards Rohestvensky's fleet with all lights blazing, when she came under attack. The crew were on deck, gutting fish. When the guns opened up, they were only a hundred yards from the *Suvoroff*. One of the *Crane*'s deck-hands, Albert Almond, ran below decks followed by the boatswain. The boatswain had nearly reached the foot of the ladder when he fell back and shouted, 'I'm shot – my hands are off!' Almond turned to help him, but another shell burst, tearing away the flesh from Almond's arm. As he fell, he was hit in the face by a machine-gun bullet. The boat's engineer, John Nixon, appeared at the foot of the ladder. 'Who are you?' he screamed at Almond's bloody face.

Up on deck, William Smith, the *Crane*'s Captain, died in the first barrage. His head was blown off by a shell. Another shell hit the Third Mate, slicing his head in half from chin to hair. The First Mate was hit in the back by a shell splinter an inch and a quarter long, but he stayed at his post. He frantically waved the red lantern as though to ward off the shower of shot and shell. When it was clear that the trawler was finished, he gave the order to launch the lifeboat. The survivors strained at the winch, but the mechanism was smashed and the boat stuck.

It was now that the cruisers from the Russian Fifth Division arrived and turned their lights on the battle. The guns of the *Suvoroff*, the *Alexander III*, the *Oryol* and the *Borodino* swivelled to face the new danger from the west. However, when the *Moulmein*, the *Gull* and the *Mino* changed course to help the *Crane*, the Russian guns opened up again on all four vessels. The skipper of the *Gull* ignored the barrage to launch his boat and board the *Crane*. The trawler was shipping water and sinking fast. The deck was a slaughterhouse, running with blood. In the middle, where they had fallen, lay the Captain's headless corpse and the Third Mate's faceless body. Wounded men lay in what shelter they could find. The wounded and the dead were taken off under heavy fire. Shortly afterwards, the *Crane* sank.

Even after he had finally recognised the trawlers, Rohestvensky still believed that the cruisers from the west were Japanese warships. The battle continued between the Fifth and the Sixth Divisions until the signallers on the *Suvoroff* recognised something familiar about the lights from the bridge of one of the cruisers. Aboard the *Aurora*, Admiral Enkvist was sending instructions to the *Donskoi* using a code unique to the Russian fleet. Rohestvensky ordered the bugle to sound the cease-fire.

The action had lasted twenty minutes. Rohestvensky barely paused to consider the chaos in the water around him. He ordered his ships to extinguish all lights and to steam south-west at full speed in the wake of Enkvist and the cruisers of the Fifth Division. There was tremendous excitement on board. The crews were convinced that they had held off an attack by a rogue Japanese fleet. Aboard the *Suvoroff* only the ship's doctor expressed any doubts. He alone was certain that there had been no Japanese – that the heroic action of self-defence had been a monumental mistake.

Surprisingly, considering the volume of fire directed against the *Aurora* and the *Donskoi* by the battleships of the Sixth Division, the Russians suffered few casualties. Both cruisers were hit above the water-line. The *Aurora* took four shells from twelve- and six-pound guns. A gunner was slightly hurt and the chaplain was struck by a 45mm shell which passed through his cabin and left him mortally wounded. The most serious casualties were on board the *Oryol*. The weight of weaponry and the huge space devoted to officer accommodation made the Russian battleships dangerously top-heavy. The ships rolled extravagantly even in moderate seas, pushing the lower gun-decks underwater. The crew of the *Oryol* tried to fire a twelve-pound gun with the muzzle submerged. The gun exploded, killing some of its crew and seriously injuring the rest.

At dawn on the morning of 23 October, the Russian fleet steamed into the Channel, keeping just outside the three-mile limit. Near midday, the battleships of the Second Division hove to opposite Brighton's New Palace Pier where they were joined by colliers contracted by the 'Hamburg-Amerika' Line. For two hours they loaded coal, watched by a curious crowd on the pier and on Marine Parade. Later in the afternoon, the *Suvoroff* and the rest of the Sixth Division arrived off

Rottingdean and they too took on coal. After the events of the night before, there is a strange sense of unreality in the picture of the Russian battleships pausing for the admiration of out-of-season tourists in the calm waters off the south coast.

It was not until early evening that the 'Gamecock' Fleet limped into Hull, led by the *Moulmein*, her flag at half-mast. The bodies from the *Crane* were carried onto the wharf amid the wailing of wives and children. That night the local MP, Sir Henry Seymour King, took a deputation of seamen from the fishing fleet to London on the night mail train. They had breakfast at the Foreign Office. The Foreign Secretary, Lord Lansdowne, was out of London and so they met with two of his officials. The officials asked for evidence of the attack.

'It's up at Hull,' replied one of the fishermen, 'two headless trunks.'

The newspapers picked up the story and named the attack the 'Dogger Bank Incident'. On the evening of the 24th, angry crowds filled Trafalgar Square demanding retribution. British public sympathy was already behind the heroic Japanese in their struggle against the barbarous Russians. The atmosphere became increasingly ugly. The Russian Ambassador was jeered in his carriage. Lord Lansdowne sent a telegram to Sir Charles Hardinge, British Ambassador in St Petersburg, ordering him to protest to the Russians – 'the fact that these vessels could have been mistaken for what they were – namely, a peaceful fishing fleet engaged in their ordinary occupations, can only have been due to culpable negligence. The indignation provoked by this incident cannot possibly be exaggerated.' The attack itself was bad enough, but what caused most anger was that the Russians had left the scene without offering help to the survivors, like hit-and-run drivers speeding from the scene of the crime.

By the morning of the 25th, with the Russian fleet heading out of the Channel in thick fog, it seemed that the British Government was being forced into war. Sir Charles Hardinge presented his note of protest in St Petersburg. The note demanded an explanation, an apology and assurance that the guilty would be punished. Count Lamsdorff, Russian Minister for Foreign Affairs, replied expressing the Tsar's 'sincere regret', but offering no apology. King Edward VII's Private Secretary sent a message of sympathy to the Mayor of Hull with a gift of 200 guineas to the bereaved families. The Queen sent a further £100. Taking advantage of the moment, the Mayor of Tokyo sent a telegram with his sincerest condolences.

In the afternoon, the Admiralty issued 'preliminary orders for mutual support and co-operation to the British Fleet'. The Home Fleet was ordered to Portland to defend the Channel, the Channel Fleet was despatched to shadow the Russians, and Gibraltar was put on a war footing. The twelve battleships and forty-four supporting cruisers, destroyers and gunboats of the Mediterranean Fleet were recalled to the mouth of the Mediterranean. The parting message from Sir Charles Beresford, Admiral of the Home Fleet, was 'Situation critical. Good Luck.' By the afternoon of the 26th, there were twenty-six British battleships at sea waiting the order to intercept and destroy the Russian Fleet. Prince Louis of Battenburg, Admiral of the Fleet, sent a telegram to foreign naval stations warning that 'war is imminent'.

On the afternoon of the 26th, the Russians put in at the northern Spanish port of Vigo for coal. Rohestvensky gave his version of the incident on the Dogger Bank. He claimed that his fleet had been 'provoked by two torpedo-boats which, without showing any lights, under cover of darkness advanced to attack the vessel steaming at the head of the detachment. When the detachment began to sweep the sea with its searchlights and opened fire, the presence was also discovered of several small fishing vessels. The detachment endeavoured to spare these boats.'

Russia supported Rohestvensky's version. The *St Petersburg Times* commented that 'the lessons of the first days of the war have not been wasted, and the new and treacherous attack by the Japanese has been met by the vigilant and pitiless eye of our Admiral and the straight fire of our guns.' The Tsar sent a message to Rohestvensky, assuring him that 'in my thoughts I am with you and my beloved squadron with all my heart. I feel confident that the misunderstanding will soon be settled. The whole of Russia looks upon you with confidence and in firm hope.'

Beresford's ships closed around the entrance to Vigo harbour, blocking the exit from the port. There was panic in the Chancelleries of Europe. For both Britain and Russia, war would be disastrous. Russia was allied with France and Germany. A conflict with both might cripple the Empire. Russia's hopes in the East rested on the Second Pacific Fleet. It could not hope to survive a confrontation with the world's most powerful navy. Eventually, Rohestvensky agreed to leave a handful of officers and men behind in Vigo to attend an international board of enquiry. On 1 November, John Fisher, First Lord of the Admiralty, wrote to his wife: 'It has been nearly war again, but the Russians have climbed down.'

On the same day, Beresford withdrew his ships to allow Rohestvensky to leave Vigo; but the crisis was still not past.

For three days and nights, as the Russians steamed down to the coast of Africa, the Channel Fleet shadowed their every move, manoeuvring in perfect formation along their flanks and across their bows. At night, British searchlights picked out one Russian ship after another. For the Russians, standing at their stations, waiting for the blow to fall, it was a wearying and humiliating journey. They had to watch helpless as the British Empire demonstrated the superiority of its seamanship and the ease with which it could destroy them if it wished. The exhibition aroused conflicting feelings in the Russian seamen. Most felt anger and frustration. 'It is disgusting to be treated like this – to be followed around like criminals,' wrote a midshipman on the *Oryol*. Rohestvensky felt only the frustration. Semenoff recalled watching the movements of Beresford's cruisers, 'like a well-rehearsed play', from the rail of the *Suvoroff*. 'Do you admire this?' asked Rohestvensky from behind him. 'Do you admire this? This is something like seamanship. Those are seamen. Oh, if only we . . . ' The Admiral left the sentence unfinished and ran, overcome with emotion, down the ladder to his cabin.

On 3 November, the Russians hove to off Tangier and the Home Fleet retired. War had been averted.

The International Commission of Enquiry was convened in Paris and reported in February 1905. It condemned Rohestvensky for opening fire on the trawlers and for leaving the scene of the crime. Great Britain was awarded £65,000 compensation. What the enquiry did not reveal was the trail of hysteria and appalling incompetence that had led to the tragedy on the Dogger Bank.

Behind the facade of the pomp and imperial glory, the voyage of the Second Pacific Fleet had been doomed from the start. Amid all the forced optimism of the Tsar's farewell visit to the fleet in September, the one discordant voice had been from Captain Bukhvostoff of the *Alexander III*. 'You have wished us a lucky journey,' he told the Tsar, 'and have expressed the conviction that with brave sailors we shall smash the Japanese. We thank you for your good intentions. You wish us victory, but there will be no victory. But we will know how to die, and we shall never surrender.' Bukhvostoff was the only man prepared to speak openly, but he was echoing the thoughts of most of his comrades. Even Rohestvensky was secretly writing that 'we should not have started this hopeless business; and yet how can I refuse to carry out orders when everyone is so sure of success.'

Many of the ships were obsolete. The *Donskoi* was built on a design from the 1870s and carried rigging for sails. Even the new battleships were past their time. Inefficiency and corruption in the Baltic shipyards had delayed completion for six years. The guns and armour were already outdated. The *Oryol* almost sank on launching, settling in the water at an angle of thirty degrees due to faulty rivets. Rohestvensky found the superstructure so top-heavy that he had to issue orders restricting unnecessary signals. As emerged in the disaster aboard the *Oryol*, the lower gun decks were useless in anything but a dead calm.

Most experienced seamen were already on duty in the Far East. The fleet was manned by conscripts and transfers from the merchant service. Revolutionary ideas were rife on the lower decks. Vasilieff, the crippled Engineering Officer aboard the *Oryol*, kept a library of anarchist and communist literature which he distributed throughout the fleet. Among the revolutionaries the feeling was that 'if we gain victory over the Japanese we shall hinder the revolution which is the only hope of the country'.

Perhaps the fleet's most damaging shortcoming was in radio communication. The ships were equipped with an experimental system developed by the German firm, Slaby-Arco. In theory it was tremendously sophisticated. In practice, it was almost unusable. It could transmit but hardly ever receive. Something more practical might have avoided the absurd misunderstandings of the night of 22 October.

Rohestvensky himself deserves much of the blame. With some justification, he trusted in no one but himself. He saw confusion all around him and believed he could resolve it by sheer force of will. He had no confidence in his second-in-command, Admiral Von Felkeram, a short fat man with a tiny mouth 'as round as the opening of a thimble', or in Enkvist, the vain little man who commanded the cruisers. Enkvist's arrival with his cruisers to join battle at the Dogger Bank when he should have been fifty miles away heading south is some indication of his competence. Rohestvensky never consulted with any of his officers and refused to share his plans. His subordinates lived in terror of his temper.

Rohestvensky cannot be blamed for the atmosphere of hysterical fear that shrouded the fleet's exit from the Baltic. The absurd rumours of Japanese naval activity 18,000 miles from home were the result of over-zealous fabrications by Captain Hartling, a Russian counter-espionage agent based in Copenhagen. Hartling created such an atmosphere of conspiracy that the smallest movement at sea was reported as enemy action by the consuls in Norway, Germany and Denmark. Lord Fisher saw behind all this the scheming of the Kaiser, working to isolate Britain in Europe.

No matter how great the provocation, nothing can excuse Rohestvensky's irresponsibility in ordering his captains to fire on any vessels which got in among the fleet. To travel through peaceful waters with these instructions was an act of piracy in itself. He was not a novice. He had been Naval Attaché in London. He knew the fishing grounds of the North Sea and his watchmen should have known their signals.

Whatever their crimes, Rohestvensky and his seamen paid for them in blood and sweat. Their voyage to the Sea of Japan was a nightmare. With British coaling stations closed to the fleet, they had to refuel in fly-blown malarial ports or at sea off abandoned shores. Coal overflowed the bunkers and had to be stored in the gangways and piled on the deck. For four months through the oppressive heat off the African coast and the Indian Ocean, they lived in a hell of coal dust, choking the lungs, blinding the eyes, coating the food. Sailors went mad. At Dakar, a sub-lieutenant on the *Oryol* ran round the deck screaming: 'The Japs are waiting for us! We shall all be sunk!' Scores committed suicide or died of suffocation or disease. At Madagascar, the crew of the *Nakhimoff* mutinied and fourteen were shot. Rohestvensky oscillated between frenzied activity and deep depression. 'More and more often there falls on me,' he wrote in Madagascar, 'complete oblivion as to my surroundings. I have such attacks of endless despair, such fancies, such horrible thoughts, that, by God, I do not know what to do or where to hide.' Rohestvensky had become the Ancient Mariner and the 'Gamecock' Fleet his albatross.

Finally, on 27 May 1905, the Russian Second Pacific Fleet met Admiral Togo's ships in battle in the straits of Tsu-Shima.

It was a cold dull day. The Japanese tore Rohestvensky's command to pieces. Only three ships out of forty made it through to the Russian Pacific port of Vladivostock. Five thousand Russian seamen died. The war was over.

The Admiral himself was captured. He was returned, an invalid, to St Petersburg on the Trans-Siberian railway. He lingered through his retirement and died in 1909. The fate of his command was revenge of a sort for the crew of the *Crane*.

3.

Our Fate Is Your Fate

China in 1926. The world's last great medieval empire has broken up in anarchy. Since the fall of the Manchus in 1912, warlords have fought over the corpse of the country. There is unimaginable chaos. For the Chinese there is torment. Millions are dead from famine, plague and war. In the cities the starving fight over dead rats. In the countryside, children scrabble in the rubbish for rotten cabbage leaves. Desperate men from disbanded and defeated armies plague the roads and the seaways. China is a living hell.

The coastal steamer *Sunning* is untouched by the surrounding anarchy. It is 15 October 1926, and the ship is bound from Amoy to Hong Kong, en route from Shanghai to Canton. Empires rise and fall, but on every sea in every corner of the globe British ships manned by British officers live in a floating cocoon of order and stability. However, it is a fragile security. In the past twelve years, piracy on the South China Sea has reached a level not seen since the Mediterranean of the Barbary Corsairs.

The bad times began in 1914 with the attack on the *Tai On*. The *Tai On* was a Chinese-owned steel screw-steamer of 700 tons, sailing under the British flag and commanded by British officers. She left Hong Kong on 27 April 1914 with

363 passengers, a crew of forty and over 100 coolies and baggage-handlers. Three hours out of Hong Kong she was passing Ki O Island, close to Macao, at the entrance to Wangmoon, in Chinese territory.

The pirates attacked in numbers in the darkness. The captain, Robert Henry Wetherell, managed to secure the bridge. The pirates smashed the steering gear and the dynamo, plunging the *Tai On* into darkness. They gathered the passengers and threatened to shoot into them unless Captain Wetherell surrendered. Wetherell refused and he, his officers and his Portuguese guards aimed a murderous barrage of rifle-fire at the attackers. The pirates spread among the passengers demanding their valuables. If they hesitated, they were shot. They forced women and children to crawl up to the bridge and beg Wetherell to hand over the ship. When they failed, the women and children were killed.

When Wetherell sent up distress rockets, the pirates realised they had run out of time. They smashed up cabin furniture, soaked it in kerosene and set fire to the ship. The blaze spread faster than they expected. Pirates and passengers were forced to jump for their lives. In the appalling conflagration, over 100 were killed. A further 150 drowned in blind panic in the water. Piracy was back in blood and Wetherell had set an example for how a British officer should respond.

The pirates established themselves at a base in Bias Bay, forty miles to the east of Hong Kong. Their leaders moved anonymously and easily in the Chinese communities of Hong Kong and Macao, posing as successful traders. They ran an organisation far more efficient than the nominal Chinese government in Canton.

The *Sunning* belonged to the China Navigation Company. She was a smaller version of the *Tai On*, built on the same coastal-steamer lines. On board were a crew of 110, six British officers and 200 passengers. Most of the passengers were Chinese labourers from the Amoy and Swatow Districts. They were on their way to contracts in Malaya and Burma where they would save every penny of their pitiful wages in the endless Chinese battle against starvation.

The *Sunning* had met pirates before. In 1923, her captain had been shot in the jaw and the safe looted. The attack was led by an immaculately-dressed Chinese man in horn-rimmed glasses. Security had since been tightened on all ships on the coastal Chinese routes. Passengers were searched before coming aboard. The bridge was cut off from the passenger decks by a padlocked iron grille and patrolled by armed Indian guards.

Nowadays, most crews are instructed to avoid violent confrontation. There are, of course, exceptions. The Russians have a reputation for resisting armed attack with enthusiasm. In 1982, according to a report in the *Asia Wall Street Journal*, a Russian vessel towed a Nigerian pirate craft out to sea, leaving one survivor to spread the word and a boatload of bullet-riddled corpses. However, most merchant ships go unarmed. In the 1920s, though, British officers were expected to act heroically. Force was to be met with force.

There was no resistance possible aboard the *Sunning* at 3.40 p.m. on 15 November 1926. The sea was dead calm in the torpid heat of the tropical autumn. The pirates came from among the passengers. Silently they overpowered and disarmed the guards at the entrance to the bridge. The officers on watch had no time to raise the alarm. Second Engineer

Orr, poking his head out of his cabin to see about the noise, was knocked out with a bottle. Cormack, the Chief Engineer, was clubbed unconscious with his own teapot. The radio was disabled. In the space of five minutes, the ship was in pirate hands. Captain Pringle, overcome in his cabin, was faced by the 'Number One Pirate'.

The 'Number One Pirate' was an old friend of the *Sunning*. He emerged from among the First Class passengers dressed in gorgeous silk robes. The glass on his tortoiseshell spectacles shone on a smooth round face. He ordered Pringle to set course for Bias Bay.

The man in the tortoiseshell glasses had gone to a great deal of trouble to hijack the *Sunning*. The leading members of the gang had travelled for months on the ship, back and forth between Shanghai and Canton, taking note of security measures, crew strength and procedures. In early November a spy at the office of the China Navigation Company had discovered that on the 15th, the *Sunning* would be carrying $500,000 in gold bullion in the ship's safe.

The safe had two keys. One was held by Captain Pringle and the other by the ship's Chinese Comprador. Pringle was forced to hand over the first key, but the Comprador could not be found.

On European vessels, the Comprador formed the link between officers and the Chinese crew. He supervised the loading of cargo, sub-let passenger accommodation and operated a private trading operation. This Comprador was a remarkable man. Among the crew he inspired utter devotion.

The official accounts of the *Sunning* piracy state baldly that five of the crew were killed for refusing to reveal the Comprador's hiding-place. One was shot and the other four were thrown overboard, one by one. The dead men are praised as a group for their gallantry. They are not named. No one who could read or write was present when they died. Their heroism was extraordinary. They were poorly-paid company employees with nothing to gain from their sacrifice. The tragedy was that their sacrifice was for nothing – so that a man in tortoiseshell glasses could be kept from opening an empty safe.

The rumour about the gold was wrong. The bullion had been switched to another company ship. The safe held nothing but the crew's wages.

The pirates never found the Comprador. He did not emerge for twelve hours, by which time the piracy was over. When he heard that the ship had been taken he ran down to the stoke-hold, smeared his face with grease and was hidden by the firemen beneath a pile of coke.

The pirates treated the officers well. They were needed to operate the ship and the 'Number One Pirate' was a gentleman. Pringle and Beatty, the Chief Officer, were guarded on the bridge while they steered the vessel. The other officers were held below in the First Mate's cabin.

Pringle was a cautious man. He was content to let matters drift. Hurst, the Second Officer, had a more adventurous spirit.

Hurst had a revolver in a drawer in his cabin. He asked the guard to let him fetch his saxophone and portable organ so that they could pass the time with a bit of jazz. It is a mystery why the Chinese agreed.

Hurst was too closely watched to collect his gun. He came back with the instruments. William Orr, Second Engineer, picked up his Hawaiian guitar. Andrew Duncan, Third Engineer, took his ukulele. Together they played for the two white passengers, Mrs Proklofiera, an elderly White Russian, and Mr Lapsley, a retired official of the Eastern Telegraph Company. They made a strange group, their syncopation rattling in the silent ship. To the Chinese ear the Western music sounded like strangled cats. The guards retreated to the gangway, leaving one man to endure the torture. Mr Lapsley and Mrs Proklofiera began to dance.

On the bridge at 5.15, Beatty sighted another vessel on the horizon. The 'Number One Pirate' warned Pringle that if he signalled he would be shot. The man in the tortoiseshell glasses was unaware, despite the thousands of Chinese dollars he had spent researching the procedures of the *Sunning*, that the other ship was the *Annui*, commanded by the Commodore of the China Navigation Company fleet.

Standing orders of the company laid down that a vessel must dip its flag when passing a sister ship commanded by a senior officer. Pringle and Beatty kept quiet, guns to their heads, as the ships closed.

Hurst, down in the Chief Officer's cabin, had also seen the silhouette of the *Annui* through the porthole. He called in the guard and told him that they were passing the *Sunning*'s flagship. The guard ran up to the bridge. While Orr and Duncan played on, Hurst fetched his pistol and ammunition from his cabin. When the guard returned, Hurst was back in his seat blowing his saxophone.

When they had passed the *Annui*, Pringle took a puzzling risk. He told the pirates about the company etiquette, explaining that in a matter of hours the British Navy, alerted by the Commodore, would be on the track of the *Sunning*. He judged that this would frighten them into abandoning the attack. The man in the tortoiseshell glasses did not seem concerned. He looked Pringle calmly in the face. 'Our fate is your fate,' he said, 'if we are to die, you too will die.'

Beatty felt that Pringle had pushed things to a crisis. He wanted to be prepared for violence. Two revolvers were kept in the chart-room adjoining the bridge. He asked that Hurst be allowed to come up to help handle the ship. While Beatty distracted the attention of the two guards, Hurst slipped into the chart-room, loaded the two revolvers and left them in a drawer alongside the weapon he had taken from his cabin. On another pretext he went down to Orr's cabin and brought up Orr's pistol to hide beside the others. Now they had to wait their moment.

As night fell the weather changed. A strong head-wind blew up, slowing progress to a crawl. The 'Number One Pirate' became anxious. He pressed Pringle for more speed. Pringle replied that already they were at the *Sunning*'s limit.

There is an air of charming unreality about the *Sunning* episode. Through all the violence and danger runs the feel of an English country house weekend. As darkness fell, the officers and the white passengers gathered to dine together, served by the Steward. While they dined they discussed their position. They agreed that they would act when they sighted a patrol vessel. Pringle had lost them any chance of pretending innocence. The signal for action would be a single whistle down the engine-room tube. Cormack, the Chief Engineer, would secure the grille at the entrance to the engine-room and give the officers control over the ship's movement.

The night wore on. The wind continued dead on the *Sunning*'s bows. As Bias Bay came closer, there was still no sign of the navy. The officers knew that, once in the shelter of the bay, the pirates would remove everything of value from the ship and escape either into the mountainous jungle of the interior or one of the thousands of creeks and inlets of the barely-charted coast. They also knew that they themselves might be included among those objects of value.

Piracy in China was an ancient and, depending whom you mixed with, an honourable, trade. Like all such professions it operated on a strict code determined by tradition. One of these traditions was ransom. There was a certain profit in hijacking cargo and stealing the valuables on board a ship. But the staple of Chinese piracy, from time immemorial, had been payment for the return of hostages. As employees of a powerful company, the officers were negotiable currency. Even if the navy did not appear, they had to act before Bias Bay. Beatty and Hurst agreed that the signal should be the first sighting of Chilang Point, the spur that guarded the bay's entrance.

At midnight Beatty saw the loom of the lighthouse on the point. He warned Hurst to be ready. Hurst went into the chart-room to plot the ship's position. He took the four revolvers from the drawer and laid them beneath a chart on the table. As he came back onto the bridge, Beatty called the two guards to the handrail and pointed over the bows towards a speck of light on the horizon. 'CHILANG POINT,' he shouted, as they leant over the rail – 'CHILANG POINT!'

The plan had been for Hurst to shoot the guards. Hurst knew that the report of a revolver would be heard throughout the ship. Instead he picked up one of the 28 lb sea-leads that held down the coconut matting on the floor of the bridge. He swung it at the head of the shorter guard as he craned over the rail. Hurst later remembered, with less-than-Christian relish, that the guard's head 'cracked open like an egg-shell'.

As the other guard turned, Hurst swung again and knocked him to the ground.

Pringle took the dead guard's rifle and stood to guard one of the two stairways up to the bridge. Hurst, armed with a pistol, took the other.

By now Mrs Proklofiera, Mr Lapsley, Orr, Duncan and Lok, the Chinese radio operator, were held in the captain's cabin, directly beneath the bridge, guarded by a single pirate armed with a rifle. The guard heard the thump of falling bodies on the ceiling and came out of the cabin to investigate. As he started to climb the port steps to the bridge, Hurst shot him dead. Beatty rushed down and took his rifle as the main body of pirates, alerted by the shot, rushed for the stairway. Beatty ran back up to the bridge and the three men barred the security gates, locking themselves on the bridge.

Beatty, Pringle and Hurst were now isolated from the officers and passengers below. However, the skylight of the captain's cabin was set in the floor of the bridge. While Orr and Duncan barred the cabin door, Beatty smashed the skylight with the butt of his rifle. Duncan, Orr, Lok and the passengers climbed up through the shattered glass and armed themselves with Hurst's revolvers.

As they took positions to repel an assault, they were unexpectedly attacked from the bridge itself. The second guard had been knocked unconscious, but his skull had not been cracked like an egg. He revived, reached for his rifle and fired across the bridge, miraculously missing everyone. Before he could collect himself for another shot, Beatty swung his rifle and clubbed him on the head. The guard fired again, at Beatty's legs, but again missed. Beatty clubbed him again, this time so hard that he broke the stock on the rifle. The pirate's head was now in questionable shape. He threw his gun overboard and jumped from the bridge onto the deck below.

For an uneasy five minutes each side reviewed its position. Hurst sent the agreed single blast down the tube to the engine-room. There was no answering signal. The officers had control of the bridge. They were armed. While they held their position, the ship would not reach Bias Bay. The pirates controlled the rest of the ship. There was no sign of help. It seemed that their failure to signal the flagship had been ignored. There would be no outside intervention. The two sides would have to resolve the drama alone.

It was a tense time on the bridge. The 'Number One Pirate' had warned them that if they resisted they would die. Pringle was too old and too experienced to feel much enthusiasm for their position. However, for Hurst and for the younger officers, it was for exactly this sort of experience that they had enlisted for service in the South China Sea.

The lull ended in the worst way possible. As expected, the pirates advanced across the open stretch of deck towards the steps. But in front of them, they pushed Cormack and the cabin-boys as human shields.

Cormack had moved too soon to secure the grille at the door of the engine-room. At ten o'clock, having received no signal, he slammed the door shut. The pirates smashed the locks on the grille and posted guards on the door.

The defenders on the bridge did not hesitate. They could not shoot through Cormack and the cabin-boys, so they shot at them, aiming for the less vital parts of their bodies. In this they had mixed success. They inflicted a variety of wounds to chests, arms and legs.

Cormack fell, severely wounded. The pirates walked over him. Later a fireman from the crew picked him up, believing he was dead. With touching care for the corpse of his chief, the fireman carried him to the stoke-hold and buried him in the coke-pile.

For three hours the men held out on the bridge while the pirates tried time after time to storm the approaches. By 3.30 a.m., ten pirates were dead and the defenders were out of ammunition. No one on the bridge had been hit, but somehow Lapsley, the retired official of the Eastern Telegraph Company, the passenger who had danced that afternoon to the jazz combo with the White Russian widow, had disappeared. He was never found.

Not realising that the defenders had run out of ammunition, the pirates tried a new tactic. They dragged up mattresses from the cabins and piled them at the foot of the bridge. They withdrew and set the mattresses alight with burning rags.

Without Cormack's attention, the engines had stopped. Through the night, the wind had increased. The *Sunning* was now pitching in a Force Six gale. As the wind swept across the deck from the bows, it fanned the flames, sending a cloud of thick black smoke over the bridge-rail, choking the exhausted defenders.

From the shadows in the lee of the wind the pirates watched and waited. No men could survive in that heat and smoke.

The boatswain and five Chinese crew members had locked themselves in the forecastle head when the officers had seized the bridge. Pringle yelled through to them, above the flames and the wind, to drop the anchor. His fellow officers looked at him in amazement.

The anchor rattled through its chains and held on the sea-bed. The ship shuddered and then, slowly at first, and then with a grating strain of the anchor-cable against the metal of the prow, the *Sunning* began to swing around, the bows blown by the gale while the anchor held the prow. As the ship turned beam-on to the full force of the wind, the deck lurched at a crazy angle; and then she was round and the wind was fanning the flames and smoke away from the bridge, back towards the pirates and the heart of the vessel.

The pirates ran back for the bows. It was too late for them to drop the bow anchor. This would only fix the ship in place. Smoke and flames spread across the deck and down into the passageways below. The timbers of the deck caught fire. The heat was so intense that steel beams began to buckle and then to melt.

The pirates' position was desperate. If they stayed where they were, they would be fried alive. They sent a deputation, with soaked rags over their mouths, through the fire and smoke to the foot of the bridge. They offered to leave the ship if the officers, as a gesture of faith, gave up their arms. Pringle smiled down from the bridge and shook his head.

It was over. Twenty of the pirates took to two lifeboats. The remainder threw away their arms and tried to melt in among the Chinese passengers. The burning ship was back in the hands of its officers.

For some time it looked as though the fire had spread too deep for the vessel to be saved. As a precaution, a boat was lowered with Hurst, Duncan, Lok, Mrs Proklofiera and two Chinese crew. The selection of passengers to be saved gives some idea of priorities aboard European vessels in the South China Sea in the first half of the century. Within minutes the rope that held the boat was burned through by the flames and the boat drifted off over the horizon.

The remaining crew set to work to fight the fire. The Comprador emerged from among the firemen and began the work of separating the pirates from the innocent on the passenger-deck. Thirteen were identified and placed under armed guard.

At 5 a.m., with the flames barely under control, the *Sunning* sighted a Japanese merchantman. She signalled for naval assistance. HMS *Bluebell* reached the scene at daybreak. Marines came aboard and helped to extinguish the last of the flames. Later in the morning the *Sunning* was taken in tow by her sister ship, the *Kaying*, and hauled to Hong Kong harbour. The piracy of the *Sunning* was over.

The same morning a Norwegian steamer, the *Ravensfjell*, picked up the lifeboat with the officers and Mrs Proklofiera. The *Bluebell* found another of the lifeboats with nine pirates aboard.

In the weeks that followed both sides received their reward. The officers and crew were thanked by the Hong Kong Government for their heroism. The colony awarded £100 to the officers and £25 to the men. Eight of the pirates were executed. It was justice of a sort. The man in the tortoiseshell glasses was never found.

4.

Menschenraub

Did the captain and owners of the steamer *Falke* kidnap their own crew and steal their own ship? It was difficult to work out who was lying and who was telling the truth – too difficult for a court in Hamburg in April 1930. With reluctance they acquitted the converted idealist, Captain Zipplitt, and the unconvertible rogues, Felix Kramarsky and Felix Prenzlau. With the trial, ended the byzantine voyage of the *Falke* and the heroic but futile dreams of General Delgado-Chalbaud. In Caracas, the capital of Venezuela, Juan Vicente Gomez, 'The Tyrant of the Andes', remained undisputed as dictator for life.

Gomez died in December 1935. In 1936, when the American journalist Thomas Rourke travelled to Venezuela to write the story of the dictatorship, he was seen off by an exile still too afraid to return to his homeland. 'Thomas,' the man told him, 'I will tell you one thing: there has never lived, nor ever will live a man as cruel as Gomez.'

The decade that followed put a new perspective on cruelty. Against the horrors of Hitler, of Stalin and of a world at war, the life of the dictator of a little-known Latin American country was quickly forgotten. Gomez's reign was shunted into the back corridors of history along with all stories of banana republics and revolutions in countries where pools of sweat spread beneath the armpits of corrupt chiefs of police. Like anything that has ever happened south of the Rio Grande, to most of the Western world the life of Gomez became an absurd curiosity – half a joke and half an irrelevance.

It is not entirely a mystery that we should dismiss huge tracts of the world like this. In a sense Latin Americans ask for their reputation. Both the country and the people are too flamboyant and unstable for sluggish western blood. We cannot handle a man as bizarre as Gomez or a country as strange as Venezuela.

Juan Vicente Gomez came from the wild mountainous north-west of Venezuela, near the Columbian border. For the first half of his life he was a typical South American feudal landowner. Until his death he remained virtually illiterate. In the late nineteenth century Venezuela had more in common with the middle ages than the age of democracy and reason. Local *caudillos* made their own law and broke it when it proved convenient. Until he was thirty-five, Gomez was satisfied with milking his peasants, upsetting his neighbours and littering the countryside with illegitimate children. On an obscure provincial scale he was already building the reputation that would later dominate the country – of savage brutality and of almost diabolical mystic powers. The Indians called him '*brujo*' – the wizard. He was obsessed with magic and superstition. He avoided anything to do with the number thirteen. He despised organised religion. His only weakness was an extraordinary sensitivity about his small delicate hands. For his whole life he wore gloves at all times, even when eating.

In 1892 Gomez entered politics in the traditional

Venezuelan way. He chose the wrong side in a revolution and had to cross the frontier to Columbia. He took with him his family and a clan of feudal dependants. Over the next seven years Gomez re-established his fortunes cattle-rustling across the border and plotting to return to his lands.

In 1899 his chance came. He crossed the border in support of a revolution led by General Castro. He operated a brilliant guerrilla campaign in the north-west. When Castro became president, Gomez became his blunt instrument.

Castro liked the trappings of power, but he was not fitted for the day to day tedium of running a country. He preferred to have fun. Almost single-handed he bankrupted Venezuela, selling her for credit with foreign banks. He was drunk for more or less the whole ten years of his presidency. He liked to swim naked in the public fountain in front of the Presidential Palace. One night, in delirium, thinking there had been an earthquake, he jumped from his bedroom balcony into the street and lay there until dawn with his legs broken. He kept twenty-two mistresses in separate houses scattered around Caracas, each one ready for a visit at any time. At least to begin with, they all had to be virgins. His agents scoured the countryside searching for suitable candidates.

While Castro was busy with his liver and his bed-springs, someone had to run the country. Gomez took the job. Castro's neglect, debts and mismanagement roused a string of revolts. Wherever trouble broke out, Gomez was dispatched with government forces. Gomez had found his vocation. With a mixture of brutality, cunning and military genius he destroyed all opposition. He became indispensable as Castro's enforcer.

For ten years Gomez showed extraordinary patience, but by 1909, he could no longer maintain the fiction that Castro was fit to rule. Castro was by now in a permanent fever from the combined effects of drink and a lethal mixture of aphrodisiacs he was swallowing in a desperate attempt to keep up with his twenty-two wives. Drugs and alcohol had eaten away the wall of his bladder. When he travelled to Europe for an operation, Gomez took the opportunity to declare himself President.

Gomez's dictatorship was to last for twenty-seven years. In many ways it was a precursor of the fascist rule of Mussolini, Hitler and Franco – a mixture of a new form of state efficiency with harsh, often wilful suppression of dissent. His apologists – the only writers published in Venezuela – saw him as the saviour of the country and spread the gospel of Gomez to anyone who was interested in the rest of the world. Certainly he balanced the books. He overturned Castro's legacy of foreign debt through clever manipulation of Venezuela's oil resources. Anyone who stood in his way paid a frightful penalty.

Some of the world's worst criminals have been excused because they loved their mothers. For all his faults, Gomez never let his family down. His brother, Eustoquio, had all of Juan Vicente's energy and cruelty but none of his intelligence. In 1907, Eustoquio had been sentenced to fifteen years in San Carlos, an island gaol off Venezuela's northern coast, for shooting the Governor of a Federal District who had tried to calm him in a drunken argument. Gomez's first action on taking power was to order Eustoquio's release.

The judges who had sat on Eustoquio's trial refused to endorse the pardon. They were imprisoned. The editors of three national newspapers criticised the treatment of the judges. They were sent to San Carlos gaol. After a thirty-six-hour voyage tied up in the hold of a ship they arrived to find that Eustoquio had been made governor of the prison. They were forced to pass through two files of soldiers who beat them with *vergas* – a peculiar Venezuelan type of swagger-stick made from a stuffed bull's penis. After running the gauntlet of the bulls' penises, the three editors were each fitted with a pair of *grillos* – and left to rot.

Venezuela's contribution to the world's art, literature and thought has largely been ignored. However, if in no other areas, they have shown considerable ingenuity in the fields of torture and crowd-control. Along with the *vergas*, Venezuela was the home of the *tortol*, a knotted rope looped around a prisoner's forehead and tightened by twisting a stick through the knot; the *cepo*, a torture too horrible to describe in detail, which separated a victim's vertebrae and ruptured his abdominal wall without leaving a single external mark, and, the universal feature of prison life – the *grillos*.

The *grillos* were a form of leg-iron – a lattice of solid iron bars weighing from between twenty and eighty pounds, all the weight resting on the prisoner's bare ankles. The prisoner had to wear these excruciating socks day and night for his entire sentence. Apart from the constant pain, the chafing of metal on bare flesh opened sores which were never given the chance to heal. With many prisoners the sores developed into gangrene. Less fatal, but more unpleasant, was when the sores became the breeding ground for the *gusana,* a fly native to Venezuela. The *gusana* laid its eggs in the wound. The eggs grew into worms which fed on the prisoner's flesh before issuing as adult flies.

Eventually, Eustoquio found San Carlos a little limited as a field for his sadistic talents. When rebellion broke out in the west he was sent to the Columbian border where he suppressed dissent by hanging captured rebels alive on meat-hooks by the side of the road.

Gomez was attracted to the trappings of European monarchy and power. He greatly admired the Kaiser and dressed up to imitate his hero in a spiked helmet and uniform of the German Imperial Navy. However, he was never a demagogue in the way of Hitler or Mussolini. In his entire political career he never made a speech. He was more of a brooding presence in the background of Venezuelan life. His intricate web of informers and agents, penetrating every corner of society, gave him a reputation for almost supernatural omniscience.

Gomez never married. The nearest he had to a wife was a woman he stole in his early days on the border from her Italian husband. He had numerous children, some of whom he officially recognised as the basis for building an enduring dynasty. When Charles Lindberg, the solo American aviator, landed at Maracay on his goodwill tour of South America, Gomez greeted him from under a canopy on the landing-field. A group of Gomez's children came forward with bunches of flowers for the pilot.

'Are they natural?' asked Lindberg.

'Yes,' said Gomez, thinking Lindberg was talking about the children, 'they are natural, but recognised.'

His favourite son was Vincentino – 'little Vincent'. Gomez intended that Vincentino should succeed him. However Vincentino had a lot in common with Eustoquio. In July 1923 another of the President's brothers, Juancho, was found dead in his bed at the President's Palace with twenty-seven stab wounds through his heart, liver and stomach. Gomez launched a thorough investigation. All suspected political opponents were rounded up and tortured to extract confessions. The methods were successful. Gomez's secret police constructed an impressive picture of a national conspiracy. Hundreds were imprisoned or died during questioning. In fact, no conspiracy existed. The investigation was an elaborate exercise to conceal the truth that Vincentino had killed his uncle in a frenzied bout of paranoia.

Castro died in the Canary Islands in 1928. His last words were 'how pleased Juan Vicente will be', but the old dictator had long since ceased to be a threat. The French authorities had arrested him some years earlier when he tried to launch an invasion from Martinique and loaded him, rolled in a blanket, aboard a steamer bound for Lanzarote. From there, until his death, he issued meaningless pronouncements to an indifferent world.

However there were other refugees who represented more of a danger. By the late 1920s they were scattered in pockets of exile across the globe. Many had a deep and burning personal interest in Gomez's downfall. No one loathed Gomez more than General Roman Delgado-Chalbaud.

Delgado-Chalbaud's hatred for Gomez was so intense that it bordered on insanity. Delgado-Chalbaud came from one of Venezuela's most aristocratic colonial families. Initially he had supported Gomez in order to rid the country of Castro, but he had soon turned against Gomez's dictatorial rule. In 1913 he was arrested for his part in a conspiracy and spent fourteen years in Caracas's dreaded Rotunda gaol, his legs imprisoned in a pair of eighty-pound *grillos*. In 1927, in one of Gomez's periodic fits of clemency, he was exiled. He travelled to Paris with his wife and eighteen-year-old son and began to plot his return. He set out to enlist the support of other compatriots.

At first the Venezuelan community in Europe was suspicious of Delgado-Chalbaud. The other exiles were republican and the General's aristocratic background and history of support for autocratic rule made him an unlikely ally. They suspected that his true aim was to set up his own dictatorship. However, he persuaded them that he had been changed by his time in prison. It was impossible to doubt the sincerity of his loathing for Gomez. He proved remarkably efficient at raising funds for revolution. When money ran short, his wife, Senora Luisa Elena, pawned her jewels for the cause.

He gathered around him a group of twenty of the regime's most virulent opponents. Among them were two members of an abortive expedition in 1927 which had set out from Europe to invade Venezuela aboard the steamer *Angelita*, but been impounded by the Cuban authorities. All of the conspirators had particular reasons for hating Gomez, but none had quite such an acute personal interest as Captain Luis Pimental, a survivor of the young officers' conspiracy of January 1919.

Gomez had received early news of the plot of 1919. The conspirators were arrested and fourteen of the principal ringleaders were driven to the Villa Zoila, Gomez's country house. Gomez himself was occupied in the capital. He entrusted their interrogation to his beloved son Vincentino. Under the junior psychopath's supervision, the fourteen were led one by one to a rope threaded through a pulley in the ceiling. One end of the rope was tied and knotted around the victim's genitals. The other end was hauled through the pulley by the investigating officers until the prisoner was suspended above the ground. Captain Entrenera, the first conspirator to undergo this torture, was enormously fat. The weight tore the rope through his scrotum, leaving his genitals hanging in the knot, and leaving Captain Entrenera to bleed to death on Gomez's parquet floor. The others escaped alive, but with their testicles squeezed out flat. None of them gave away the names of their fellow-conspirators. Pimental refused to cry out with pain. For his defiance he was strung up four times.

Delgado-Chalbaud and his group of revolutionaries approached Felix Kramarsky and Felix Prenzlau, two businessmen at the seediest end of the European arms trade. According to Kramarsky's later testimony at the Hamburg court, the Venezuelans put in a $200,000 order for 2,000 rifles and one million rounds of ammunition to be delivered to an as yet unnamed island in the Western Atlantic. The dealers were taking a considerable risk. Payment was to be made from the Exchequer in Venezuela after the success of the revolution.

Kramarsky approached the Polish Ministry of War. He bought 2,000 obsolete 1888-model rifles which he described rather kindly as 'bored out, but still fairly serviceable'. He had more trouble in finding ammunition within his price-range. Finally he made do with 200,000 rounds purchased through a German bank from Albania where they had been stock-piled for an abortive attempt by a pretender to regain the Afghan throne.

At the beginning of June, 1929, Felix Prenzlau bought the *Falke*, a 119 ton coal-burning steamship from the Hamburg Mercantile Marine Company. The *Falke* had been built in 1902 at the Earles Shipbuilding Yard in Hull. The Hamburg Mercantile Marine Company had their suspicions about

Prenzlau and Kramarsky. They assumed they intended to use the *Falke* for some illegal purpose. They suspected it was liquor smuggling. They did not imagine it would be revolution.

On 7 June, the *Falke*, with a German crew of thirty-five, left the North Sea port of Altone for Gdynia on the Baltic. They arrived on 12 July. On 19 July, General Delgado-Chalbaud, his son, and their twenty co-conspirators arrived in Gdynia from Paris.

Much of the speculation over the *Falke* episode centred on whether the crew understood the ship's mission. The crew maintained that they believed they were on a legitimate trading trip. At the subsequent trial, they gave various versions of the deception. Some claimed that they believed the ship was carrying a consignment of plum sauce. Others, rather more realistically, admitted that they knew the cargo was armaments, but believed they were destined for the legitimate government of Brazil.

Kramarsky and Prenzlau maintained that the crew were thoroughly aware of the purpose of the voyage. At Gdynia they loaded the arms and ammunition. The crew, seeing the nature of the cargo, demanded double pay for the loading. Kramarsky points to this as proof that the crew were prepared to set a price for their cooperation. The crew argued that this was a reasonable demand for handling a load that might explode in their faces. Whatever the reasons, Kramarsky refused the demand, but Delgado-Chalbaud, watching the loading from the wharf, stepped in and paid the demand in cash. The Third Engineer claimed he was so excited by the news of double pay that he completely forgot to wonder why his employers were being so generous. On 28 July they left

Gdynia with their twenty-two South American passengers and rusting assortment of cut-rate armaments.

As soon as the *Falke* reached international waters the mood aboard changed. The Venezuelan flag was raised on the stern. Relaxed merchant marine discipline was replaced by military rule. A machine-gun was set up on the stern. The ship's name was changed to the *General Anzoategui* in honour of a Venezuelan Republican hero. The revolutionaries carried out firing-practice on the deck for an hour each day. Most unexpected of all, the *Falke*'s German captain, Ernst Zipplitt, took an oath to the new Republic and was appointed the First (and, as it proved, only) Admiral of the New Republic of Venezuela, invested with his authority by General Delgado-Chalbaud in a special ceremony in front of the passengers and a somewhat dazed crew.

Equally extraordinary was the behaviour of the General himself. 'The nearer we approached to Venezuela,' the Third Engineer recalled in court, 'the wilder the General became. He would bare his teeth and grind them together. As he grew more enraged, he began hacking at the water casks and other wooden parts of the ship with his sabre.' At this stage in his testimony, the Third Engineer started to suit his actions to his words and had to be forcibly restrained by the court ushers.

In the first week of August, the *Falke* reached the Caribbean. Off a deserted island east of Curacao, they rendezvoused with a rebel sloop and took aboard further arms and ammunition along with 300 more revolutionaries. Whatever the crew's expectations, none of them, with the exception of Zipplitt, had anticipated forming the spearhead of a military invasion. However, they had no option but to follow orders and head for the Venezuelan coast.

On 10 August the *Falke* arrived off the coast of Venezuela at the Araya Peninsula, 200 kilometres east of Caracas. Venezuela, like all the South American republics, is a country of huge geographical diversity. To the west and the east it is mountainous, but the centre of the country is dominated by the vast plains of the Orinoco basin – the *llanos* – the main areas for oil and food production. Delgado-Chalbaud's plan was to seize the town of Cumana, across the bay from the Araya Peninsula and gain control of the eastern seaboard, the delta of the Orinoco and the entrance to the *llanos*.

He had arranged to meet with local forces under Pedro Arestigueta at an isolated beach east of Cumana. From there, Arestigueta was to make his way along the coast and attack Cumana from the east. The *Falke* was to land Delgado-Chalbaud and his men at Puerto Sucre to assault Cumana simultaneously from the west. According to the plan, the two forces would meet at dawn on 11 August at the narrow bridge which separated Cumana from Puerto Sucre. On the afternoon of the 10th the *Falke* unloaded arms and ammunition for Arestigueta and he and Delgado-Chalbaud parted with the words 'until tomorrow on the bridge'.

At 10 p.m., Delgado-Chalbaud issued final orders to his men. They dispersed to clean their rifles. It was a calm, warm, velvet night, the moon and the stars obscured by a layer of low cloud. The German crew, cut off by language and ignorance of South American politics, stuck to their posts and hoped for the best. At 3 a.m., the *Falke*, steaming without lights, anchored off the wharf at Puerto Sucre. They waited for the sound of Arestigueta's attack from the east of the town. By 5 a.m. there was still no sound. Dawn would reveal their position. Delgado-Chalbaud gave the order to attack.

The invading force landed from small boats. They were accompanied by the German Third Officer and two Polish seamen. The crew testified at the Hamburg enquiry that the three crew-members were forced at gunpoint into the boats. It seems strange that Delgado-Chalbaud should have gone to such trouble. He had enough of a task that morning without having to watch over a group of reluctant seaman conscripts. He may have been trying to ensure that the steamer did not abandon the revolution. If so, he over-estimated the selflessness of the *Falke*'s crew. It seems more likely that, like Captain Zipplitt, the Third Officer and the two Poles had become infected with the romance of Latin revolution. By the time of the Hamburg hearings, it was clearly in the crew's interests to portray the rebels as brutal monsters. Apart from Zipplitt, the only people in a position to contradict their version were either dead in the dusty streets of Puerto Sucre or locked in a Gomez gaol.

The rebels split up and attacked the garrison at the Puerto Sucre Customs House on the wharf. The garrison put up stiff resistance. In the darkness and confusion certain units mistook each other for government troops. They suffered severe casualties, but overran the garrison. Still with no sign of Arestigueta's support they fought their way to the bridge. The main garrison at Cumana had moved machine-guns to cover the narrow approach to the bridge. In the first assault, General Delgado-Chalbaud was killed. It was as well that his dream should end there when there was still hope of victory rather than later in a prison cell with *grillos* back round his ankles. The Third Officer of the *Falke* also fell, mixed up in the unreality of another country's cause.

The rebels maintained the assault on the bridge until 9

a.m. By then there was hardly an officer left standing. The defending forces had also suffered. The Federal Governor, General Emilio Fernandez, Gomez's right-hand man in the east, was dead.

Arestigueta and his men, meanwhile, had become hopelessly lost among the bogs, the tidal lagoons and the rocky headlands of the coast. It was midday when they arrived at the eastern approaches to the town. In the pitiless heat, they were exhausted, dispirited and half-dead with thirst.

When Gomez had heard by telegraph of the invasion, he had ordered two planes from the tiny Venezuelan air force to Cumana. Venezuela was short of home-grown pilots. The planes were flown by Belgians. They arrived as Arestigueta's men entered the evacuated eastern suburbs and machine-gunned the men exposed on the road.

By now it was obvious that the invasion had gone terribly wrong. Still Arestigueta carried on with his planned attack on the main barracks of Cumana. The battle continued for two days. The rebels fought with desperation. As they had approached Cumana, they had seen no sign of the *Falke*. Their line of retreat to the sea was gone.

During the initial attack, the *Falke* had stood out from the wharf, at the limit of effective rifle range from the defenders on the shore. The crew became restless as bullets flew across the deck. Delgado-Chalbaud had left his least effective lieutenant, Jose Pocaterra, in control of the ship.

By 9.30, when the battered attackers pulled back from their assault on the bridge, it was clear that the enterprise was doomed. Zipplitt, clinging to his Admiral's baton, was determined to remain and provide what support he could. However, the crew, free of the restraint of armed Venezuelans,

seized their opportunity. The Chief Mate declared that the
Captain was unfit to command. Pocaterra dithered between
loyalty to his comrades and desire to put the sea between
himself and the disaster on the shore. While he hesitated the
crew steered the boat out of the lee of the Araya Peninsula.

The *Falke* steamed to Grenada and then, running out of
coal, south to the British colony of Trinidad. Her arrival at
Port of Spain was an embarrassment to the British authorities.
Gomez had denounced the ship as a pirate vessel. Trinidad
lies only a few miles from the Venezuelan coast and the
British had no desire for a diplomatic incident. They barred
all contact between the ship and the shore while they made
enquiries about the *Falke*'s ownership and plans. The crew
appealed to the German consul, claiming that they had been
forced at gun-point to accompany the rebels. In Germany,
Prenzlau and Kramarsky denied all involvement in the
invasion. Zipplitt meanwhile telegraphed to the owners that
his crew had mutinied.

In Europe there were confused reports: Cumana was in
the hands of the rebels; the *Falke* had sailed from Trinidad
and was roaming the coast, threatening government shipping.

The truth was less exciting. By the 13th, Cumana was
securely back in Gomez's hands. A thousand reinforcements
sent from the capital had mopped up the final resistance.
The *Falke*, far from terrorising the coast, had run out of money
for coal. The owners had to send $5,000 to bring her and her
crew back to Germany.

The trial of Zipplitt, Kramarsky and Prenzlau began in
Hamburg on 9 April 1930. They were charged with the crime
of Menschenraub – stealing men. It was alleged by the
prosecution that they had 'played with the lives of their

fellow-citizens for money'. The State Prosecutor demanded sentences of eighteen months hard labour for Kramarsky and Prenzlau and twelve months for Zipplitt. The trial, however, left the jury bewildered. No one could give them a convincing picture of what had occurred aboard the *Falke*. The defendants were acquitted.

Back in Venezuela, those rebels who were not butchered were sent to the citadel of San Antonio. Gomez had barely blinked. He survived to die in his bed at the age of seventy-eight. He was mourned by Vincentino.

5.

The Mountain Of Wealth

In real life it is rare to find a story with a beginning, a middle and an end. This is why murders are so fascinating. If a killer is found and punished, then fact takes the shape of fiction. The death forms the beginning, the investigation the middle and the trial the end.

The trouble with reality is that the ends are never neatly sewn. Life is a messy and inconclusive business. The characters who flit in and out of the bizarre tale of Aleko Lilius leave a tangle of inconclusive threads. We never know what finally became of Ko Leong Tai, the man who walked like a dog, or of the grinning shopkeeper with the single ear or of Lai Choi San, 'The Mountain Of Wealth', Queen of the Macao pirates. We know what happened to Weng, Lilius's faithful interpreter, because we see his death, but the fate of the rest is left to our imagination. It may be better that way. The people Lilius described in his obsessive search for pirate life on the South China Sea are the stuff of dreams.

Aleko Lilius was an American journalist – one of a desperate breed who infested the trouble-spots of the world between the wars. In 1929 Lilius arrived in Hong Kong, sent by his American newspaper to discover exactly what was going on in the South China Seas.

83

In the three years since the attack on the *Sunning*, piracy had become international news. In November 1926, Britain demanded action from the Chinese Government in Canton. The Chinese, with the country crumbling to pieces around them, dithered and did nothing. When the British steamer *Hopsang* was overrun and plundered in March 1927, the Royal Navy took matters into its own hands.

The pirates still operated from their base at Bias Bay, sixty-five miles east of Hong Kong. The minesweeper *Marazion* towed three hundred marines in small boats across the ten miles of shallows that protected Fan Lo Kong, the main Bias Bay settlement. The alarm was raised and the pirates themselves faded into the hills. The rest of the inhabitants were ordered to gather their belongings on the seashore and watch as the marines destroyed their houses, along with forty junks and sampans in the harbour. The Chinese Government protested at the invasion of sovereignty. The British Government ignored the protests. The pirates rebuilt their charred homes and returned to business.

The next two years saw more pirate attacks and more British reprisals. In October 1927 the SS *Irene*, with 238 passengers aboard, was seized and the Chinese steward killed. As the pirates made away with the vessel, she was torpedoed by a Royal Navy submarine. The *Irene* caught fire, but miraculously all of the passengers survived. The following September, the *Anking* was pirated and the Chief Engineer killed.

Still, by 1929, no one outside the Chinese community knew who financed and organised the pirates or how they operated. Lilius wanted the answers to these questions. He wanted to enter the pirate world.

Aleko Lilius was born in Southern Russia and brought up in Finland. His parents had emigrated to the United States when he was a teenager. By 1929 he saw himself as the heroic ideal of the roving correspondent – half Hemingway and half Errol Flynn. Physically he resembled a rather fleshy advertisement for a patent body-building course. In the years before television, the American public had a hunger for foreign sensationalism – for stories of grinning, opium-crazed yellow devils with knives clenched between their teeth. Lilius's job was to feed the hunger.

He started by exploring official channels. He spent frustrating weeks interviewing Hong Kong Government officials and naval officers, ploughing through reports in the Colonial Secretary's office. Everywhere he was told that direct contact with the pirates was impossible. The pirate world was closed to westerners. It was the province of a group of desperadoes in Bias Bay. They had no contact with the civilised European settlements in Macao and Hong Kong. He was wasting his time.

Finally in Hong Kong he met up with a Portuguese who suggested he travel to the Portuguese colony of Macao. He might find some answers in the Sun Tai gambling house. He sailed for Macao aboard the *Sui An*. The *Sui Ann* had a history of her own. In 1922 she had been hijacked to Bias Bay, her master shot in the back and her cargo looted.

The Sun Tai was a huge, three-storey *fan-tan* house, the largest casino in the colony. *Fan-tan* is an obsession wherever Chinese gather. It is played with *cash* – an old Chinese copper coin with a hole in the centre. A pile of *cash* is hidden beneath a bowl on the *fan-tan* table. Bets are laid and then the bowl is removed and the croupier lifts off the coins in groups of four with a pair of chopsticks. The gamblers bet on how many coins will remain after the last set of four has been lifted – one, two, three or none. The game has taken on mythical status. It has spread wherever the Chinese have travelled. In Korea there is a tradition that a man can only father a child if he wins three successive *fan-tan* games in the interval between his wife's periods. *Fan-tan* is not just a game.

Lilius was lucky at the Sun Tai tables. He became so involved in the game and the excitement generated by the mass of half-naked players, that he forgot why he was there. When a man standing beside him put a hand on his arm, he shook it violently away.

The man grabbed his sleeve again. He was a small Chinese dressed in a long, blue silk gown, felt slippers and dirty sun-visor around a shaven head. Lilius noticed that the hand laid on his arm was abnormally small, with yellow-stained fingers.

'Stop gambling when luck smilee,' said the small man, 'lose monee, makee heavy heart.'

Lilius turned back to the table. 'Portuguese man, gleat fliend,' the man went on, 'sent this Chinaman talkie talkie flip top-side Hong Kong.'

Lilius had entered the world of the Chinese pirate.

The small man led him out of the *fan-tan* house to an English-pattern house in an oriental garden. The door was opened by a servant. The servant had the meanest face Lilius had ever seen. A single knife-scar ran from the right corner of his mouth to the lobe of his ear.

Among the Chinese, negotiations can be a complex process. Lilius wanted to be shipped directly aboard a pirate vessel. The small man said that he knew nothing of piracy.

He would ask among his acquaintances. Lilius would have to wait a week.

He returned to Hong Kong. He had no confidence that this contact would be any more reliable than previous ones, so he continued his search.

In the market he bought jade from a man with a dirty hole in the side of his head. The man laughed when Lilius asked how he had lost his ear.

'Chinee pirates choppee off ear,' he said, 'send him by my blother. He! He! He!'

Westerners tended to forget that attacks on European ships were a tiny irrelevance within the huge business of Chinese piracy. The deaths on the *Sunning*, the *Irene* and the *Anking* led to international protests and reprisals, but the core of the piracy trade was then, as it had been for centuries, attacks on ordinary Chinese fishing vessels and passenger craft. Any Chinese who travelled regularly would expect, at least once in his life, to be captured by pirates and held for ransom.

When a Chinese was kidnapped, intermediaries presented the bill to his family. If there was a delay in payment, it was customary to offer the prisoner the choice of losing a finger, the tip of his nose or an ear. The amputated protuberance would be delivered to the relatives as proof that the pirates were serious. The negotiations were regulated with respect for custom and tradition. There was no ill-feeling on either side. The kidnapped person was a '*p'iao*' – literally a 'ticket'. Attempts to retrieve the ticket by force went against pirate etiquette and the pirates responded by crumpling the ticket and throwing it away.

When Lilius showed interest the shopkeeper burrowed beneath his counter and, still laughing, brought out a package wrapped in dirty silk. Inside the package was 'a dried and blackened human ear – his own'.

Lilius asked the man to keep his remaining ear open for any contacts among the pirate world. He left the man still laughing, tying the shrivelled lump back in its filthy scrap of silk.

He spent the rest of the week trawling fruitlessly through the *sing-sing* houses, opium-dens and brothels of West Point and then returned to Macao, expecting further delays and evasions. Instead, the small man with the felt slippers had kept his word. The following morning he was aboard the flagship of 'The Mountain Of Wealth', Lai Choi San, Queen of the Macao pirates.

The ship was a junk, armed with twelve smooth-bore medieval cannon. The crew were bigger and more muscular than the normal southern Chinese, with hard impassive faces. Instead of the normal wide-brimmed Chinese hats they wore red handkerchiefs wrapped around their heads. However, the most impressive sight was Lai Choi San herself.

The Chinese had a tradition of woman pirates. The early years of the nineteenth century had been a similarly unsettled time. Then, as in the 1920s, famine raged in Southern China. The people of the coast, faced with starvation, turned to crime. Ching-Yih, an obscure hunch-backed fisherman with a genius for command, built a pirate fleet of 1,800 vessels and 70,000 men. When Ching-Yih was killed in a typhoon, his place was taken by his young widow. It was said of her that 'before the beauty of her face, the eyes of men become confused'. But there was nothing soft about Mrs Ching. Among the list of rules that regulated her fleet were that any man raping a woman without his superior's consent would be executed;

that any pirate advancing or retreating without orders would be beheaded. A bounty of $20 was paid for the head of an enemy. Her pirates destroyed the Imperial battle fleet under the 'Invincible' Admiral Kwolang-Lin, undefeated in fifty-five years at sea. With a crescent of 3,000 boats she sank all but nine of a fleet of ninety-nine Portuguese and Imperial vessels sent to trap her in the mouth of the Yangtse.

Lai Choi San's photographs show a slim short woman in her early forties, jet black hair held by jade pins in a knot at her neck, dressed in black. The overall impression is of a maiden aunt or a small-town librarian. She was always attended by two older women who chattered with her about domestic matters and were continually at work, even during battle, on intricate embroidery samplers. She communicated her orders to the crew and her fleet only through the ship's captain. Her word was absolute law. Her husband, Lilius learned, had gone to his ancestors 'after a short and lively dispute over a trivial domestic matter'.

Over the next two days Lilius saw a great deal of the routine drudgery of pirate work. Lai Choi San ran a racket providing protection for the Macao fishing fleets. She collected tribute from each vessel they encountered. On the first day they attacked a rival pirate junk and took two prisoners. There was talk of shooting them. Lilius, always enthusiastic for local colour, begged Lai Choi San for permission to watch. In the end, much to his disappointment, she kept the men for ransom.

Lilius wanted to see at first hand the pirate base at Bias Bay – to be the first European to enter Fan Lo Kong without a gun-boat. Lai Choi passed him on to one of her captains who had an uncle at Bias Bay. They moored off the town and

Lilius was put in a boat with a guard of five armed pirates. He asked the captain why he was remaining behind. The captain mumbled something which Lilius could not understand.

The first impression of Fan Lo Kong was of utter drabness. It seemed like any dull Chinese fishing village. As they passed through the dirt streets, he began to sense hostility among the groups of sullen faces gathering on the doorsteps. Men began to murmur and point at the white man and his camera-case. To them all foreigners were British, and feeling against the British was strong. Legend had turned the 1927 raid into a massacre. Even those who had witnessed the attack now claimed that 1,000 men, women and children had been slaughtered as the blood-crazed Royal Navy bombarded and looted the coast.

Lilius had heard through an informant in Hong Kong that there was a 'House of Torture' in the main square. Here, prisoners were kept while their ransom was negotiated and those whose families refused the price were tortured and killed. As a tourist, his tastes were predictable. He wanted to see the house. If possible he wanted photographs of prisoners and instruments of torture.

The guards were becoming increasingly uneasy. A crowd had gathered at their backs. Lilius photographed the outside of the 'House of Torture', but when he made to go in, the crowd started to throw stones. One of the guards was hit on the head. He raised his rifle and aimed into the villagers. The gun misfired and the mob turned and ran while the guards hustled Lilius, complaining loudly at the missed opportunity, to the boat.

Back on board, Lilius sought out the captain.

'Well, Captain,' he asked, 'aren't you going to visit your uncle in Fan Lo Kong?'

The captain laughed. 'No,' he said. 'No, I no think my uncle likee me. I think he shootee me if he see me again. No, my uncle no likee me at all.'

Back in Hong Kong Lilius returned to his frustrating round of official evasions and secret but useless rendezvous in seedy night-spots. He had caught a glimpse, but not reached anywhere near the heart of the piracy business. He knew, from snatches of rumour, that Hong Kong itself was the main controlling point of piracy in the South China Seas, but the world seemed closed to him. He continued to visit the laughing man with the missing ear. Eventually his persistence brought results. The jade-trader had the names of certain pirates held in Hong Kong Gaol.

Lilius tried to get official permission to visit the prison, but his requests were refused. He was becoming a nuisance. The Hong Kong authorities liked to deal with the piracy problem in their own way. They had no use for publicity, particularly from a bumptious American with a craving for first-hand experience of blood. To add to his problems he could not reveal the names of those he wanted to interview. Piracy was a capital crime. The men were being held for other offences. If he asked to see individuals, they would be executed.

The bumptious American took matters into his own hands. He is a little coy on exactly how, but he managed to have himself sentenced to two months in Hong Kong Gaol.

Conditions in the prison were abominable. Cockroaches three inches long swarmed over the inmates, sucking the saliva from the corners of their mouths as they slept. At night he was wakened by screams of torture and the sickening swish of whips on flesh, the screams growing fainter and fainter with each blow. In the yard he watched as a special category of prisoner was forced, for hour after hour, to walk in a narrow circle, lifting a heavy iron cannon-ball to their waists at every third step, turning madder and madder as their sentences wore on. Every morning on his way to exercise he crossed the gallows bridge outside his cell door. Five times he heard, in the hour before dawn, the muffled thud as a prisoner was dropped through the trap and the rope tightened around his neck.

Eventually Lilius too, even with his abnormal appetite for human suffering, turned a little mad. Segregation inside the prison was strict. He had little opportunity to speak to the Chinese prisoners. He was making no progress in his search for piracy contacts. He had regular contact with only one Chinese – a man convicted of highway robbery who made a daily round of the prison corridors to empty the spittoons from each cell into a huge wheeled bath.

The prison food was disgusting. Lilius caught dysentery and finished his sentence in the sanatorium. In the next bed was a feeble-minded Scotsman who claimed to be a sleepwalker. One day, so he said, he had woken up on the top deck of a bus. Another time he had resurfaced in a restaurant being served a meal. His present predicament arose from waking up in a jewellery shop with his hands full of watches.

Lilius got nothing from his time in gaol, apart from bedsores, a bad stomach and uneasy dreams. Once released he went once more in search of 'The Mountain Of Wealth'. He picked up an interpreter named Weng in Hong Kong and travelled back to Macao. In a *fan-tan* house he came across one of Lai Choi's lieutenants who agreed, for a fee, to take him north where Lai Choi was engaged in 'some business'.

A day out of Macao, however, the lieutenant's junk grounded on a sandbank in the bay of an uninhabited island. The stranded ship was joined by two other pirate junks. The captains came aboard and the atmosphere changed. Lilius and Weng were put ashore and locked in an abandoned temple. The pirates had decided that he was more valuable as a prisoner than as a paying guest. As a white man he would fetch a worthwhile ransom.

They were kept in the temple for three days. However, their kidnappers were too slow. Another group of pirates arrived and laid claim to Lilius. They overpowered his kidnappers, lined them up against the wall of the temple and shot them. Lilius got his execution photograph. He managed to persuade the new arrivals that he had friends in high places and they took him back to Macao.

He went back to hanging around in bars. In the lounge of Macao's Riviera Hotel, listening to the conversation of a group of Chinese customs officers, he heard for the first time the strange tale of the Dog-Man of the South China Sea. At the time he barely registered the story. It seemed too far away from reality.

In 1898, in the village of Chung King, far up the Yangtze River, lived a merchant called Ko Leong Tai. Like all prudent travellers, Ko had laid aside money to settle any future ransom demand. When he was taken by pirates on the Yangtze, he sent a letter to his brother back in Chung King, asking him to forward funds for his release.

For some time there was no response and then an answer

arrived, offering the pirates a small monthly sum to keep Ko shut up for life. The brother had announced Ko's death, appropriated his property and married his wife.

Ko was locked in a bamboo cage which was just large enough for him to squat. The roof and floor were rigid, but the walls of the cage were made from loosely woven bamboo leaves. The pirates piled boulders on the roof so that, once inside, Ko had to support the weight on his shoulders.

Ko stayed in his cage for fourteen years, through the final throes of the Manchu dynasty. In the anarchy of 1912, the pirate band broke up and Ko was released. By that time he was so deformed that he could only walk on all fours like a dog.

Ko's brother had now moved to Macao and joined the syndicate that held the colony's gambling monopoly. From the moment he heard of Ko's release the brother never left home without an armed guard. According to the rumour of the South China Seas, Ko had joined another pirate group. In the years since his release he had been gradually moving down the coast in search of his treacherous sibling.

Lilius was making no progress in Macao. His editor was becoming restless. He decided to try the Chinese mainland. On board ship for Canton he met an old acquaintance.

In the autumn of 1927 Lilius had been covering the campaign by Marshal Sun Ch'nan Fang against the Bolsheviks on China's northern border. Among the Marshal's army were a number of White Russians. On an armoured train heading towards the front he had come across a White Russian captain. Since their meeting, the captain's fortunes had turned for the worse. Following the defeat of the North Chinese army he had fled with other White Russians to Mukden in Manchuria, then to Harbin and finally jumped ship in Hong Kong. He was now a guard on the Hong Kong to Canton ferry.

The captain told Lilius that Wong Kiu, the chief of the West River pirates, was recruiting White Russians as bodyguards. He had fought with Russians during the Sino-Japanese War and he trusted and respected them. He wanted a group of men who owed allegiance only to him.

Through his parents Lilius was fluent in Russian. Impersonating a refugee ex-combatant, he met a representative of the pirate chief on a flower-boat on the Canton River. A flower-boat was a floating brothel used by junk-men, pirates and foolish tourists. While girls barely in their teens sang in a droning monotone on deck to attract custom, Lilius made his proposal. His offer was accepted. In exchange for his services as strong-arm man, he was to receive a daily ration of rice, a few dollars when business was good and clothing off the back of any six-foot captives. Lilius had finally made it. He was a pirate.

Wong Kiu was based in the village of Fu San two days sail up the Canton River. He lived the life of a feudal baron. In the village his word was law. He was the local hero. He had two loves in his life. He smoked opium incessantly and he kept pigs – not ordinary pigs in a sty, but huge black glossy pigs in his living-room.

The new business relationship was uneasy from the start. Wong Kiu was an ugly badly-scarred man of middle age with piercing eyes. The eyes measured Lilius and his story and found both wanting. Wong Kiu, like many Chinese, had nothing but contempt for Europeans. He suspected Lilius of being a British spy, but was unsure of how to treat him. It might be useful to send him back with intimidating stories of

Wong Kiu's power and influence. It might be useful to keep him. It might save trouble to kill him. For a week, Lilius and Weng were left to hang about Fu San, every movement shadowed by armed guards, while their fate was decided.

On the trip up the river from Canton, Lilius had befriended a Chinese 'song-girl'. He refers to her only as 'my little Chinese girl'. She had been sold by her parents to Wong Kiu's pirates in settlement for a gambling debt. She was used to 'keep company' with important hostages while they waited for ransom payments. In his memoirs Lilius is rather vague about his relationship with the girl and rather romantic about her role among the pirate crew. However, there is no reason to believe that their relationship was in any way innocent.

Lilius's position at Fu San became more and more uncomfortable. He decided to escape. Along with Weng and the girl he slipped out of his hut at night and stole a sampan. At dawn in the open river they hailed a junk and asked for passage. They were taken below deck and led into a windowless cabin dimly lit by sunlight through the ill-fitting planks of the ship's beams. As his eyes became accustomed to the light, Lilius saw Weng squatting on the floor. 'Before him a man crouched on a chair, knees bent up under his chin, long monkey arms clasping his legs.'

They were in the cabin of the dog-man.

The man's body was appallingly thin. For five minutes he sat silent staring at them with eyes that held a terrible sadness. Then he spoke to Weng. His voice was the most unpleasant sound Lilius had ever heard. It was not human. 'It was like a whisper mingled with a crow's cawing.'

The dog-man agreed to give the castaways passage, but he wanted something in return. Through Weng he asked Lilius if he would ever be prepared to kill a man. Lilius said he would only do such a thing in self-defence. In that case, said the dog-man, how much would he charge to kill a man in self-defence? Would he be prepared to kill a man in Macao in self-defence?

They moored that night among a fleet of pirate junks at the mouth of a river. In the still darkness each boat was lit by flaming torches. The sound of strange unchanging melodies from single-string guitars came over the water from neighbouring decks, drowned at intervals by the explosion of fire-crackers. Swarms of hundreds of bats flew low between the masts in search of insects that hung in clouds above the yellow water of the estuary. Beside Lilius the song-girl smoked a seamless chain of cigarettes, blowing the smoke across his face to ward off the mosquitoes.

Over the next two days, Lilius moved from junk to junk, peddling his services as a White Russian acting as the agent for 100 stranded comrades looking for work. He roused the interest of another Wong – Wong To Ping – pirate chief and an enemy of Wong Kiu. Lilius's previous employer had killed two of Wong To Ping's sons. They left the girl with a trader who promised to hand her on to respectable friends in Hong Kong. She passed out of his life.

Wong To Ping took them to his village where Lilius's Russian was tested by a veteran of the northern campaign. The veteran's own Russian was so execrable that he had to bribe Lilius to pretend to understand it. From there they sailed out into the open sea, to Wong To's prison island where he held 200 of Wong Kiu's men guarded by two junks perpetually circling the rocky shore.

Wong To Ping needed a man to carry profits to his sponsors

in Macao. Lilius was ideal for the job. No one would suspect that a European was acting as bag-man for a Chinese pirate. However, before Lilius could be trusted, he had to be bound inextricably to the pirate cause.

Much like the Mafia in Sicily, Chinese crime traditionally has been, and still remains, closely linked to a network of secret societies. As with the Mafia, the origins of these societies are often political, and even benevolent, rather than criminal. In hard times, it pays to stick together.

To win the trust of Wong To Ping, Lilius had to join Wong To's society, the 'Hall of the Righteous Heroes'. For a day before the initiation ceremony he was forbidden food and drink. When the cock crowed at dawn, a gong sounded. Five men entered his room each holding a bunch of white feathers. They handed him the feathers. They led him to the gate of a hut he had never before entered. He gave a feather to the man at the gate and was ushered inside with his five companions. They removed their coats and each held a dagger over a bowl of smoking incense while Lilius swore to 'obey the rules of the benevolent society whose members sat in the Hall of the Righteous Heroes'. He was warned that to break the rule of the Hall was death. To follow the rule of the Hall was also death, but an honourable death. The gong sounded once more.

The five Chinese made cuts in their left shoulders with their daggers. With the feathers, they wiped away the blood from their wounds and placed the feathers in the incense-burner. Lilius did the same. There were two bowls on a table in the centre of the room, filled with some unidentifiable liquid. Lilius was ordered to carry the bowl out to the courtyard where he was surrounded by a circle of members of the society. He was then bombarded with questions. To each question, none of which he understood, he answered 'Hon!'

His five 'guardians' now dipped a bunch of feathers in the liquid from the bowls, told Lilius to open his mouth, and tickled his throat with the feathers. He was violently sick. Wong To Ping told him to drink the liquid in the two bowls. The liquid was thick and dark, sticky, salty and sickening. It tasted like bad blood.

As the mixture settled, congealing in his stomach, a yellow-robed priest emerged from the circle carrying a bucket covered with a cloth. Lilius was given back his dagger and told to pull back the cloth. Inside were two roosters. They crowed into his face in fright. He was instructed to bend back their heads and cut their throats while Wong To caught their blood in the emptied bowls. As the blood gurgled out Lilius was overcome with nausea. 'I knew,' he wrote later, 'that if they requested me to drink this blood I would not be able to do it. The whole thing was becoming thoroughly disgusting.'

Fortunately he had only to cut up one of the roosters and give the heart to Wong To Ping. Wong To swallowed the heart, put a white feather into his mouth and pulled it out red with blood. Lilius blew the feather into the air. The priest picked it from the floor and burned it. The initiation was over. Lilius had entered the 'Hall of the Righteous Heroes'. Weng followed him, faithful to the last to his employer's thirst for a story.

As a righteous brother, Lilius was admitted to low-level society secrets. There were 140 members. The money they extorted from kidnapping was distributed among the poor. Some of the members drank the blood of executed prisoners and ate their hearts but Wong To himself rather disapproved of this practice. Lilius was given a block of wood on which was inscribed the seal of the society and the Chinese characters of his name within the organisation. His name was 'Li Lai Assi' which means 'Benevolent Scholar'. For an awkward moment when Wong To pronounced the name, Lilius feared that his true identity had been revealed, but the similarity of sounds was pure coincidence.

Lilius was given the money he was to carry, the address of a house in Macao, and half of a chit which would be matched by the man to whom he made the delivery. He was given an escort of four guards and in the late autumn heat they set off in a sampan across the pirate-infested waters for Macao.

At sunset on the first night they sighted a junk on the horizon. They took refuge in a hut on a deserted island. At dawn they saw the junk in the island bay. As they watched, four long war canoes slipped from the junk's side towards the shore. The four guards ran for the undergrowth and Weng and Lilius hid beneath the floor of the hut while the attackers riddled the walls with bullets.

The hole in which they sheltered also held a nest of fire-ants. As they itched and rolled they heard a fresh sound of shooting from further away. Wong To had not entirely trusted his new brother. He had sent twelve of his band to keep watch on his progress. Lilius and Weng emerged from hiding to see the attackers fleeing for their junk. As they ran they shot wildly back towards the hut. Lilius turned to see Weng fall to the ground.

'Are you shot, Weng?' asked Lilius.

'A little,' replied Weng.

The wound was in the chest. It took a day to sail to Macao. Lilius tried to tend to the wound, but his companion died before they reached the harbour. The pirates threw the body overboard.

Lilius, of course, survived. Others might die in pursuit of his stories, but not Lilius. He honoured Weng's memory in his own way. His account of life among the pirates is dedicated to the man who was shot 'a little'. The dedication says much about both men and not a little about the gap in understanding between East and West:

'Dedicated to the memory of plucky Weng. Only a Coolie, But a Faithful Friend Who Died In My Service.'

6.

East Meets West

It was a cold clear spring morning. In Manchuria, the province on China's north-eastern frontier, there are only a few brief days between the bitter cold of winter and the furnace heat of summer. The sun was bright on the waters of the estuary of the Liao River, the cold rising off the water, the surface dotted with ice-floes from the river's upper reaches.

The *Nanchang*, a British steamer of 2,480 tons, had anchored in the estuary on the night of 28 March 1933 to wait until morning to enter the port of Newchwang on the Gulf of Po-Lai. Newchwang was only nineteen miles to the east, but the water between was riddled with sand-bars and shifting shallows. The *Nanchang* needed a pilot and several hours of daylight.

At dawn on the 29th, Captain Robinson, commander of the *Nanchang*, turned down the offer to share a pilot with another vessel. He needed time to get up steam. As dawn turned into morning, no other pilot appeared. He and his six British officers and thirty-seven Chinese crewmen waited and gazed over the flat silted landscape towards the distant hills of the Liaotung Peninsula.

The horizon was dotted with fishing junks crossing the bar. It was a peaceful scene on a peaceful day. When two junks approached there was no hint of alarm. In 1933, Manchuria was not the safest place on earth, but attacks against foreign vessels were unknown this far north. Piracy was a plague in the South China Sea, but up here the problems were limited to the land.

Since the Chinese revolution of 1911, Japan had extended her economic influence over Manchuria. The province became, in all but name, a Japanese colony. Then, in 1928, the Chinese Nationalists under Chiang Kai-Shek set out to win back control over the old empire. The Japanese army, determined not to lose its new territory, invented a crisis in September 1931 and used the excuse to invade Manchuria and set up the 'independent' puppet state of Manchukuo under Japanese 'protection'. While the League of Nations dithered and denounced, the Japanese bombed the Chinese into submission. By March 1933 when the *Nanchang* rested at anchor in the Gulf of Po-Lai, the Japanese were in complete control of the government and the tattered remnants of the Nationalist army had retreated as bandits into the backwoods.

As the two junks made to pass close by the bows of the *Nanchang*, they altered course and pulled up against the ship's side. The hatches of both junks opened and men swarmed out from the holds onto the *Nanchang*'s deck.

The pirates were dressed in a variety of clothing – some in the padded blue cotton jackets of the north, but most in tattered remnants of uniform. They carried a startling variety of firearms, from antique flintlocks to modern Japanese-issue Mausers. They shot wildly across the deck. Two Chinese crewmen fell wounded.

The officers, recovering too late from the shock, were cornered below in the Second Engineer's cabin. The only crew-members to escape capture were Captain Robinson and Jeffrey, the Chief Engineer. Robinson made undetected for the radio-room, looking for a chance to send off a distress signal. Jeffrey hid in the engine-room.

The captive officers were herded onto the deck along with the rest of the crew. The pirates spoke no English. They suspected that there were other Europeans on board and tried to force the Chinese crew to reveal their hiding-place. The Chinese pretended ignorance and the pirates, scared that help might be on the way, looted the cabins of valuables, loaded their European captives into a narrow locker in one of the junks, and set sail for the mouth of the Liao River. The attack lasted twenty minutes. Its aftermath was to last six long months.

As soon as the pirates had left, Captain Robinson appeared on deck and steered off in pursuit. However, within minutes, the shallow-bottomed junks were over the sand-bar where the *Nanchang* could not follow. At midday, Robinson radioed news of the attack to the authorities in Newchwang and limped after his message into the port.

In the hold of the junk were four British officers: Johnson, the thirty-year-old Welsh Chief Mate; Hargrave, the twenty-five-year-old Second Mate; Blue, the twenty-eight-year-old Scots Second Engineer; and Pears, the Third Engineer. The space was four foot high, five foot long and six foot wide. The deck and the beams crawled with thousands of tiny black beetles. For the next twenty-four hours, unable to stand or lie down, with no protection against the bitter night cold, they shivered and wondered about their fate.

Robinson's message took five hours to reach Grant, the sole representative of Butterfield and Swires, the ship's owners, in Newchwang. He immediately contacted the Peking office and the British Embassy. A team gathered in Newchwang to handle the incident.

Newchwang was a place of faded glory. In the middle of the nineteenth century it had been no more than a gaggle of fishermen's huts at the mouth of the Liao River. With the opening of trade to Manchuria, the Europeans had arrived, and with them the baggage of European civilisation. The ubiquitous European Club was built to offer the comforts of home – cricket and football pitches and a badminton court. A grassless golf course was carved on the mud-flats outside the town. Now the clubhouse roof had fallen in, the pitches were pot-holed and the golf course was abandoned, a field of operations for bandits from the defeated Nationalist army.

The men sent to resolve the *Nanchang* piracy were a representative group of Empire-builders. Denzil Clarke, Vice-consul at Mukden, the Manchurian capital, was made acting Consul. In the Great War he had been the youngest battalion commander in the British Army. He spoke fluent Chinese and Japanese. The embassy representative was J.V. Davidson-Houston, the young Assistant Military Attache at the Peking Embassy. Representing Butterfield and Swires were Grant and Burton, the company's Manchuria man. The final member of the team was Bertie Hemingway, the laconic agent for the Asiatic Petroleum Company, loaned for the crisis for his knowledge of the region.

The negotiators had clear but contradictory instructions from the company and the British Government. They had to ensure that no risks were taken which threatened the safety of the hostages, but at the same time they must avoid agreeing to any ransom demands. If Europeans were seen as a source of income, no white man in Manchuria would be safe. Clarke and Davidson-Houston set off into the tangle of Manchurian Government armed with their equivocal mission.

The first problem was to discover where power lay in Newchwang. In theory, the Manchukuo Government was the highest authority, but early on it became clear that the Japanese ran things here as much as in the rest of Manchuria.

They first visited Lieutenant-General Wang Tien-Chung, the Commander of the Manchukuo garrison. Like many Chinese officials, the Lieutenant-General was a former bandit. Banditry, as an honourable profession, was an acceptable rung on the Chinese career ladder. Wang was a hamster-cheeked man in his early thirties with a Chaplin moustache and a disconcerting dribble of long straggling hairs falling from a mole on his left cheek. Wang's office was reached through a seemingly endless succession of doorways and courtyards. The magnificence of the entrance was an old Imperial Chinese device to reflect the importance of the official. In Wang's case, as he cheerfully admitted, the appearance was an illusion.

Wang's room had no doors. He was spied on continually. To protect himself, he spoke in code. As a Chinese he was only a 'Secondary Devil'. The Japanese were the 'Primary Devils'. Whenever he referred to the Japanese he made a sign with his right hand at waist height. Power was in the hands of 'small men'. The only suggestion he could give was that, since the pirates were obviously redundant officials of the Japanese-controlled Fishery Protection Bureau, they might be persuaded to give up their hostages by the offer of reinstatement at a generous salary.

General Pai, the Chinese Chief of Police, was equally

powerless. He regarded the whole affair as a huge joke far beyond his capacity to resolve. He shook his huge yellow marshmallow-shaped head and sent them on to the Japanese police.

Considering the eminence of the ranks of the Chinese, it was odd to find the garrison of the Japanese gendarmerie, feared for its brutality throughout Manchuria, in the hands of a sergeant-major. Sergeant-Major Saito began by making a detailed inspection of the military attache's uniform. He lingered over the grenade badges on Davidson-Houston's lapels, stroking their outline with appreciation. 'Very pretty,' said Saito, 'very gentle.' He spoke with the slightly sinister intonation of all Japanese officials, sucking in breath with a whistling sound before each phrase in the characteristic Confucian desire not to exhale over someone who might prove to be a social superior. Apart from his interest in lapels and inhalation, he offered no practical advice.

The consensus was that they would have to wait. While they waited, Wang Tien-Chung offered to provide a regiment of his troops to cover the Europeans from hole to hole on the Newchwang golf course.

Bertie Hemingway suggested that they set up some line of communication to the pirates. He arranged a meeting between Davidson-Houston and the only Englishman in Newchwang with contacts among the Chinese fisherman – a smallholder called Farmer. Farmer had settled in Manchuria fifty years before and had married a Chinese wife. The two men met in a cabaret bar owned by a French Armenian where three bored Russian prostitutes saw to the needs of what little European carriage trade now passed through Newchwang. Over a bottle of 'Queen George Whisky – Brewed at

Buckingham Palace under the personal supervision of His Majesty', Farmer agreed to find fishermen to pass a message to the pirates.

After raiding the *Nanchang*, the pirate junks had sailed into the maze of marshy inlets that made up the Liao Delta. For a day the four captives were left alone in the hold. On the morning of the 29th, two Chinese dropped down through the hatch, sat facing them and smiled. The most senior was wearing Johnson's overcoat and watch. He rubbed his fingers to indicate money and then, still grinning, pointed a revolver at the head of each captive in turn to show what would happen if no money appeared. Then, with a shriek of laughter, he fell backwards in a charade of death. Still laughing, the two pirates hauled themselves back onto the deck.

At mid-morning on 30 March they were let out of the hold for the first time to walk on the deck and meet their captors. The junks were beached by the receded tide on an inlet amidst a huge expanse of mud-flats littered with chunks of ice. The pirates were led by Hsin-Chun, a deserter from the Manchukuo army, still dressed in the tatters of his uniform. Most of the crew were Chinese peasants, forced off their lands by the turmoil of war.

The captured officers were accustomed only to the kow-towing townsmen of the Trading Ports with their superficial subservience and pidgin English. These Chinese not only spoke no language they could understand, but they also had no respect for Europeans. In fact they had very little respect for anything. After years of unrewarded toil in the fields they were enjoying the freedom of piracy. Their main sport was to shoot indiscriminately across the deck. In the first week two were wounded by their own colleagues. They joined two others who had been shot during the assault on the *Nanchang* – one through both hands and one through both feet.

To the pirates, the officers were ridiculous figures from another planet. The pirates prodded them and laughed at their long noses, hairy faces and deep-set eyes. As a reward for giving so much entertainment, the officers were given dog-skin blankets to keep away the night chill.

During the whole time of their captivity, they were rarely treated particularly badly. They lived more or less the same life as their captors. The experience was abysmal not because of cruelty, but because the life of the ordinary Chinese was so crushingly hard – sleeping on bare boards in the cold and the heat, infested with lice and cockroaches, eating a bowl of plain rice and drinking a cup of hot water twice a day.

On 31 March they were allowed out again to gaze across the mud and have their noses pulled. When they were shut up at night, they found that the hatch was unlocked and the deck was deserted.

They had noticed that the mud flats seemed to melt into firmer ground on the horizon. They lowered themselves over the side of the junk and set off in the starless night in what they hoped was the direction of land. Their legs sunk up to their thighs in the freezing slime. Quickly they lost all sense of direction. The night was pitch black, the sky overcast, with no moon or stars. After two or three hours, they had seen no sign of land. Their footsteps began to fill with water. They realised that the tide was coming in. It looked as though they would end there, drowned in a muddy delta eight thousand miles from home because a group of amateur pirates had assumed that not even a white man would be stupid enough to escape across tidal mud in total darkness.

The four men tried to retrace their steps, but the incoming water filled the tracks and smoothed the mud. They blundered on, their legs numb with cold. After another hour, with the water up to their waists, they made out the deeper black of the hull of their junk in the first light of dawn. They were too exhausted and too bewildered to be grateful for deliverance. They levered themselves up onto the deck and slunk back to shiver the remainder of the night in their freezing cupboard.

Their captors had slept through the escape and the return, but in the morning they saw the mud-caked clothes. For an hour the pirate leader shouted at them in Chinese, making ominous gestures with his revolver. From then on they were guarded closely and their rice ration was replaced by *ping tzu*, a particularly filthy sort of flapjack made from millet dough.

The pirates were as keen as Davidson-Houston to establish contact with the other side. They ordered the officers to choose one representative as a messenger. The Englishmen played poker with cards made from empty cigarette packets to select the messenger. Johnson was by now keeping a diary on scraps of paper collected from their pockets. He described the game as 'the most nerve-wracking we had ever played'. Blue won. When they informed the pirates, they were told that Pears had been selected instead. When captured he had been dressed in overalls and the pirates assumed he was the least important.

On the night after the attempted escape, Pears was led across the marsh, given a letter and set on the railway line to Newchwang. He had lost his shoes in the escape attempt and in the morning he arrived with bleeding feet at Newchwang Station.

The letter that Pears delivered to the British consul showed a surprising level of sophistication for a group of backwoods bandits. In return for the release of the hostages, they demanded enough arms to equip a small army. They wanted 100 light machine-guns, 3,000 Japanese rifles, 120 German rifles and 20 heavy trench-mortars along with one million Chinese dollars, the equivalent of £50,000. Alternatively, they would be happy if the League of Nations threw the Japanese out of Manchuria. If neither was forthcoming, and 'if Japan sends troops to attack us and shots are fired, we shall shoot your three foreigners without any doubt whatever.' The letter was signed by Hsin-Chun, leader of the band, and by Wild Wolf (Vice-Chief), Wild Cat (Company Commander), and Tiger The Second, Great Might and Heavenly Dragon (Detachment Commanders).

The first ten days of April passed in exchange of letters through the messengers recruited by Farmer. The pirates were offered jobs at the Fishery Protection Bureau, but they stuck to their wider political demands; the captives were sent delousing powder, preserved sausages, adventure novels and cigarettes; the pirates passed on the novels, sniffed the delousing powder and smoked the cigarettes. On board the junk, life took on a routine. The ships retreated each day further into the delta, hiding from the Japanese spotter-planes in jungles of fifteen-foot high reeds. The prisoners sat on deck and watched the pirates crack lice and pop them into each others mouths. The Chinese were adorned in a bizarre collection of looted clothes. One wore Johnson's dress suit and another carried Johnson's empty suitcase wherever he went. Blue entertained the crew by spitting out his false teeth until reminded of an earlier kidnapping where pirates had confiscated a captain's false eye because they believed it watched them while he slept.

On 6 April, conditions in the hold deteriorated. They were joined by the man who had been shot in both feet. His wounds had begun to fester and the smell was overwhelming. By now the dog-skin blankets were a moving mass of lice.

On 11 April, the boredom was broken. Spring had come in earnest. The evening was warm and they were on deck slapping the fat marshland mosquitoes. Three strange junks were sighted approaching around a bend in the creek. The captives were pushed into the hold. For ten minutes they heard the confused sound of gunfire. The hatch opened and two strangers dropped down into the hold to inspect them. The pirates had been pirated. Blue, Hargrave and Johnson had changed hands.

Hsin-Chun had been killed and his men had fled into the marshes. Their new owners were part of a fleet of ten junks. They were less genial than the previous band. They carved a square hole to the adjoining hold and a particularly unpleasant, dead-eyed opium-addict called Yung-Lu watched them through the hole day and night, belching and farting and occasionally spitting at them through the hole. The captain of their junk was a youngish man with part of his right ear missing and a scar across his mouth. To emphasise his importance he appropriated Johnson's dress suit. Every evening, when the junks shifted position, he jumped down into the hold and removed the suit. With great care he put on Blue's engineer's cap and a camel-hair dressing-gown with fancy cording on the cuffs which Pears had left behind. Then he jumped back on deck to issue his orders.

The little fleet moved further into the tangle of reeds. The weather grew hotter. The lice, the cockroaches and the mosquitoes multiplied. The hostages made some progress with the pirate crew. They sang Edwardian music hall songs and the Chinese accompanied them, howling like dogs. 'A Long Way To Tipperary' was the crew's favourite. They insisted on repeating it again and again long into the night. They called it 'Toots A Long Way'.

The captives brightened the hold by plastering the beams with pictures of the girl on the packet of 'Knit Girl' cigarettes. The cigarettes were vile, but the girl was beautiful. In an old copy of the *Strand* magazine, the pirates found their own pin-up – a photograph of a rhinoceros. They cut it out and spent hours gazing at it through fists bunched like binoculars.

Meanwhile, the pirates dropped the idealistic side of the ransom demands and offered to settle for four million Chinese dollars, eighty gold rings and 200 pairs of shoes.

In response to the new demands, Denzil Clarke arranged a meeting of all the interested parties in Newchwang. The ransom was out of the question. Clarke went round the table asking for suggestions. Only General Pai, the moon-faced Chinese Commissioner of Police, had anything new to offer. He felt that the chief problem was that the Liao Delta was too full of junks. It was impossible to distinguish which one held the prisoners. His solution was to send the pirates a Japanese flag to hoist on their mast. It would then be possible for the Japanese air force to bomb all the other junks in the delta 'and thus isolate that on which the Englishmen are living'. There was a long silence. Pai made a deprecatory gesture. 'That is just my humble advice,' he concluded.

The trouble with Pai was that it was impossible to tell from his marshmallow face whether he was joking or not.

When this suggestion failed to rouse enthusiasm, he made another. He thought that they could impregnate the next gift of cigarettes with poison gas. 'But would not the Englishmen themselves be poisoned by the gas?' asked Clarke. 'Regrettably there would be some danger,' conceded Pai, 'this is just my despicable suggestion.'

The only positive thing to come from the meeting was the news that the Japanese were sending a more senior officer, Captain Obata, to take charge of the hostage crisis. This raised hope of action, but at the same time suggested that the Japanese were planning a direct military attack which would mean death for Blue, Hargrave and Johnson. By the unusual etiquette of Japanese honour, Obata was not given specific orders to obtain the release of the hostages since failure to do so would mean he would have to commit suicide.

While they sent delaying messages, unpoisoned cigarettes, Butterfield and Swires boiled sweets, opium and morphine to the pirates, the negotiators had to amuse themselves as best they could in Newchwang. A British Navy sloop, the *Cornflower* had arrived in the harbour. The crew challenged the pupils at the Newchwang school to a football match. The Chinese wore tennis eye-shades, padded trousers and long cotton underpants. They put up a good defence considering they had never before played football. They lost 4–1.

On a more solemn note, the Japanese garrison held a memorial service for the dead of the Manchurian Campaign. Not satisfied with this, they held another for the dead horses, dogs and pigeons which had served in the Imperial Army. And so May slipped away.

Life improved slightly for the captives. They were moved to bigger quarters aboard the pirate flagship. Here they could all lie down at once. However, since the mast came through a hole in the roof, the cabin became a lake in the rain. Their bodies began to moulder.

The food, the vermin, the damp and the constant ogling of the guards wore them down. It is a tribute to the spartanness of a British public school upbringing that they stayed alive. Even so, they suffered from constant fever. The pirates, not wanting to lose their investments, showed a certain solicitude for their health. Their heads were shaved with broken glass to keep down the lice and they were offered opium to reduce aches and pains.

The Chinese used more direct treatment for their own ailments. When one complained of a sore throat, he was stripped naked and laid face-down on the deck. For fifteen minutes his companions lifted him again and again into the air by the flesh of his shoulders and dropped him onto the wooden boards. They then kneaded the bruises until his back was a mess of blood.

The worst part of the captivity was boredom. What excitement there was, was unwelcome. On 20 May, Li Wen Chi, the pirate leader, a sinister figure with a face like a length of hardwood, dressed in a long black robe, gave them a lesson in what to expect if the ransom was refused. They were led to a clearing on the shore and made to watch as a peasant, suspected of spying for the Japanese, was laid out, face down, in a crucifix position, his hands and feet held by ropes. Chi whipped the man until he lost consciousness, then revived him to beat him again. The skin on his back was flayed to pieces. He was then dragged from the clearing. There was silence and then a single shot.

The pirates became tired of the delays from Newchwang.

They started to issue bloodier and bloodier threats. At the end of June, 500 Japanese troops arrived at the port and it became clear that Captain Obata was preparing to force the issue. The British, both on the ship and in the port began to wonder how the farce would end.

On 5 July the pirate fleet was attacked by Japanese bombers. Blue, Hargrave and Johnson were thrown overboard to swim for the shore. They tried to escape, but the pirates had kept their shoes. They were recaptured, but not before Blue and Hargrave had cut their feet to ribbons running across fields of reed-stubble.

The pirates now decided that the water was too dangerous. On 6 July, they set out on what was to be a nightmare two month trek through the swamps and sweltering heat of the Manchurian hinterland. The walk had no purpose. They headed first for the north.

Throughout July, they walked by night and rested by day. On the third day it began to rain. The Chinese refused to move in the wet. For five days it rained. They sheltered in a hollow – the three Britons and 100 Chinese, building pathetic reed shelters which were swept away in the torrent. Afraid of pursuit they built no fires. When the rain eased, the mosquitoes came in thick clouds and with them came tiny land-crabs which nipped their legs, arms and faces. When the rain stopped they set off again. Hargrave's feet, cut in the reed stubble, swelled and began to ooze pus. The Chinese treated the sores with toothpaste. He had to continue on mule-back.

By 19 July, Hargrave was feverish and could go no further. They holed up in a peasant village. While Hargrave groaned in a quinine stupor, the pirates brought a group of giggling

117

girls into the prisoners' hut. They suggested that the Englishmen might like to have sex with the girls for everyone's amusement. When the officers refused, the pirates were offended. The Englishmen tried to explain that public sexual intercourse was not a usual practice in the United Kingdom. 'In England,' commented one pirate rather sniffily, 'they seem very particular.'

Each village was built on the same model – a mud wall around eight or nine huts. The huts were made from mud and plastered with dry cow-dung with wooden window-frames and windows of rice-paper. Beneath the windows were swill-tubs for pigs. The troughs bred flies which swarmed thick in the huts, cramming into peoples' mouths when they slept. There was a sophisticated form of central heating. A flue-pipe led from the mud-grate at one end of the hut beneath the single large bed. In midsummer the heat inside was unbearable. Outside in the spaces between the huts was a constant reminder of the fragility of life. On his sixtieth birthday each Chinese man was given a coffin by his children. The old men occupied their days lovingly dusting and polishing their future resting-places.

In every village the pirates were welcomed and fed. However, at the end of July they came to a farm where the family refused them shelter. The pirates killed everyone except for the young son who was tied to a tree and tortured until he revealed where the family had hidden their rice store.

At the beginning of August the party turned back south and began to travel by day, feeling they were in less danger of pursuit. On the 9th they came to a village where 300 people had gathered to watch the foreigners have their hair cut. When they refused to allow their heads to be shaved, the barbers plucked the hairs from their eyebrows, ears and nostrils. The journey was becoming increasingly bizarre. Here they came across a group of bandits leading twelve old men who they had captured for ransom. Hours behind the old men trailed their wives, hobbling painfully on tiny bound feet over the rutted path.

By the end of August they were back within thirty miles of the Bay of Pan Shan where they had originally been captured. Blue's throat was so inflamed that he could not swallow and it was feared that he would die. This did not worry the pirates too much. They had high hopes that the ransom would soon be paid. They slaughtered a pig, tossed the intestines to the hostages, and settled down to wait. Nothing happened. No one arrived with the ransom. By now patience was wearing very thin. Autumn was approaching and with it the harvest and the dying of the reeds. They would no longer have cover for their movements. The Chief muttered darkly about thrashing the three with bamboo canes and taking them back up north to end life as slave labour in the interior.

At the start of September the various factions in Newchwang finally reached a compromise. Butterfield and Swires, still insisting that they were not prepared to pay ransom, gave Captain Obata 20,000 Chinese dollars 'incidental expenses' and he set off with a company of soldiers to Pan Shan Bay.

From 2 to 7 September the hostages festered in a village a few miles from the sea. Again they were offered the local women. 'When we refused,' Johnson wrote, 'they suggested we should sleep with the men. They say that they do this very well in China.' By now both hostages and captors were bored with each other. Both sides had wasted six months of their lives wandering around the reeds. In return the Chinese had learned the chorus to 'Will Ye Stop Yer Tickling, Jock . . .'

On the morning of the 7th, a fat Korean in a western suit arrived at the village, sitting uneasily on the back of an ill-tempered horse. His suit was mud-splattered and torn. It had been his first attempt at riding and had not been successful. The Korean was a go-between from Captain Obata. He had come to check that the officers had not been swapped for White Russians who were common as beetles in the ragged debris of the Chinese Empire in the thirties. He satisfied himself that Blue, Hargrave and Johnson were in fact Blue, Hargrave and Johnson and departed, leaving them a tin of cigarettes. The pirates stole the cigarettes.

The next day, Captain Obata arrived. He handed over the $20,000. They had to wait through the day while each man was given his share.

The farewell, when it finally came, towards evening, was a touching affair. The pirates insisted on shaking hands with each of the hostages. The final words as they were escorted from the village were 'please join us next year, and together we will kidnap others.'

7.

The Fat Man
In The Radio Room

George White Rogers was a fat man. Had he been thin, he might have had no urge to kill 125 fellow human beings off the coast of New Jersey. Life and death can often hinge on the smallest thing.

Had it not been for Rogers' twisted dreams, the *Morro Castle* would have sunk into history as a footnote to the years of Prohibition. The liner would have ended its days rusting in some New England dockyard or sold for scrap beached on a Caribbean coast. As it was, the ship died at the peak of her tawdry splendour.

In 1920, Congress passed the Volstead Act, making manufacture, sale and consumption of alcohol illegal within the borders of the United States. Private enterprise adapted to satisfy the American thirst. Most effort went into importation – the bootleggers developed a lucrative trade across the Canadian border or up from Mexico and the Bahamas. The cruise lines offered another option. Instead of bringing the booze to the customers, they carried the customers to the booze. There was no Volstead outside territorial waters.

The Ward Line operated liners between New York and Havana, Cuba. Fun-seekers could drink on board, buy Cuban rum at $5 a gallon and drink all the way home. It was a successful route. The company expanded. In August 1930 it launched the *Morro Castle* to siphon more profit from the 'floating gin palace' trade.

The *Morro Castle* was the fastest turbo-electric vessel in the world. On her maiden voyage she cut twelve hours from the record time between New York and Havana. Over the next three years she shuttled 174 times over the same route – three days out, a day in Havana, three days back and seven hours to change the sheets and stock the kitchen. She was a floating, money-minting, alcohol-hazed shuttle-cock, a tribute to American ingenuity in a time of crisis.

In 1933, Prohibition was repealed. This had no effect on the *Morro Castle*'s account-sheet. She still retained the glamour of illicit pleasure without risk. Those who had an income despite the Depression still wanted a good time. Three-quarters of the passengers were single. Women usually outnumbered men by two to one. The fare was affordable for the new breed of white-collar American with a steady job and a week's holiday. A cruise to Havana offered one long party on the waves.

For the crew of the *Morro Castle* the dream was a little sour. The Depression had affected the waterfront badly. For the ordinary sailor, work was scarce. The owners exploited the glut of labour. While a deluxe cabin cost $160 for the return trip, deck-hands earned $30 a month. For the crew, the food and accommodation were filthy. They had to work double shifts. The officers used the seven-hour turnaround in New York for a quick glimpse of their wives and children. The crew were forbidden to leave the ship. They were fully occupied restocking the bar and the saloon. If they went

Lai Choi San, 'The Mountain of Wealth', the woman who introduced Lilius to piracy on the South China Seas. (British Library)

Aleko Lilius, obsessive American journalist, flanked by his rescuers after his imprisonment on Temple Island. (British Library)

Hargrave, Blue and Johnson, the three hostages from the *Nanchang*, pose after their release. (British Library)

George Rogers (centre left), 'the fat man in the radio room', next to William Warms (centre right) at the *Morro Castle* enquiry. (From *The Strange Fate Of The Morro Castle* by Gordon Thomas and Max Morgan-Witts. HarperCollins Publishers Ltd)

The burnt-out wreck of the *Morro Castle* cast up on the beach at Asbury Park, New Jersey. (See acknowledgement for previous photograph)

Henrique Galvao, unlikely pirate of the Portuguese liner *Santa Maria*. (Hulton Deutsch)

Mario Maia, Captain of the *Santa Maria*. (Hulton Deutsch)

A US naval patrol aircraft shadows the *Santa Maria* as she approaches the Brazilian coast. (Hulton Deutsch)

Dr Antonio Salazar, Dictator of Portugal, mobbed by fans as he welcomes the *Santa Maria* back to Lisbon after Galvao's escapade. (Hulton Deutsch)

ashore, they lost their job. In America in 1934, losing your job meant the bread-line.

The poor conditions meant that only those who were desperate shipped on the *Morro Castle*. Some were forced to it by hard times and others because they were unemployable on a decent ship. On her second to last voyage, in August 1934, forty deck-hands and twelve stewards were sacked for drunkenness, theft or assault. These were typical numbers. There were always bums on the quay ready to take their place. The ship never left New York undermanned.

The officers were of a different class. The Captain, First Mate and Chief Engineer were dedicated professionals. They were company men, wholly committed to the Ward Line. Captain Robert Wilmot was fifty-two years old. In thirty-two years at sea he had not made a single reported error. Command of the *Morro Castle* was the peak of his professional ambition. He was a large, solid, teak-faced man with slit shaded humourless eyes.

The *Morro Castle* set out on her final voyage on the afternoon of Saturday 1 September 1934. Every cabin was full. Aboard were 230 officers and crew and 318 passengers, including all 102 members of the Concordia Singing Society of East New York.

The journey out followed its normal pattern. The only unusual thing was the strange behaviour of Captain Wilmot. Normally, Wilmot spent as much time as he could spare entertaining the First Class passengers. He had a story from every ocean and he adored an attentive audience at the Captain's Table. On this voyage, though, he kept to his cabin, refusing food and drinking only bottled water. He communicated with the bridge by telephone and would see only the First Mate and the Chief Radio Officer.

Wilmot was afraid. He suspected that someone was trying to kill him. Something had gone wrong with the dream of the *Morro Castle*. In July he had almost died from food poisoning. He had been the only person affected. Then, on 27 August, there had been a fire in the hold. The source of the fire was never discovered, but Wilmot believed that it had been caused by a bomb.

A fire in the hold is a nightmare for any ship. The *Morro Castle*, on the face of it, was better prepared than most. The fire had been detected immediately by a sophisticated system of smoke-detectors. Automatic extinguishers had put out the flames with pressurised jets of carbon dioxide. However, Captain Wilmot knew just how dangerous a fire could be in the hold of this particular vessel. The *Morro Castle*, unknown to its passengers and most of its crew, was a floating arsenal.

The United States regarded Cuba as within its sphere of influence. For $2,000 a year it rented two military bases on the island to guard the approaches to the Gulf of Mexico and protect the huge US commercial interests on the island. However, Cuba's stability was under threat.

As early as 1919, Communist insurgents had landed on Cuba from Haiti. Since then they had carried on a sporadic guerrilla campaign against a succession of US-backed dictators. In 1933 the United States had tried to ease popular discontent by supporting the overthrow of the brutal General Gerardo Machado. However, his replacement, Fulgencio Batista, was equally oppressive. Human rights were a secondary consideration to the State Department. The important thing was to keep out the Communists. Open arms sales to a dictatorship were unpopular in the United States, so the Government had to use less orthodox means to supply Batista. On each of its voyages, the *Morro Castle* carried in its hold a number of crates labelled 'Sporting Goods'. Inside these crates, sometimes as many as a hundred on an individual trip, were powder, shells and ammunition for the Cuban Government.

Wilmot suspected that the insurgents had found out about the 'Sporting Goods'. They had poisoned his food and bombed his ship's hold. He was well aware of the nature of his cargo. He believed that he was the target of a Communist conspiracy.

The passengers were unaware of the danger. For the three days from New York's East River dock to Havana, they amused themselves with bingo, deck-tennis, shuffleboard and booze. The sun shone alike on morning hangovers and underpaid deck-hands.

The *Morro Castle* arrived at Havana on schedule on 4 September. Wilmot went straight to visit Captain Oscar Hernandez, the harbour Chief of Police. He may have wanted reassurance. Instead, Hernandez confirmed Wilmot's suspicions. The Chief of Police had reliable information that the guerrillas were planning an assault on the *Morro Castle*.

Wilmot was near hysteria. He had not eaten and hardly spoken for three days. He could do nothing about insurgents in Havana, so he turned his paranoid suspicions on his own crew. The most likely saboteur was George Ignatius Alagna, the First Assistant Radio Officer.

Alagna had committed the one unpardonable sin – he had tried to organise a strike aboard the *Morro Castle*. Alagna, like the rest of the crew, was disgusted by the working and living conditions on board. However, his main grievance was an order from the Captain that junior radio operators should polish the ship's woodwork when not on radio duty. In response to this indignity, he had stood at the gangplank before the sailing on 4 August and tried to persuade the junior officers to withdraw their labour. No one had joined his action, but he had succeeded in delaying sailing for two hours. From then on he had been marked as a Communist agitator.

All radio officers on American ships were subcontracted from the Radiomarine Corporation of America. Shortly after leaving New York, the Corporation had telegraphed to Alagna with the news that his contract was terminated with effect from his return from Havana. At the age of twenty-two, it looked as though his career was over. In Wilmot's mind, this made him a desperate man.

Before leaving Havana, Wilmot called in his Chief Officer, William Warms. Wilmot wanted Alagna clapped in irons for the journey home. Warms advised caution. They had no excuse to imprison Alagna. It might make the ship a target for union activists. Instead, Warms promised to keep a close watch on Alagna's movements.

There were two other radio operators aboard. The most junior was Charles Maki, a nineteen-year-old Finn. His photographs show a blond, blue-eyed Aryan ideal. Maki was obsessed with his physique. He used to gaze for hours at photographs of body-builders taped above his bunk. As a hobby, he and another Finn took turns hitting each other with bare fists until one knocked the other senseless. In his work, Maki was slow and ponderous. He had insufficient imagination to cause trouble.

The Chief Radio Operator was George White Rogers. Rogers was a strange man who had lived a strange life.

At the time of the *Morro Castle*'s last voyage, he was thirty-three years old. From birth he had suffered from a pituitary disorder known as Frohlich's Syndrome which retards sexual development and causes excessive retention of body fat. His parents both died when he was six and he went to live with his maternal grandparents. At the age of seven, following a near-fatal bout of pneumonia, he put on fifty pounds of weight in a little over a month. By the age of twelve he weighed 170 pounds, most of it in fat, packed around his wide blubbery hips. Not surprisingly, boys being boys, he had a hard time as a child. He was savagely mocked for his shape and for his whining, high-pitched voice. As a compensation for his unpopularity, Rogers turned to petty crime – to anything that would earn him either respect or a secret sense of superiority.

From fourteen to sixteen, Rogers passed through two reform schools. He was thrown out of the first for theft and 'moral perversion'. The 'moral perversion' was unspecified but may have been connected to his habit of continually rubbing his genitals to encourage the growth of pubic hair. At the second school he was found sodomising a younger boy. They put him aboard a ship out of San Francisco as an Assistant Radio Operator. Through the twenties, after a short and unhappy four months in the US Navy, he drifted from job to job, pursued by minor scandals. In 1923 he lost his job as technician on a New York radio station for stealing a pair of 50 watt transmitters. In 1929 a mysterious fire destroyed the offices of the Wireless Egert Company. Rogers was suspected, but released for lack of evidence.

Rogers had one consistent consuming interest. He was fascinated by methods of triggering explosions. In a back room in his house he experimented with chemical reactions and delayed-action fuses. He concentrated particularly on development of an ingenious device, the size of a fountain pen. At the bottom the device contained combustible powder and, at the top, acid. The two were separated by a copper membrane. The thickness of the copper acted as the timer. When the acid ate through the copper, the device ignited.

During this time, Rogers also showed signs of mindless cruelty. When his wife insisted, against his wishes, on attending the funeral of a distant aunt, she returned to find that he had poisoned her dog.

By 1934, Rogers was still a very odd figure of a man – 250 lb of fat, wedge-shaped head melting into narrow sloping shoulders, a fixed blubbery smile on his loose wet lips.

The Radiomarine Corporation of America knew nothing of the stranger side of his character when he applied for work as an Assistant Radio Operator.

Rogers joined the *Morro Castle* in June 1934. Soon after his arrival, Stanley Ferson, the ship's Chief Radio Operator, began to receive a series of anonymous letters warning him that his life was in danger if he remained on board. These letters have been traced to one of Rogers's acquaintances, a radio ham in Bayonne, New Jersey. When, in August 1934, Ferson walked off the ship in New York, Rogers took his place.

Rogers was addicted throughout his life to certain patterns of behaviour. He would go to great lengths to achieve something and then wilfully throw it away. He had gone to a great deal of trouble to get the post of Chief Radio Operator, but had then made a stupid mistake which he knew would be detected. He had been caught stealing cash paid by passengers for sending personal radio messages. On 5 September, his position on the ship was the same as Alagna's. He had been given notice to quit by the Radiomarine Corporation.

On 5 September, shortly before the *Morro Castle* left Havana, Rogers went to Captain Wilmot's cabin. He told him that he had found two bottles of acid on the shelf above Alagna's bunk. Rogers claimed that he had thrown the acid overboard. The news seemed to confirm Wilmot's suspicions about Alagna and the Communist conspiracy. He told Rogers to keep a careful watch on Alagna and report anything suspicious directly to him. Wilmot knew nothing about Rogers' past or about his interest in explosives. Alagna had brought nothing aboard from Havana. Rogers himself had purchased the acid and he had not thrown it away.

That evening, Wilmot continued to behave very oddly. During the regular round of inspection with Chief Officer Warms, he insisted, for the first time, on visiting the galley. He had decided to eat that night at the Captain's Table. The hors d'oeuvre for 5 September was dressed crab and the plates were laid out in the galley ready for serving. Wilmot carefully inspected the line of crabs and picked out one particular specimen for himself. The Chief Steward promised that he would mark the plate and ensure that the Captain received no other. Wilmot thanked the Chief Steward and proceeded with his inspection of the ship.

It is strange, given Wilmot's obsessive concern for his own safety, that he paid so little attention to that of his ship. The fire precautions aboard the *Morro Castle* were less than primitive.

The last fire-drill had been in June. A woman passenger had broken her ankle during the excitement and successfully sued the Ward Line for $25,000. Wilmot's position depended on avoiding inconvenience for his employers. To avoid further accidents he cancelled all drills and ordered the deck fire-hydrants to be sealed and the fire-hoses to be locked away.

Arthur Pender, one of the ship's watchmen, secretly logged all of the liner's safety hazards. He found that there were no sirens on the fire-doors, that air-ducts had been painted over, that plugs in the lifeboats were not fastened and four of the lifeboats were placed so they could only be boarded by breaking thick glass windows.

However, Wilmot's biggest mistake was his decision to move 20 lb of explosives to a space above the ceiling of the First Class writing-room. The *Morro Castle* had a Lyle Gun – a cannon designed for firing ropes to other ships or to men overboard. Normally, it was kept on the bridge. From a distance the Lyle Gun looked like a more orthodox cannon. Given the tense situation in Cuba at the time, Wilmot thought it was wiser to move the gun out of sight. The one place that was both concealed but also accessible was the locker between the deck and the ceiling of the First Class writing-room. Along with the Lyle Gun went its accompanying charge – 20 lb of explosives stored in a pretzel can.

Wilmot could be forgiven for not imagining a sequence of events where the Lyle Gun proved significant. What was less forgivable was his decision to close down the ship's smoke-detecting system – the mechanism that had saved the *Morro Castle* from the August fire.

The cargo loaded in Havana included a consignment of salted hides. They smelt revolting. Several passengers who witnessed the loading commented that the smell would ruin the return voyage. The smoke-detector system circulated air from the hold to the main body of the ship. Wilmot decided to shut off the system, seal the hold and contain the smell. This prevented a great deal of embarrassment and avoided a boatload of dissatisfied customers. It also helped to send 125 of the customers to the bottom of the Atlantic.

The ship left Havana at 6 p.m. on the evening of Wednesday 5 September, loaded with Cuban rum and exotic Caribbean memories. The weather was still fine and the sea calm.

Captain Wilmot emerged for dinner on the Wednesday night, but by Thursday morning, he was back in hiding, locked in his cabin. He opened the door only to Warms and babbled incoherently about a plot to destroy him with acid. In the evening he appeared briefly on the bridge. He looked out at the ocean and then returned to his cabin. He said that he felt ill. He would take an enema and lie down.

On the night of Thursday 6 September the barometer began to fall and the wind stiffened. At 3 a.m., the boat was hit by a tropical storm. For the passengers, it was a miserable night, but by dawn on Friday the weather had cleared and it was warm and sunny. The passengers emerged onto the deck and dived again into crazy golf, deck-dancing and clockwork horse-racing. At the centre of every entertainment was Robert Smith, the *Morro Castle*'s cruise-director. Smith – huge, muscular, blond-haired, bright-eyed and shovel-jawed – had the job of ensuring that everyone had a good time. While the sun lasted, his work was easy.

By late afternoon the *Morro Castle* was entering another storm. The ship began to pitch and roll. Half of the passengers threw up their lunch and retired to their bunks. The storm continued all night, winds gusting up to Force Eight across the deserted shuffleboard court.

The passengers stayed in their cabins or mooched in sulky groups at the bar. They revolted against Robert Smith's tireless smile and muscular enthusiasm as he pursued them from deck to deck and resisted any of his attempts to interest them in party games.

Captain Wilmot emerged from his bed on Friday night. It was traditional for the captain to host a cocktail party on the last night of the voyage for a select group of First Class passengers. The affair was sober and subdued. The guests arrived at 5.15 and had all left by 6 p.m. No one noticed anything peculiar in the Captain's behaviour.

At 7.45, Chief Officer Warms knocked on the door of Wilmot's cabin to report that the weather had again worsened. The ship was entering patches of dense fog. There was no answer. Warms entered the cabin. There was no sign of the Captain. He walked through to the bathroom. He found Wilmot slumped over the bath, his trousers round his ankles, his eyes open and staring.

A lot of speculation has surrounded Wilmot's death. At the time Dr Van Zyle, the ship's doctor, diagnosed 'indigestion and heart failure'. There were six more doctors on board. During the course of the evening, Van Zyle led each one through the captain's cabin to inspect Wilmot's body. By then the corpse had been laid out in dress uniform on the bed. On superficial examination, all of the doctors agreed with Van Zyle's assessment of cause of death. Later events made it impractical to carry out an autopsy.

The Chief Steward removed a bowl of half-eaten fruit from the cabin. The remains were never analysed. If Wilmot was murdered, we will never know. Because of what happened later, suspicion has fallen on George White Rogers. However, there is no evidence. Rogers was responsible for so much death that it might be charitable not to blame him for the Captain's.

Friday was the night of the final explosion of fun aboard the *Morro Castle* – the farewell fancy-dress ball. Many passengers were too sick to think of dancing, but the rest were set to party until dawn. When Robert Smith announced that festivities were cancelled out of respect for the Captain, feelings were mixed. Some passengers dutifully retired to their cabins after dinner. Others collected in rebellious groups and ordered mixers for their Havana rum. Smith, with an acute sense of decorum, patrolled the decks like a bitter school-matron, dampening fun wherever he found it – closing the lid on the piano in the saloon and disabling the record player in the palm-laden Verandah Cafe.

Warms took command of the ship. He had been afraid that life had passed him by. This was his chance to stake a claim to the captaincy of the *Morro Castle*.

William Warms had the pinched, knobbly face and sad spaniel eyes of a straight-man comic. He was a dry humourless man dedicated to the sea and desiccated by a life of thwarted ambition. He had been a sailor since the age of twelve. In 1918, after nine years' service with the Ward Line, he was given command of a fruit boat. Seven years later he took over the *Yumari*, a small passenger steamer. With the *Yumari* a pattern emerged in Warms's life. Other captains might be careless about safety, but Warms was seen to be careless. He lost the captaincy of the *Yumari* and was suspended from sea-duties for a year for failure to hold lifeboat and safety drills. In 1928, he was given another chance with command of the cruise liner *Agwistar*. The ship was hit by a series of mystery fires and he was reprimanded for failure to take precautions. He lost his command and was demoted to Chief Officer.

Opinions varied on Warms's competence. Many of the crew respected him as a 'real seaman'. Others were concerned by his safety record. Eban Starr Abbott, the Chief Engineer, hated him. Abbott was a dandy – an excellent engineer, but despised by Warms as a 'chocolate sailor'. There was so much tension between the two that Wilmot had recommended transferring Abbott to the *Morro Castle*'s sister ship.

While Warms was discovering Wilmot's body, Abbott was on the way to the captain's cabin to report another problem. One of the ship's three boilers had broken down. Abbott could not repair the damage until they reached New York. In normal circumstances this was a trivial problem. The voyage might be slightly delayed. Events that night, though, were not going to be normal.

With the weather worsening and speed reduced, Warms took his place on the bridge. He decided not to leave his post until arrival at the East River dock on the morning of the 8th. He wanted to do nothing to jeopardise his chances of keeping command.

As the night wore on, the weather abated a little. The wind was still strong from the north-east, but the forecast storm had not materialised.

At midnight in the radio-room, George White Rogers handed control to Maki the muscle-bound Finn, and walked out 'to get a breath of air'.

By 2.45 a.m. only four passengers were left drinking in the bar. The stewards prowled around them, exhausted and bored, anxious to close the bar and get to sleep. The passengers showed no signs of leaving. One of the women suggested they stay up to watch dawn over the New York skyline. The stewards cursed her under their breath.

At 2.50 a.m. the night watchman reported smoke rising from a duct leading to the First Class writing-room. Two seamen were sent to investigate. The smoke was coming from a locker in the writing-room. When the seamen opened the locker door, they were faced by a wall of blue-white flame. Clarence Hackney, the Third Officer, was sent down with a small fire-extinguisher. By now the whole writing-room was on fire, the flames licking the ceiling. Hackney was forced back into the corridor by the heat. In panic he forgot to pull down the steel fire-door behind him.

Warms immediately gave orders to uncap the hydrants and fetch the hoses from below. Following normal procedure, he turned the ship head-on to the wind. At 3 a.m., as soon as he realised that the situation was serious, he sounded the alarm.

The hours that followed were a catalogue of terror and confusion. Vital time was wasted uncapping the hydrants and lugging the hoses to the deck. With one boiler out of action there was insufficient water pressure to fight the flames. Below decks there was panic as the lights flickered on and off, plunging passengers into darkness and confusion. Neither passengers nor crew knew the emergency procedure or lifeboat stations. They ran wildly through the corridors searching for escape.

The decision to turn head-on to the wind was disastrous. Instead of reducing surface for the wind, the manoeuvre channelled a concentrated draught below decks to fan the flames. Shortly after 3 a.m. there was a huge explosion. The powder for the Lyle Gun had exploded. The flames spread rapidly across the deck. Hydrants were abandoned and fire ate through hoses. Water leaked uselessly onto the deck, reducing pressure to the hoses still in operation.

Up on the bridge, Warms must have felt the injustice of his position. He was paying for another man's mistakes. He issued a stream of frantic orders in response to the crisis. Amidst the confusion, he made only one culpable mistake. For thirty minutes he refused to give permission to send an SOS. Rogers sent Alagna to the bridge again and again to ask for instructions, but each time Alagna was ignored.

As soon as Warms raised the alarm, the crew set to work to wake the passengers. They banged pots and pans in the passageways and blew bugles and whistles. Some women died because they stayed to dress properly before leaving their cabins. One man died because he left his cabin without his false teeth. As he tried to reach the deck, his ankle was trapped by burning debris. He was too embarrassed to open his mouth to call for help. One passenger had fallen asleep in a friend's cabin, too drunk to reach his own. He was woken from his stupor by a steward shouting from the corridor. 'Get dressed, Mr Brady,' yelled the steward, 'the ship's on fire!' He almost stayed there to fry. 'All I could think of,' he remembered later, 'was that my name wasn't Brady – that the message wasn't for me.'

Soon the superstructure of the ship was a bonfire. The bows were split from the stern by a wall of flame. Crew-members began to throw deck-chairs into the water to serve as life-rafts. Passengers and crew began to throw themselves overboard.

The clear duty of the Chief Engineer was to see to the engine-room. In the first moment of crisis, Abbott had sent his assistant in his place. He clothed himself in full-dress uniform and went up to the bridge where he cowered in a corner, overwhelmed by terror and shame.

The first lifeboat to be launched landed stern-first, almost vertical in the water. Two passengers were spilled into the sea. Abbott ran to the second lifeboat. As he ran he tore the gold braid from his uniform. He stepped aboard and ordered the seamen to cast off. The boat was launched with only eight aboard. Many of the crew followed Abbott's example. They were underpaid, badly-fed and treated like scum. They owed no loyalty to the company or the passengers. Of the first eighty people aboard lifeboats, seventy-three were members of the crew.

At the same time, there were countless acts of heroism. Often the least likely people took the greatest risks to save lives. The Chief Steward gathered a group of his waiters and led them time and again to rescue passengers in the flaming corridors of the cabin decks. Robert Smith, the entertainments officer, threw himself into the thick of danger. Eventually, trapped by the flames, he threw himself into the sea, his arms wrapped around a small boy. He carried on holding the boy's head clear of the water long after the child was dead from cold.

Panic spread as more and more were cut off by the flames. A man was trapped in a corridor with his pyjamas on fire. He broke a window with his cane and squeezed through onto the deck, cutting his back on the broken glass. Other passengers watched horrified as he jumped about the deck, skin peeling from his back, hair on fire, screaming in pain. Finally he ran to the stern and threw himself overboard into the wake of the propeller. As he was pulled down into the churning water he was shouting 'I'm here! I'm here!'

When the first rescuers arrived in the cold wet light of dawn they saw a sea littered with corpses. Battered survivors, half-dead with cold, clung to floating debris. Two desolate groups remained on the ship – on the stern a group of passengers huddled around the head stewardess; on the forepeak, the captain and what was left of his crew.

In the aftermath of the disaster there were several enquiries. Rumour from Havana spoke of Communist sabotage. However, there was no evidence that the fire was more than an accident. A federal jury convicted Warms and Abbott on charges of criminal negligence, but they were released on appeal. Several of the crew and passengers were feted for their heroism. Among them was George White Rogers, the fat man in the radio-room.

Rogers had remained at his post in the smoke-filled radio-room waiting for Warms's order to send the SOS. Later he had made several attempts to rescue trapped passengers. Throughout the night he had showed an uncanny coolness. He had seemed actually to be enjoying himself.

After the drama of the *Morro Castle*, Rogers returned to his old life. He set up another radio repair shop in Bayonne New Jersey. The shop ran into financial problems. In February 1935 he nipped out 'for a breath of air'. When he returned, the shop had burnt to the ground. He was suspected of arson, but there was no proof. He collected the insurance.

In June 1936, Rogers joined the Bayonne police force as a radio technician. In the police station he worked closely with another old seaman, Vincent Doyle. Doyle was fascinated by Rogers. Rogers talked obsessively about explosive devices and the mechanics of the perfect crime. Doyle looked into Rogers's past and asked him questions about the *Morro Castle*. Rogers was surprisingly forthcoming. He put forward his own theory on the disaster. Step by step he came close to admitting that he had been responsible. When he had 'stepped out for some air' at midnight on September 7, he had slipped into the deserted First Class writing-room. He had placed an incendiary device shaped like a fountain pen into the breast pocket of a jacket hanging in the locker, then he had walked back to his post and waited to become a hero.

By 1938, Doyle had almost enough evidence to charge Rogers with setting fire to the ship. The Bayonne police technicians did occasional electrical work for other policemen. One afternoon, Rogers went home early, leaving a fish-tank heater for Doyle to repair. When Doyle plugged the heater into the wall-socket, the ensuing blast destroyed the room and left Doyle in hospital for eighteen months. Rogers was charged with attempted murder and sentenced to twelve to twenty-five years in prison.

The war saved George White Rogers. In 1942 he was released on parole to join the forces. Turned down by the navy, he set up another repair shop in Bayonne. This shop too ran into difficulties and he borrowed $7,500 from an elderly neighbour and the neighbour's spinster daughter. When they wanted the loan back, they were found battered to death. Rogers went back to prison. He died of a brain haemorrhage in 1958.

The circumstantial evidence against Rogers is over-whelming. It is impossible to fathom his motives. There is probably no sense to be made from the terrible end of the

Morro Castle – just an act of wilful madness by a man whose body never fitted.

8.

The Glory Of Living

At 1.45 a.m. on 22 January 1961 the Portuguese liner *Santa Maria* was fourteen hours out of Curacao on her three-day voyage to Port Everglades on the Florida coast. It was a hot, calm, clear night. The Companhia Colonial de Navigacao had spent $17.5m on the *Santa Maria*. She was a symbol of Portugal's constant struggle to be taken seriously as a civilised western nation. Like her parent country, the liner was magnificent in many respects, but technically she was something of a joke. That night the air-conditioning had failed.

The heat between decks was almost unbearable. Many passengers had abandoned their cabins and were sleeping on the deck to catch the slight westerly breeze from the open Atlantic.

In a small sweaty cabin on the Third Class passenger deck, Henrique Galvao, a sixty-five-year-old escapee from a Portuguese gaol, was preparing to make his personal mark on the decade of revolution and love. He had a tall, spare frame that retained much of its youthful athleticism and the swarthy face and hollowed cheeks of an ascetic monk or a horror-film extra. Physically, he was in terrible shape. He had a history of nervous illness and six weeks earlier he had suffered a heart attack which might have killed a man less consumed by a sense of mission. As he sat on his bunk in the final moments before the assault he was utterly convinced that he was the man chosen to liberate his country and that the hour of that liberation was at hand.

Over the past two hours, twenty-three men had passed through Galvao's cabin. They had collected weapons and final instructions. By 1.30, only one of the conspirators had failed to appear. Galvao sent his second-in-command, Captain Jorge Sotomayor, former officer in the Spanish Navy, in search of the missing man. Sotomayor found him, motionless and bathed in sweat on the bunk in his cabin, a wet handkerchief wrapped around his head, paralysed by a combination of terror and heat. It is hard not to sympathise with the man's loss of nerve. Galvao was asking a lot of his handful of 'commandos'. He was asking them not just to pirate a ship, but to conquer an empire.

At 1.45, the commandos moved into action. Captain Sotomayor led the first section to secure the radio-room, the bridge and the pilot-house. Galvao took the remainder to occupy the officers' quarters.

Galvao had reached the door separating the officers' accommodation from the empty main passenger saloon, when he heard shots from the deck above. He raced with his men up to the bridge. There he found the *Santa Maria*'s Third Officer dead on the floor in a pool of blood and a young officer-cadet stunned, slumped against the doorway with two bullets in his chest. Sotomayor held a gun to the head of the terrified seaman at the wheel.

Sotomayor claimed that the crew on the bridge had opened fire as he entered the room with his men. Galvao later wrote that he himself picked up the crew's weapons and threw them overboard. The captain of the *Santa Maria*, Captain Maia, swore on his return to Portugal that there were no weapons on board the liner and that Sotomayor and his nervous commandos had opened fire indiscriminately in a fit of hysteria. Certainly it is odd that Galvao, with only fourteen firearms among his gang of twenty-four should throw the crew's guns into the sea.

Whatever the truth behind the killing of Third Officer Joao Jose De Nascimiento Costa and the wounding of Cadet-Officer Antonio Lopez De Souza, the events on the bridge were to lead to the ruin of Galvao's plans.

Galvao was not the only one who had heard the shots. The telephone rang on the bridge and Captain Maia's voice, dopey with sleep, demanded to know what was going on. 'Nothing is going on,' replied Galvao, 'except that I have just taken over your ship. Resistance is quite impossible and I invite you to surrender.'

By the time Galvao finally reached the officers' quarters, Maia and his subordinates were gathered in the Captain's cabin in their pyjamas and dressing-gowns. They looked like guests in a country house murder mystery woken by a scream from the west wing. Galvao, who had little time for anyone who lacked his own instincts for suicidal bravery, described them as a 'group of sub-humans, one of them whimpering like an abandoned calf'. The only crew-member for whom he had any respect was the Third Officer. This may not have been a huge consolation to Joao Jose De Nascimiento Costa's corpse, cold on the floor of the wheel-house.

Galvao presented the officers with three alternatives. They could either be clapped in irons in a store-room, throw in whole-heartedly with the conspiracy or continue to run the ship under protest, following his orders. Much to Galvao's disgust they chose the third alternative – the compromise, in his eyes, of cowards.

At 2.30 a.m., the 600 passengers and 350 crew were gathered in the First Class lounge. Armed men guarded the doors. The heat and dense smell of sweat were overpowering. Galvao stood up on the bandstand and announced in Spanish, Portuguese and English that the *Santa Maria* was now the property of the Free Iberian People, that the vessel was engaged on a secret mission to depose the dictatorships of Salazar in Portugal and Franco in Spain, and that no harm would come to anyone who obeyed his orders. As a finale to his speech, the ship's loudspeakers blared out the strains of Tchaikovsky's '1812 Overture'.

By 3 a.m., Portugal's most luxurious cruise-liner was in the hands of a sixty-five-year-old hospital case, a retired Captain of the Spanish Navy and a bizarre collection of exiles, most of whom had never before in their lives handled a firearm. Apart from the Third Officer, the only resistance had been from a group of stewards who, fuddled with sleep, had convinced themselves that there was a mutiny among the passengers, armed themselves with knives from the kitchen and set out from the galley in search of adventure. They had been disarmed without bloodshed.

Galvao's first order was to set course eastward. Instead of heading due north for the Yucatan Channel and the Gulf of Mexico, the ship was now headed directly out of the Caribbean, towards the open Atlantic and the west coast of Africa. Galvao had a plan and he needed to move quickly. The plan, of course, was extravagantly mad.

* * *

Henrique Galvao was born in Barreiro, Portugal, in 1895. Throughout his life he remained a nineteenth-century figure, someone strangely out of place as a symbol of the Swinging Sixties. He described himself as 'a writer, a student of African problems, an African explorer, a sportsman, a playwright, a naturalist, a big-game hunter, a politician and a high government official.' Certainly he was a man of many parts.

Galvao was educated at a military college and entered the army. His early years coincided with turbulent and confusing times in Portugal. The monarchy was desperately trying to cling to absolute power in the face of the rise of Republicanism. In 1908 King Carlos was assassinated after a failed coup and in 1910 the Royalists were finally thrown out, King Manuel 'The Unfortunate' leaving for exile in England and a suburban house in Twickenham where he lived out the rest of a miserable life. Over the next sixteen years there were forty-five military coups as petty factions tried to make some sense of democracy. By 1926, the country had been battered more or less to a standstill. In desperation, the army turned for direction to an obscure thirty-seven-year-old Professor of Economics at Coimbra University – Dr Antonio de Oliveira Salazar.

Salazar came from Santa Coimba, a small town in the Dao valley celebrated for its wine and for not much else. He was absorbed in the drier recesses of economics, making his name with a series of papers on gold and wheat production. He was given the job of sorting out Portugal's chaotic finances, but his ambitions went far beyond the Treasury. The country wanted stability and was prepared to accept a strong man. Democracy had not been the paradise they had expected. By 1932, when Salazar was elected Prime Minister, he had already been five years in undisputed control of Portugal. He was to remain dictator until his death.

Of all the Fascist and semi-Fascist dictators who strutted across Europe in the thirties, Salazar was perhaps the least dangerous. Portugal never had the resources to threaten world-domination. Stuck away on the fringes of Europe, her political opposition was rarely enough of a threat to goad the state into mass terror.

Salazar did have his moments. Until 1945, when the dreams of Hitler and Mussolini turned sour, he hedged his rule about with shabby imitations of fascist ceremonials. He adopted the Roman salute and sent bands of volunteers to fight with Franco in the Spanish Civil War. In his personal life he was puritanical. He never married or showed any inclination for the sleazier sorts of fun that absolute power can buy. His eccentricity went more in the other direction. The Portuguese Catholic church was horrified by the priest-killing and nun-raping excesses of the Spanish Republicans across the border and seized on Salazar as a soldier-saint. Photographs of his grey, vulture features were sold at the doors of churches, printed on the back with 'Indulgences' granting the bearer exemption from a certain number of years in purgatory.

Galvao at first supported the coup of 1926 which brought Salazar to power. He was attracted by the dictator's anti-corruption slogans and the new drive to balance the books. From the army he went into colonial administration in Angola and steeped himself in Africa. He produced a stream of books with titles ranging from *Packaging In Colonial Trade* to *Lands of Witchcraft, In the Land Of The Blacks* and *Kuriha – A*

Story Of Wild Beasts, a 'political study of animal psychology'.

A lot about Galvao was ridiculous. However, by the mid-1940s, when he was elected as a Deputy for Angola in the National Assembly, he was one of the few Portuguese who not only understood the corruption and brutality of colonial rule in Africa, but also had the courage to speak what he knew.

In March 1949, Galvao presented to the Assembly a report on forced labour in Angola which uncovered an appalling web of slavery, disease, poverty and oppression. When the report was shelved, Galvao went into opposition. He directed the campaign of the anti-Salazar candidate in the Presidential election. When his candidate lost, Galvao complained of electoral corruption and was sentenced to seven years in prison for slander. While in prison he published a secret newspaper. As a result of this he was tried for libel and sentenced to a further eighteen years.

In 1958, Galvao was in a prison hospital in Lisbon. Since his arrest five years earlier he had suffered from periodic attacks of partial paralysis. He heard only indirectly of the Presidential campaign launched by General Humberto Delgado, the strongest threat so far to Salazar's dictatorship.

Delgado was an air force officer driven by intense ambition. He had the wide, white-toothed grin, the heavy complacent face and the slicked black hair of a classical Latin political operator. He introduced, for the first time, American techniques of political campaigning into a Portuguese election, travelling across the country in an open-top limousine with a cavalcade of flags and bunting. Wherever his trail went there was frenzy and violence. For the first time there were signs of a loosening of the Salazar strait-jacket. However, in the end, the election went the way of all elections under Salazar. In a rigged ballot, Delgado gained only twenty-five percent of the vote and he had to take refuge in the Brazilian Embassy in Lisbon to avoid arrest.

The popular success of Delgado's campaign and his escape from the security police spurred Galvao to make his own gaol-break. In a false moustache, with a hat pulled down over his eyes, he lowered himself onto a ledge outside the sixth-floor window of his hospital cell. He described his escapade in characteristically humble terms: 'Using my ability as a gymnast and my immunity from dizziness caused by heights I passed on the outside from window to window until I reached the one that I wanted and then, with the cold blood that God gave me, I walked out of the main entrance past the unsuspecting guards.'

Dressed as a porter, Galvao sought asylum in the Argentinian Embassy and in May 1959 he was given safe conduct to Buenos Aires.

For the next two years, Galvao lived the dispiriting and pathetic life of a political exile. He failed to raise any enthusiasm in Argentina for action against Salazar and at the end of 1959 moved to Venezuela. He had been promised financial help from wealthy Portuguese exiles in Caracas, but the promises came to nothing. He was reduced to making a living as a salesman for speculative real-estate, hawking from door to door the deeds for plots of jungle earmarked for the new Brazilian capital, Brasilia.

Through the hard times, Galvao kept his dreams alive. Delgado was now in exile in Brazil. In 1960, with a group of Spanish exiles, the General formed the Iberian Revolutionary Directorate of Liberation, which made up by the grandeur of its title for the hopelessness of its cause. Galvao, the Venezuelan salesman of dubious real-estate, was appointed head of the Portuguese armed forces 'to exercise supreme command over Portuguese territories, ships and aeroplanes'.

Galvao had no money and no influential supporters. As far as the Western powers were concerned, a stable dictatorship under Salazar was infinitely preferable to a shaky democracy that might slip into Communism. The Latin American governments were too far away to care a great deal about a small state on the fringes of Europe. For all his self-dramatisation, Galvao was a determined and resourceful man. While those around him formed committees, issued directives and sat drinking cheap booze in the sun, Galvao searched for some way to strike at Portugal. He came up with the one route that needed neither wings nor powerful friends. If Galvao could not get to Portugal, then Portugal would come to him.

Every month, the Portuguese transatlantic liner, *Santa Maria*, docked at La Guaira, the port of Caracas, on its way to Florida and Lisbon. Galvao's plan was simple. He would recruit, equip and train 100 'commandos' from among the Portuguese exile community in Venezuela. He would smuggle them aboard the *Santa Maria*. In international waters they would seize the ship. Undetected, they would sail eight days across the Atlantic to Fernando Po, a tiny Spanish dependency off the coast of West Africa. To avoid concern at their failure to arrive in Florida, they would radio to Port Everglades that there were problems with the engines. Once arrived at Fernando Po, they would capture the island, take the Spanish officials hostage, seize a gunboat, bomb Luanda, the capital of Angola, with captured Spanish planes, seize Angola in coordination with an internal uprising in Mozambique, and use control of Portuguese Africa as a springboard to topple Salazar's dictatorship, helped by mutinous Angolan and Mozambiquan troops.

Galvao's plans were hampered from the start by shortage of cash. He had to rely on Portuguese exiles who feared that they would face extradition if things went wrong. Given the ambition of the plan, their caution was not entirely inexplicable.

Instead of 100 commandos, Galvao recruited twenty-four Spanish and Portuguese refugees. In August 1960, he set them up in an abandoned holiday camp near Caracas where they practised calisthenics and judo. Few had any experience of this sort of thing. There was a bricklayer, a clerk, a carpenter, a builder, an electrician and a blacksmith; there was a sports promoter, a forty-six-year-old chauffeur and a forty-year-old anaesthetist.

While his men trained, Galvao collected intelligence and tried to raise funds. A woman sympathiser took a job as a telephone operator aboard the *Santa Maria* and memorised the ship's communication system and the positions taken by the watch. Publicity leaflets from the office of the Companhia Colonial de Navigacao in Caracas included a map of the ship and the numbers of passengers and crew. In the window of the agency was an exact scale model of the vessel. Galvao spent nights on the pavement outside until he had memorised the exact layout of decks, cabins and passageways.

The attack was first set for 14 October. However, by the time the *Santa Maria* docked in Caracas, the conspirators were still $2,000 short of the money they needed to buy tickets for the voyage. Between them they had only five pistols and a single sub-machine gun. Galvao was even having trouble feeding his men at their holiday camp. His wealthier supporters had drifted away altogether. Each day he had to go from house to house among the poorer Portuguese exiles, scraping together 100 Bolivianos to buy enough beans and rice to keep his commandos from fainting at their calisthenics.

The weeks dragged on. Finally everything was prepared for 20 December. On the 10th, Galvao collapsed with a sharp pain in his chest. The strain of conspiracy on top of seven years in prison had told on a man who should have been rocking on a porch instead of leading desperadoes up a gangplank.

Galvao's heart attack immobilised him for ten days. The assault was postponed again until the *Santa Maria*'s return on 20 January 1961. In the meantime, his men sold all they owned and begged and bullied the balance to buy thirteen more sub-machine guns and four hand-grenades on the Caracas black market. Those without guns armed themselves with knives.

At 8 a.m. on the 20th, the *Santa Maria* docked at La Guaira. On the same day, Galvao flew with three companions to join the ship at Curacao, leaving Sotomayor to embark with the remaining twenty.

In Curacao, Galvao booked into a cheap hotel on the waterfront. Curacao is an oil port, a strange mixture of Dutch order and tropical decay. Through the night of the 20th, he waited at the window, looking over the stinking moonlit scum of the harbour towards the neat row of waterfront houses designed to remind Dutch merchants of home, their long sloping roofs built for the northern winter, waiting for snow that would never fall.

The *Santa Maria* was due to pass beneath the hotel window at eight in the morning. When it did not appear, Galvao imagined all that could have gone wrong: the arms had been discovered; the plot had been leaked to the PIDE, Salazar's vicious secret police; the conspirators had been arrested. Galvao's whole life had led to the *Santa Maria* adventure. The wait was unbearable.

At 8.30, the liner sailed past into the harbour. Two hours later, Sotomayor reported to the hotel room. The embarkation had gone with barely a hitch. Half the men had boarded on passenger tickets and the remainder on visitors' passes. Security, though, had been tighter than expected. They had taken aboard the guns, but had to leave behind a box of materials for improvising hand-grenades.

On the afternoon of the 21st, Galvao and his three companions were sneaked onto the ship. By dawn on the following day, the ship was in their hands and they were sailing due east at a steady twenty knots for the Saint Lucia Channel and the coast of Portuguese West Africa.

The sea was calm and the skies were blameless blue. The routine of the ship was oddly unchanged. The passengers, mostly Portuguese, but including a number of American and Dutch tourists, accepted the change of ownership philosophically. Galvao fostered rumours that his force numbered over 100, most of them spread incognito among passengers and crew. Even without the threat of a fifth column, there was little enthusiasm for resistance. On the whole the passengers were less concerned at being the spearhead of an Iberian Revolution than at the closure of the recreation deck which was sealed off as a buffer between paying guests and pirates. One American passenger complained to Galvao at being deprived of access to the shuffleboard court. 'He had one painted for me right outside my cabin,' he later reported, 'I think he's nuts.'

Nuts or not, Galvao was a man of strict honour. It was this that sunk his African adventure. On the morning of the 23rd, the ship was approaching the Saint Lucia Channel. No news had reached the outside world. There was every hope that, once out of the Caribbean, they could lose the liner in the open Atlantic. The ship's doctor, Cicero Campus Leite, came to warn Galvao that, without hospital care, the wounded cadet would die.

Galvao was faced with a difficult decision. Either he could land the cadet and give away his course and position, losing all hope of reaching Fernando Po undetected, or he could hang another murder round his neck. One of Galvao's endearing qualities was that, though capable of more or less anything in the heat of action, he found it impossible to make cold calculations of ends and means. He was happily launched on an enterprise that might lead to thousands of deaths, but he could not watch a wounded seaman die.

At 9 a.m. on 24 January, the *Santa Maria* hove to in sight of Saint Lucia Bay. A motor launch cast off for the harbour containing the wounded man, a sailor suffering from hepatitis, a medical attendant, the Assistant Purser, three crewmen and $2,500 to cover medical expenses.

Up until this moment, there had been serious intent behind the enterprise. From the morning of the 24th, the piracy of the *Santa Maria* became a circus with Galvao as ringmaster and the navies of the Western world as performing seals. Galvao opened up the radio-room so that passengers could reassure friends and family they were alive and well. He himself broadcast a string of misleading messages, trying to divert attention from his true objective.

Aboard the *Santa Maria* all hint of tension evaporated. The swimming-pool and shuffleboard courts were reopened and dances were resumed in the First and Second Class lounges.

At first it was assumed that Galvao was headed for Brazil as part of an elaborate plot engineered in Rio de Janeiro by General Delgado. The British destroyer *Rothesay* and the US ships *Wilson* and *Damato* headed for the Western Atlantic to search the waters east of Saint Lucia. US planes quartered the ocean from bases in Puerto Rico. The Venezuelans placed their navy and air force on general alert.

In Lisbon, Salazar was furious. He demanded that the world condemn 'this criminal act of piracy'. The PIDE spread the rumour, not entirely unfounded, that Galvao was mad, along with the less credible rumour that he was an agent of international communism. The American press picked up claims that he had travelled secretly to Cuba in 1960 to plan the assault with Fidel Castro and that the *Santa Maria* was being refuelled at sea from a Cuban tanker. In fact, Galvao's communism was limited to merging the Second and Third Class kindergartens and eating his lunch with the chambermaids.

Despite the squeals from Lisbon, world opinion swung rapidly behind Galvao. On 25 January, four Dutch ships joined the search, but they were quickly withdrawn under public pressure. In the House of Commons, Hugh Gaitskell, the leader of the Labour Opposition, demanded to know why the Royal Navy was being used to shore up a Fascist dictator. The Macmillan Government quickly withdrew the

Rothesay because of 'lack of fuel'.

The *Santa Maria* could not stay undetected for ever. In mid-afternoon on the 25th, she was seen by a Danish merchant vessel and at 6 p.m. she was sighted by a US military plane.

For two more days, tracked day and night by spotter planes and shadowed by US destroyers, the liner sailed circles in the Western Atlantic.

Galvao had a problem. He had started out with a clear, if improbable, plan. There was now no chance of reaching Africa in secret. He had a thousand people aboard a 21,000 ton lump of metal and nowhere to go. The Spanish cruiser *Canarias* and the Portuguese warship *Pedro Escobar* had been despatched to block the approaches to Fernando Po and Angola. Without a storm, the *Santa Maria* could not hope to evade US surveillance; and the sea stayed benignly calm beneath a blue sky.

On the 27th, the passengers had their first taste of the privations of piracy. To save water, Galvao banned baths between 10 a.m. and 5 p.m. Salazar, meanwhile, bombarded an increasingly sceptical world press with claims that Galvao was inflicting 'savage beatings' on passengers and crew.

In Washington, J.F. Kennedy, less than a week into his Presidency, wanted to avoid bloodshed. He ordered Admiral Denison, Commander in Chief of the Atlantic fleet, to hold off from confrontation and to search for a compromise to remove the passengers, particularly the Americans, from danger.

Over the ship's radio, Denison offered Galvao a way out. The US navy would not interfere with the *Santa Maria* if she entered a Brazilian port to discharge her passengers. Galvao seized on this as the only alternative to drifting for ever in the Western Atlantic. He ordered Captain Maia to set course for Pernambuco off the north-eastern coast of Brazil.

With the prospect of an end to the hijack, Galvao's men became more tour-guides than pirates. The American passengers took endless photographs and arranged over the ship's radio to sell their stories to the press. Galvao was flooded with offers for his own story, including a proposal to star in a television film of the adventure. He was devoting more and more of his time to preventing love affairs between his men and the single female passengers. He was a little afraid that the whole thing would deteriorate into a floating cocktail party.

On the 29th, Salazar announced that Galvao and his godless communist crew had desecrated the chapel on board the *Santa Maria*. Reports from Lisbon were now so absurd that only the most imaginative right-wing press took any notice. It was a little hard that Salazar's announcements on religious affairs should be ignored. He was, after all, a direct representative of The Almighty since his investiture in 1945 as a 'Political Saint' in the Church of Sao Domingos in Lisbon.

As the *Santa Maria* approached the coast of Brazil, its voyage took on the trappings of a triumphal procession. In private, Galvao was a sick man, virtually sleepless since the night of the 20th, taking constant cold baths to keep himself awake, still feeble from his heart attack. In public he was a cheer-leader for liberation. He stamped every passport with a disembarkation visa from the Independent National Council of Liberation. On the night of the 30th, he held a ball for First and Second Class passengers, his wiry gaunt figure sat in the captain's chair signing special souvenir menus.

By the morning of the 30th, when the liner hove to at the

limit of Brazilian territorial waters, she was surrounded by a huge flotilla of US and Brazilian warships and private vessels. The skies teemed with military and civilian planes. There was a moment of tension when the American warships uncovered the guns broadside to the *Santa Maria*, but it was a gesture of pointless bravado and, on protest from Galvao, the guns were covered again.

At 10 a.m., Rear-Admiral Allen Smith came across from the battleship *Wilson* to negotiate the terms of Galvao's surrender. He was followed by 300 journalists who swarmed aboard from small boats hired at exorbitant rates in Recife harbour. Gil Delamare, a reporter from a French news agency, tried to parachute onto the deck of the *Santa Maria* from a light aeroplane. He fell in a sodden bundle of silk into the shark-infested water and had to be rescued by one of the liner's boats. Galvao gave him an exclusive interview. Delamare's gesture was the sort of action that appealed to Galvao's instincts for hopeless dramatics.

Galvao demanded conditions for his surrender. He insisted on keeping command of the *Santa Maria* and on freedom to leave Recife harbour without interference. He had to wait a day for agreement to his demands. Brazil was in a period of transition. The right-wing pro-Salazar President Kubitschek de Oliveira was handing over to the Liberal President Janio Quadros. The transfer of power was not complete until 1 February.

Even after the handover, there were irritating administrative delays. As 1 February wore on, floating in the wet stifling heat, the good-humour on board began to fray. The crew began to fret about their future. Galvao's insistence on keeping the ship implied that he might need hands to sail her. Even if they were released, their fate was uncertain. Salazar might not be sympathetic to a crew of 350 who had submitted to twenty-four amateur 'commandos' led by a convalescent geriatric. As a gesture they organised what Galvao described as a 'small riot' which culminated in Galvao himself being thrown through a plate-glass window.

Captain Maia saved his heroism for the very last moment. With the final problems resolved, the *Santa Maria*, decked with party streamers, finally made its way into Recife harbour on the morning of the 2nd. As the ship passed the breakwater separating the harbour from the Bay, Maia ordered the Brazilian pilot to steer the ship onto the rocks. The pilot was not impressed. 'Steer it yourself, if you want,' he suggested. Maia later claimed he had cooperated with Galvao only because the rebels had primed 600 lb of explosives to sink the vessel at the first sign of mutiny. He implied that it was only concern for the passengers which had prevented him from acting and that, on the night of the 1st, the crew had sworn to die rather than take the ship out of Recife Harbour.

Moored 300 yards from the quay on the morning of the 2nd, the liner finally unloaded the passengers and crew into waiting tug-boats.

The night of the 2nd, Galvao, Sotomayor and their commandos slept alone aboard the *Santa Maria* while Galvao and Sotomayor discussed a final swan-song. They planned, the two of them, to sail the ship out of the harbour and sink her in the Bay, departing in a final glorious flurry of bubbles. 'The sinking of the ship,' he wrote later, 'seemed to me and Sotomayor the most dignified conclusion to our adventure.' With anyone else, such talk could be dismissed as bravado. Galvao, however, was magnificently mad enough to have done it. He was finally dissuaded by a Brazilian Admiral who argued that 'the glory of dying is highly decorative in the dead pages of history, but it is only the glory of living that makes history.'

At 1 p.m. on 3 February, Galvao handed the ship over to the Brazilian authorities. He was met on the quayside by General Delgado and by the Mayor and the entire Recife Legislative Assembly. The delirium of the crowd outdid the reception of the Presidential election. At least in that obscure seaport on the coast of Brazil it felt as though enthusiasm alone might batter down the doors of Salazar's dictatorship.

At 2 p.m., the Brazilians officially handed the *Santa Maria* back to the Portuguese authorities. Galvao's crazy dream was over.

Galvao carried on the struggle. He was granted asylum in Brazil. A Lisbon court sentenced him to twenty-two years in prison *in absentia*. In November he organised the hijack of a TAP airliner on a regular flight from Casablanca to Lisbon. The plane was diverted to drop leaflets urging abstention in the Presidential elections over Lisbon, Barreiro, Beja and Faro. Galvao intended to join the flight, but once again his health let him down. He was arrested in Morocco and deported. Arrested again on his return to Brazil, he was given limited asylum on the condition he did not leave the isolated state of Belo Horizonte. Even his friends turned against him. In October Delgado, who had milked all possible publicity from the *Santa Maria* hijack, disclaimed involvement, claiming that 'as a military man, I disapproved of such a crazy enterprise.' Delgado went on to expel his former supreme military commander from the National Liberation Movement for the crime of 'self-dramatisation'. Finally, alone, insane, and far from home, Galvao died in a Sao Paolo paupers' hospital in June 1970.

General Delgado had a brief final flourish. In December 1961 the Beja Garrison rebelled, declaring him President. For a few days it seemed possible that the movement might sweep Portugal, but it was quickly suppressed.

Delgado was expelled from country after country. He wandered through Europe and North Africa in a variety of disguises, at times dressed as an Arab, at others with a stone in his shoe to simulate a limp. He fomented wilder and wilder dreams of revolution until, in February 1965, he travelled with his Brazilian secretary to Badajoz on the Spanish/Portuguese border. He expected to make contact with a group of revolutionaries who would smuggle him to the long-awaited uprising. Neither he nor his secretary were seen alive again. Their decomposed bodies were uncovered by the winter rains buried in shallow graves in a river-bed on an isolated stretch of frontier. The contacts had been PIDE agents.

And Salazar? Portugal's 'Political Saint' finally fell, but to nothing as dramatic as a sea-borne invasion. In 1968 he suffered brain damage when his deck-chair collapsed. Although left virtually a vegetable, he continued to inspire such fear that no one dared tell him he no longer ruled the country. He died two years later, still controlling his imaginary empire from the bed of a Lisbon sanatorium.

9.

Double Indemnity

On the afternoon of Monday 13 November 1961, the lookout on the tanker *Gulf Lion* noticed a patch of colour on the smooth surface of the Caribbean. From a distance it looked like floating debris. As he watched, the debris seemed to flicker. Through binoculars it took on the shape of a man waving from an inflatable dinghy.

The tanker altered course to come alongside the dinghy. The man was gaunt, his eyes rimmed red, his face blistered by salt and the sun. Beside him on the raft was a small bundle wrapped in tarpaulin. He stood up, balancing with difficulty as the dinghy rode the tanker's swell. 'I have a dead baby on this dinghy,' he shouted. He formed each word carefully, as though mouthing at an idiot.

The crew of the *Gulf Lion* lowered a basket over the rail and the man laid the bundle inside. They hauled up the body and let down a ladder. The man climbed up unsteadily, his legs working like rusted pistons. He seemed dazed and distracted, his eyes looking straight through the seamen who hauled him over the side. Inside the bundle was the body of a young girl.

The tanker's Captain, Oscar Verhouille, ordered the man to be brought to his cabin. The man sat down, asked for a cigarette and told his story.

His name was Julian Harvey. He had been a lieutenant colonel in the US Air Force. Since being invalided from the service he had scraped by on the fringes of the sea, working as a charter skipper on yachts along the Eastern Seaboard.

Harvey had been recommended to a charter firm run by Harold Pegg of Hollywood, Florida. In mid-October, Pegg gave him a commission to captain a cruise for Dr Arthur Duperrault, an optometrist from Green Bay, Wisconsin and his family. They wanted a month in the Bahamas. Harvey had been uneasy about the charter. Pegg's yacht, the *Bluebelle*, was an old 60 ft ketch, built in 1928 in Sturgeon Bay, Wisconsin. Harvey was unfamiliar with the boat and had no opportunity to follow his normal practice and take a 'shakedown' cruise to get used to her foibles.

The *Bluebelle* left Fort Lauderdale on 8 November bound for the Bahamas. On board was the doctor, his thirty-eight-year-old wife Jean, their son Brian, fourteen, and their two daughters: Terry-Jo, eleven, and Renee, seven. In July Harvey had married his third wife, Mary Dene Smith. Mary came along as deck-hand and cook.

The Duperraults were looking for an escape from the onset of the long vicious Green Bay winter. At the start it was everything they had hoped for. Nowhere on earth is more lotus-eating perfect than the Bahamas in a calm late autumn. The days were sunny and bright. The nights, which they spent anchored in deserted sandy tropical bays, were gentle and warm. They swam and they fished and they sailed. In Green Bay, Duperrault was making big money from the new demand for contact lenses. This was his reward. You work hard. You live well. The Duperrault slice of the American Dream.

On Sunday 12 November, the *Bluebelle* left Great Abaco

Island for the fifty-mile run to Great Stirrup Cay. At 8.30 p.m., Harvey was at the wheel and the Duperraults and Mary were lounging on the after-cockpit after dinner. Without warning, out of the gentle westerly breeze, came a line squall – a sudden gust of wind of terrible force. The wind tore away the boat's rigging, pulling away the mizzen-mast and knocking down the mainmast, sending it crashing through the deck to rip a hole in the hull. The motor cut out and Harvey lost all control of the yacht. He started the auxiliary engine and ran down to his cabin to fetch wire-cutters to free the mizzen-mast which was flapping dangerously. When he re-emerged, the cockpit was on fire and the auxiliary motor was out, its fuel line cut by the fallen mast. He ran back down to the cabin to fetch a fire-extinguisher. By now the boat was sinking. He had to wade through two feet of water to reach the cabin. Back on deck the fire had taken hold, cutting the yacht in two. The small extinguisher was useless. Harvey was separated from his wife and the Duperraults by a wall of flame. He heard confused screams above the roar of the fire.

It was clear that the *Bluebelle* was finished. As the fire reached him, Harvey cut through the guard-rail and launched the yacht's dinghy, intending to manoeuvre it around the burning yacht and reach his trapped companions. Before he could make his way alongside towards the after-cockpit, the *Bluebelle* sank sizzling beneath the water.

In the dark he paddled among the debris. He found the limp body of one of the girls and hauled her onto the dinghy. He tried to revive her. She flickered into life, but by dawn she was dead.

Verhouille remembered afterwards Harvey's strange

impassiveness as he told his story. He broke down only once, when he seemed to realise he would never see his wife again. When Verhouille asked him the name of the girl he had rescued, it took Harvey an hour to remember that she was called Terry-Jo. As far as Verhouille could tell, the deaths of the Duperrault family made no impression on Harvey at all. He talked of them in the same dazed monotone as he used for the sunken yacht. It sounded like indifference, but shock can take many forms.

The *Gulf Lion* dropped Harvey at Nassau in the Bahamas and from there, on Wednesday the 15th, he was flown to Miami. On the Thursday, the Miami Coastguard began its investigation of the sinking of the *Bluebelle*. Harvey was called in to repeat his story to Captain Barber, the investigating officer.

As he was completing his evidence, a coastguard came into the room with good news. Another survivor of the *Bluebelle* had been picked up. The other Duperrault daughter was alive. The coastguard asked Harvey to come to the phone. The girl had been picked up on a life-float. She had not yet spoken and they needed Harvey to confirm the make and type of float used aboard the *Bluebelle*.

Harvey came back into the room smiling. 'Ain't that wonderful!' he said to Captain Barber. He was perfectly steady as he gave the rest of his evidence.

It was normal procedure to interview the owner of any yacht lost in unusual circumstances. Harold Pegg followed Harvey into the interviewing room. As Pegg entered, Harvey lost his composure. He paled, got to his feet and made for the door. Captain Barber called after him that he had the right to question Pegg on his evidence. Harvey shook his head and walked out into the car park. He started his car and drove to the Miami motel where he was registered under the name of John Monroe of Tampa, Florida.

The following morning the maid received no answer when she came to clean the room. She opened the door with her pass-key. She found Julian Harvey dead on the blood-soaked sheets of the bed. He had slashed the veins of his arms, wrists and throat with the blade of a safety razor.

It was only by the slimmest chance that the Duperrault girl had been found alive. The coastguard had instructed all ships in the area between Great Abaco Island and New Providence Island to look out for survivors of the *Bluebelle*. On the afternoon of 16 November the freighter *Captain Theo* was headed for the Northwest Providence Channel. The weather was closing in, the wind freshening and the visibility falling, the surface of the water breaking into whitecaps. Ten minutes later and they would have missed the tiny figure on the life-float.

The girl's hair was bleached almost white from three days unprotected exposure to the sun, the skin on her face a bright painful red. She was dressed in pink corduroy slacks, white woollen socks, a white cotton blouse and a white undershirt. She was half-dead from thirst and sunstroke.

The *Captain Theo* put the girl ashore at Nassau and she was flown by coastguard helicopter to the Sisters of Mercy Hospital in Miami. From the moment she had been lifted from the sea, she had fallen into a deep, trance-like sleep. On arrival at the hospital she roused herself briefly to murmur her name. Dr Franklin Verdon thought he heard her say 'Jerry'. Her age suggested she was

Terry-Jo, the elder Duperrault daughter. It seemed that Harvey had confused the names of the two girls. Dr Verdon thought that she would live. 'The things we have to worry about now,' he said, 'are pneumonia and her heart. Her body chemistry is bound to be a little haywire.' The thing that most worried him was her mental state. 'She is,' he told reporters, 'full of shock.'

Terry-Jo was in no state to talk about the sinking of the *Bluebelle*. However, Harvey's behaviour at the coastguard inquest led Rear-Admiral Theodore J. Fabick, Head of the 75th Coastguard Division, to take an unusual precaution for an eleven-year-old girl saved from a shipwreck. He stationed an armed guard at the door of her hospital room for the night of the 16th. With the news of Harvey's suicide the next morning, the guard was removed.

Harvey left a note on the bedside table of his blood-spattered motel room. The note was addressed to James Boozer, a Miami advertising salesman. Boozer had been a friend of Harvey's since the Second World War. They had gone through pilot training together at the Thunderbird Field base in Phoenix, Arizona in 1941. In the note Harvey asked Boozer to take care of Lance, Harvey's fourteen-year-old son from his first marriage. He asked that his body be buried at sea. The note ended: 'I am tired and nervous and can't take it any longer.'

The press descended on Boozer. He described his old friend as another innocent victim of the *Bluebelle* tragedy. Boozer believed Harvey had killed himself 'because of his intense love for the girl he had met and married . . . she was the dream girl of his life.' Harvey had blamed himself for her death. Although he was obsessed with safety, throughout his life he had been dogged by bad luck. It wasn't his fault, he was just 'accident-prone'.

Over the next few days, as the details of Julian Harvey's life emerged, it became clear that Harvey had been 'accident-prone' in much the same way that it is slightly uncomfortable to take a bath with a crocodile.

His early adult life was a succession of triumphs. He was decorated as a bomber pilot in the Second World War and as a fighter pilot in Korea. In 1946, at the end of the Second World War, he completed a degree in Aeronautical Engineering at Purdue University. In 1953, after Korea, he joined the elite group of air force test pilots. He was a rising star. However, already things had begun to go askew in Harvey's life. After a brief wartime marriage ended in divorce, he married again. In 1949, stationed at Eglin air force base in north-western Florida, he crashed his car through the railing of a bridge on Fort Walton Beach, killing his wife Joan and mother-in-law, Myrtle Boylen. In 1953 he was forced to bale out of a jet trainer at Edwards air force base in California. It was his last act as a hero. With the jet plunging out of control, he stayed on board long enough to eject his passenger. The following year he crashed again, this time in the Arizona desert. He injured himself so badly that he was invalided out of the service.

Harvey tried to make a new life as a charter skipper. With his air force pay-off he bought a yacht, the *Tabatross* and hired himself out to trippers off the North-East Coast. In 1955 he ripped the hull of the *Tabatross* on the submerged hulk of the US battleship *Texas* in Chesapeake Bay. He collected $14,256 damages from the Federal Government and bought an 81 ft ocean-racing yacht, the *Valiant*. The *Valiant* was so luxurious that it had an open log fireplace in the mess-room. Four years later, Harvey duly wrecked the *Valiant*, fireplace and all, off the coast of Cuba.

Harvey had a taste for the expensive life. By the autumn of 1961 his savings were gone. He was heavily in debt and reduced to hiring himself out to crew other people's yachts. On 27 July in Tijuana, Mexico, he married Mary Dene Smith. For her it seemed like a new start.

The couple had met years before in Miami. Mary was a stewardess with Transworld Airlines. At the time of the marriage, she was thirty-two years old. After the wedding she had carried on working, but she hoped to give up the job and start a family. She wanted to enter into Harvey's world. She knew nothing about sailing, but wanted to learn.

In the *New York Times* on 17 November, beneath the report of Terry-Jo's rescue, the paper carried a half-page advertisement for the first New York television showing of *Double Indemnity*, the film of a James M. Cain novel starring Fred MacMurray, Barbara Stanwyk and Edward G. Robinson. In the film Stanwyk plays Phyllis Nirdlinger, a bored but psychopathic housewife, and MacMurray plays Walter Huff, a fatally susceptible insurance salesman. Together they murder the inconvenient Mr Nirdlinger and claim on his life insurance. The title of the film comes from a strange feature of the insurance policy – the company pays double in the event of accidental death. To take advantage of this provision Walter Huff goes to a tremendous amount of trouble and effort to stage Nirdlinger's death on a moving train.

In late October 1961, ten weeks after his marriage and two weeks before setting sail on the *Bluebelle*, Julian Harvey took out a $20,000 life insurance policy on his wife. The policy contained a double indemnity clause. In case of accidental death it would pay $40,000.

For two days after admission to the Sisters of Mercy Hospital, Terry-Jo Duperrault remained in a semi-coma. On 18 November her condition improved. On the 19th she was strong enough to be interviewed by the police. In America, the big news stories of trouble in the Congo and segregationist violence in the Deep South were pushed into footnotes. On 20 November the news came that the youngest son of Nelson A. Rockefeller, Governor of New York was missing, alone and adrift on a canoe off the coast of New Guinea. He had been on a hunt for examples of primitive art among the Willigiman Wallallas, a tribe of reputed head-hunters. On the 21st Terry-Jo's statement was released to the press. It elbowed the Governor's tragedy from the headlines. The girl's story bore no relation to Julian Harvey's version of events.

On the night of the 12th, the *Bluebelle* was under sail in the North West Providence Channel. Julian and Mary Harvey and the Duperraults were lounging, relaxed and easy in the balmy night, in the after-cockpit. The yacht was sailing itself. At 9 p.m. Terry-Jo and Renee went to bed; Renee to a bunk in the main cabin amidships and Terry-Jo to the port stateroom.

Some time later, Terry-Jo was woken by the noise of screaming and running feet. The sounds were confused, but among them she made out the voice of her fourteen-year-old brother Brian. She got out of her bunk and made for the companion-way stairs outside the door of her cabin. Looking through to the central cabin she saw the bodies of her mother, Jean, and her brother lying motionless at the foot of the starboard side-ladder. She ran up the companion-way stairs to the main deck. There was no one in sight. There was no one at the wheel. There was something slippery underfoot. It looked like blood.

The children called Harvey 'Captain'. It added to the sense of adventure of their first expedition on the ocean. As Terry-Jo stood horrified, not knowing where to go or what to do, the Captain appeared from the forward deck carrying something in his hand that looked like a bucket. 'What's happened?' she said.

Harvey didn't answer. 'Get down there!' he shouted. When she didn't move, he hit her with his free hand and pushed her down the stairs. She ran back into her cabin and got up into the bunk, pulling the covers over her head.

A few minutes later she heard the sound of water sloshing on the deck. She thought he must be cleaning the blood from the deck. Then she saw that water was running from the bilges into the cabin. The water was dirty and thick. It smelt of oil.

She heard footsteps descending the companion-way stairs. The Captain appeared at the door of her cabin. He was carrying a rifle. He looked at her on the bed and hesitated. Then he turned and went back up to the deck. She heard sounds like hammering and then as if a heavy unevenly-shaped object was being dragged across the deck.

The water continued to rise in Terry-Jo's cabin. When it reached the mattress on her bunk, she waded back to the stairs and went up again to the deck. She was confused and terrified, but she trusted in adults and the Captain was the only adult standing. She could not entirely believe he wouldn't help her. Harvey was by the rail. The yacht's dinghy was in the water, floating free. She asked Harvey if the boat was sinking. He said 'Yes.' He gave her a long appraising look, jumped over the side and swam to the dinghy. He disappeared from sight into the darkness.

By now the water was up to the deck. There was no one else in sight. She loosened a life-float from its bracket on the cockpit wall, climbed onto it and floated clear of the *Bluebelle*.

The coastguard prompted Terry-Jo for details that might corroborate any part of Harvey's story. Nothing fitted with his version. There had been no fire. She remembered that the mainmast had been slanting at a slight angle, but it had not been broken. The rigging hung slack, but intact. There had been no sudden squall. Somehow Harvey had killed Dr Duperrault, Jean Duperrault, Brian Duperrault and his own wife, Mary. Only Harvey knew how Renee Duperrault died. Perhaps he picked her up drowned from the sea. Perhaps he drowned her himself. Perhaps he was too sick of death to kill Terry-Jo. He must have calculated that she had no chance of survival. He had the dinghy. She was a child lost at night in a sinking ship.

The coastguard conclusion on hearing Terry-Jo's story was 'mass murder by a berserk man'. There is much that is inexplicable in the story of the *Bluebelle*. Terry-Jo remembered no bad feeling aboard the boat before the night of the 12th. It is hard to see how a sane man, no matter how desperate, could plan to kill three adults and three children to collect $40,000. People have killed for less, but not often with such wanton waste. Perhaps something happened on that night to push a disappointed man over the edge into madness.

On 20 November, Julian Harvey had his final wish. He had asked in the note he left for Boozer to be buried at sea. His body was taken out off the Florida coast aboard the

Huckster, a luxury yacht owned by Jason Whitney, a Miami yacht broker and old friend. He was accompanied by a crew of six, a Protestant minister, Boozer, Whitney, an unidentified woman and an unidentified boy. They may have been his first wife and his son, Lance. His friends consigned his body to the sea, bound with a blue ribbon. On the ribbon they wrote 'Bon voyage, Julian.'

On the 23rd, Dr Verdon at the Sisters of Mercy Hospital broke the news to Terry-Jo that her parents, her brother and sister were dead. When reporters asked for her reaction he told them that 'she is definitely down in the dumps', but she hadn't cancelled her Thanksgiving dinner of roast turkey and pumpkin pie. She had the resilience of youth. On the 27th she flew back to live with her aunt, Mrs Robert Scheers in a suburb of Green Bay, Wisconsin to try and carry on with her childhood. On the same day, Governor Rockefeller headed back to the States, finally admitting his son was lost. In Mineola, Long Island, Mate Ivanov, a disturbed mental patient on the run from the Central Islip State Hospital was the main suspect in the killing of five at an isolated farmhouse. Police found a French military bayonet near the scene of the crime. A madman on the loose. This was the sort of crime that people could understand.

The events on the *Bluebelle* were soon forgotten. On 25 April, the Miami Coastguard finally produced its report on the tragedy. The conclusions contained no surprises. Harvey, down on his luck and with a hefty insurance on his wife, had killed her and three members of the Duperrault family who happened to be in the wrong boat at the wrong time. The report was relegated to the back pages beneath an advertisement for May's edition of *Reader's Digest* – 'Have

172

You Ever Felt Like Shaking Your Fist At God?' – and the report of $90,000 damages paid to a seven-year-old girl after a mailbox had fallen on her head.

10.

Boats To Hell

The United Nations completed a form for each Vietnamese refugee arriving at a holding camp on the coast of Thailand. By 1979, so many refugees told the same story that UN officials developed a shorthand. In the space on the form for 'experience since leaving Vietnam' they wrote the three letters 'RPM'. The letters stood for 'Rape, Pillage, Murder'.

The scale of the tragedy of the boat people is too great to pick only one account. It is too great to pick a hundred or a thousand. The three recorded here can only give some tiny idea of how mad and bad the world can be.

In 1978 English *Vogue* reported that 'the body is back. Waists exist. There's a legginess that hasn't been seen for years – ankles are suddenly sexy.' The twentieth century had become thoroughly civilised. In London, Punk Rock was dead, replaced by the 'New Romantic' Movement, a style modelled on Hollywood films of the buccaneers of the Spanish Main. As far as Europe was concerned, piracy was an antique curio – an inspiration for a new brand of shirt. Eight thousand miles away, in the waters between the Mekong Delta and the coast of south-eastern Thailand and north-eastern Malaysia, the genuine article was back with terror on a scale never before seen or conceived.

The Vietnam War left a terrible legacy. By 1975, when South Vietnam finally fell to the Viet Cong, 7.5 million tonnes of bombs had fallen on a country the size of Italy – over three times as much explosives as were dropped by all sides in the Second World War. Over two million were dead and half the country's arable land had been destroyed. However, for many Vietnamese, the cease-fire was only the beginning.

Over the two years that followed, a trickle of refugees fled the country in boats across the Gulf of Thailand. At first they were given asylum in Thailand and Malaysia. Some left Vietnam because they feared persecution as supporters of the fallen regime in the south. Some were looking for a better life. Some were ethnic Chinese, escaping racial persecution.

In October 1977, Thailand and Malaysia announced that they could no longer cope with the tide of Vietnamese refugees. They began to turn boats away from their coasts, forcing them back out into the sea. Vessels that reached Singapore were refuelled, re-supplied and firmly sent on their way. Only the governments of the Philippines and Indonesia continued to provide official sanctuary. However, these countries were hard to reach from Vietnam in small boats.

Relations between Vietnam and China deteriorated rapidly after the Vietnam War. Both had interests in Cambodia. The Chinese wanted to sustain the homicidal Khmer Rouge regime under Pol Pot, and the Vietnamese to overthrow Pol Pot and set up a government in line with their own brand of communism. As the tension increased, so did discrimination against Vietnam's ethnic Chinese.

Between the seventeenth and the nineteenth centuries, pressure of population in China had led many to emigrate to Vietnam. By the 1970s there were nearly two million ethnic

Chinese in Vietnam. Hostility between China and Vietnam is traditional. Like ethnic minorities throughout history, the Chinese in Vietnam were easy scapegoats in times of trouble.

The discrimination of the mid-seventies took many forms. In the cities the ethnic Chinese were replaced in skilled jobs by North Vietnamese. They were forcibly moved to New Economic Zones hundreds of miles away in the north. If they refused to go, their ration cards were withdrawn. When Vietnam finally invaded Cambodia at the end of 1978, they were conscripted en masse into the armed forces.

The Vietnamese Government was happy for its Chinese citizens to emigrate. Before 1978 all refugees caught escaping from Vietnam were imprisoned, but with the growing xenophobia, any ethnic Chinese who could afford $2,000 for an exit permit was free to leave. Many were dumped onto rackety 'slave-boats' and set adrift in the Gulf of Thailand.

From 1978, the gradual flow of refugees gathered pace. In the first six months of the year, 20,000 boat people took to the sea. By the end of the year, 5,000 were arriving every week in neighbouring countries. In all, until the flow slackened in the mid-eighties, 600,000 escaped alive. It is impossible to tell how many failed to reach safety. The very lowest estimate of deaths is 60,000. The true figure is probably much nearer a quarter of a million.

These were poor, frightened, hopeful people. They took to the sea often with no idea of navigation, in overcrowded, unseaworthy boats with pathetic supplies of food and water. They were unarmed. They carried with them all they possessed. For pirates they were easy targets.

There are many cases, at least in the early days of the exodus, of kindness shown by Thai fishermen to the boat people. However, as the numbers rose, they were increasingly seen as a fifth column – a device to undermine the Thai economy. The Thais had always mistrusted Vietnamese expansionist ambition. Mistrust had grown to hatred with bitter disputes over rights to the crowded fishing waters off the Thai coast. More and more, encouraged by official connivance, the Thai fishermen turned sea-bandits.

The story of Than-Hung is typical of the Chinese refugees in the early years of the exodus.

Than-Hung left his home town in May of 1979 with his wife Lang and their five-year-old daughter Li. They were Chinese, though their families had lived in Vietnam for generations. For Than-Hung the alternatives were to leave or slowly to sink into destitution.

On 31 May at seven on a balmy evening, along with thirty of their relations, they boarded a ship in the far south bound for Indonesia. It was a wooden-hull boat, 24 metres long, 3.2 metres in the beam, powered by a single Ray 6 Block engine. On board, crammed into every crevice, were 467 men, women and children. At nine o'clock they sailed. It seemed to everyone on board that their problems were over. They had found a passage. The next stop was freedom.

The ship took two days to reach international waters. The wooden boat bobbed in the swell. The decks ran with vomit. By then it was clear that the voyage was not going to be easy. The helmsman, with no navigation aids, had lost his way. After five days they were running short of food and water.

At nine on the morning of 6 June they sighted a German merchant vessel. The ship signalled them to follow, but after a day and a half they lost sight. All day the sun beat down on the bare decks. By night on the 7th, thirty of the passengers were dead from thirst.

On the evening of the 8th they flagged a large unmarked fishing vessel. The ship approached. The passengers waved in hope of salvation. The crew of the fishing ship looked on unsmiling. The ship drew alongside and the vessels were roped together. The fishing crew boarded the refugee boat, armed with knives and clubs. Without a word, in a nightmare of silence, the refugees were herded onto the fishing boat.

The pirates split into two groups. While one group tore the refugee boat apart searching for valuables, the other group stripped and searched the refugees, prying in armpits and anuses for money and jewels. Anyone who resisted was beaten.

When the search was completed, the refugees were herded back onto their vessel. By now the boat was shipping water badly, holed where pirates had ripped up boards and pried open seams looking for valuables. Fifty of the refugees, seeing the state of their ship, tried to stay on board the fishing boat. The pirates cut the refugees adrift, threw the fifty overboard and sailed away into the gathering dusk.

With nightfall came the first bad weather of the voyage. The sky clouded, the wind began to blow and the waves battered the flooding boat. Than-Hung and his companions made desperate efforts to plug the holes in the hull, but the attempt was useless. The ship began to list badly. Then she capsized.

In the first shock of immersion Than-Hung and his daughter Li were separated from the child's mother. Than-Hung entrusted Li to a man clinging to the capsized hull and swam in search of his wife. Battered by the waves he circled the boat screaming Lang's name. There was no answer, only the panicked cries of other survivors. When he returned there was no sign of the man or of his baby daughter. At three in the morning the sodden rotten hull of the refugee boat sunk beneath the waves.

The day dawned calm. Of the 467 refugees only sixty remained alive, clinging exhausted to whatever of the debris that remained afloat. The sun of the day was worse than the storm of the night before. Than-Hung, numbed to everything by the loss of his wife and daughter, kept an instinctive hold on a wooden float while his tongue swelled and his lips cracked. One by one the weaker refugees lost their hold and sunk beneath the water. At sunset the thirty survivors were picked up by another Thai fishing boat and put ashore at Kelantin on the Malaysian coast. Than-Hung had lost not only his wife and child, but all thirty members of his family.

The survivors were kept in a holding station with 118 other Vietnamese refugees. After seventeen days they were all loaded aboard a boat and supplied with 200 litres of water and three days' supply of canned food. A Malay naval tug towed the boat into international waters. The tow-rope was cut and they were left to drift with the current. The boat's engine had been disabled. Freedom had not proved so free after all.

Than-Hung had only hazy memories of the nineteen days that followed. The weather turned bad again. They were lost helpless in a world of wind and spray. Some went mad and killed themselves. The survivors had to drink their own urine. When the weather calmed they were attacked five more times by Thai fishing boats. They were stripped of their clothes and anything of value that could be prised from their bodies.

The last pirate attack saved their lives. Finding nothing but a skeletal heap of dying men and women, the pirates took nothing and left them with water and a thin rice broth.

The ultimate irony of Than-Hung's journey was his final destination. The currents took the boat back to the Vietnamese coast. He was arrested along with the other survivors. He had lost everything and ended up where he had begun.

The fate of Than-Hung and his family has a nightmare quality. However there is one small island in the Gulf of Thailand where the tragedy of the boat people went far beyond nightmare.

By 1980 groups of Thai fishermen had formed into pirate fleets. In a sense they had become privateers – the first line of defence against what was seen as a sea-borne Vietnamese invasion. The most brutal set up their base on the island of Koh Kra.

By 1980 the United Nations had established camps in southern Thailand to protect and control the influx of boat people. Theodor Schweitzer, a thirty-eight-year-old American, arrived as UN representative at the Songkhla Camp in early 1980. He brought with him his Thai wife Wannah and their young daughter.

Schweitzer was besotted with the East. He had met Wannah in 1974 when he was teaching at the American College in Bangkok. From Thailand they had gone to Iran until all Americans were thrown out in 1979 on the fall of the Shah. The job in Songkhla was a chance to return to the part of the world he loved the most.

Early on, Schweitzer began to hear stories from refugees at the camp of terrible experiences at a pirate base thirty-five kilometres out in the Gulf of Thailand. He decided to investigate for himself.

His first attempt to reach Koh Kra failed. He borrowed a pilot and a helicopter from a US offshore oil-prospecting company. As they approached the island they saw strange-shaped lumps floating in the blue sea of the bay. The pilot flew low. The lumps were corpses. The unnerved pilot refused to land.

For his return journey Schweitzer hired a fishing boat. They arrived at night at the entrance to the bay. Because of the reefs and the unpredictable currents the Captain insisted they hold off until dawn. Schweitzer heard screams of agony coming across the bay from the beach. He is an extraordinary man. He stripped and dived into the water. A rip-tide carried him from the bay around the headland. He managed to swim out of the current and was thrown by the waves onto the rocky far shore. With body and feet badly cut he made his way back across the island towards the beach.

As he stumbled across the headland, two figures emerged from the thick brush beside the path. They were boat people who had seen him washed up on the shore. They had a hideous story to tell.

Nineteen days before, a convoy of four refugee boats had been wrecked at night on the reefs around Koh Kra. Of the 238 aboard, eighty were now dead. In the moonlight, the Vietnamese pointed out a row of bodies hanging from makeshift gibbets on the shore-line, beyond a line of camp-fires on the beach.

The two refugees left Schweitzer on the edge of the beach, too frightened to approach the fires. Schweitzer crossed the sand. In the light from the flames he saw young girls dancing naked, goaded on by blows from bamboo canes. He passed more women lying spent on the sand, faces burned from the fires. They threw themselves at his feet and begged to be rescued.

The pirates were gathered round the fires, dead drunk. Their faces were daubed with war-paint, like Red Indians. God knows what they thought of Schweitzer – a white man, his feet caked in blood, dressed only in his shorts. He singled out the leader and demanded an explanation. He told them he was a representative of the United Nations and that if they harmed him they would be in deep trouble. He might as well have told them that he was an alien from Pluto.

Schweitzer's arrival unnerved the pirates. They assumed that he was not alone. It also gave courage to the refugees. The men began to emerge from the shadows and jostle their tormenters. The pirates retaliated with ice-picks, knocked Schweitzer unconscious with an iron bar and made for their boats.

Dawn revealed the full desolation of the beach of Koh Kra. Dismembered limbs littered the sand. There were signs of cannibalism. The women were in a pitiful state. Some had tried to escape into the undergrowth. The pirates had set fire to the brush and the bodies of the women were scarred with untreated burns.

The early light also showed the pirate boats waiting out in the bay. Schweitzer gathered the survivors together and ferried them to his ship before the pirates realised how little support he had.

In the six months that followed, Schweitzer returned twenty-eight times to Koh Kra. Through a mixture of nerve and effrontery he saved 1,250 refugees and brought them back to Songkhla. When he tried to pursue charges against the captain and the owner of a pirate ship he was threatened with death. He hired an armed bodyguard and sent his wife and child to safety in Bangkok.

Schweitzer became obsessed with the enormity of the suffering he witnessed. The Thai authorities were obviously colluding with the pirates. However, the United Nations could say nothing. They needed to tread carefully with the Thais or risk being expelled from the country. The boat people themselves were refugees with no status and no voice. Schweitzer was alone in his crusade.

For the pirates, a major source of income was the trade in women refugees. They sold those they kidnapped to brothels on the coast. Schweitzer was told by a refugee family that their daughter was held in a brothel in Phattalung in communist-insurgent controlled territory. The girl was called Mai. The family had a photograph.

Schweitzer went from brothel to brothel asking to see the foreign girls. Most were from Laos, running from economic chaos under the Pathet Lao. Finally he found Mai in the village of Ban Na Thom. He paid for a night of her company.

Mai's story was a sadly familiar one in Thailand. The pirates had sold her for $250. She was kept as an unpaid slave. The procession of clients started at ten in the morning and continued for up to sixteen hours.

In the morning, Schweitzer offered to buy her. When her pimp refused, he returned with his bodyguard and took her by force. Fired by his mission, Schweitzer was now magnificently out of control.

Mai knew of another house where fifteen Vietnamese girls were kept against their will. He took Mai to the local police station and asked them to take care of her. He stormed on to the other brothel, but the girls had been sold on. When he returned to the police station, the officers politely explained that Mai's husband had arrived and claimed back his wife. Mai was never seen again. Schweitzer ranted, but was met by blank official smiles.

After a year, Schweitzer finally secured a permanent Thai military presence on Koh Kra. However, he had antagonised too many people. The Thai authorities registered an official complaint with the UN over his interference and lack of respect. He had become a diplomatic embarrassment. The UN offered him a job in Geneva. He refused the transfer and returned bitter to his home in Missouri.

Ted Schweitzer's courage was extraordinary, but he was not alone in trying to stem the tide of human misery in the Gulf of Thailand. The UN camps have saved many thousands of lives. While most sailed on regardless, captains of many merchant ships made huge efforts to rescue distressed refugees at sea. However, the pirate problem remained largely untouched.

Two years after Schweitzer had returned to Missouri, Ngoyen Phan Thuy, a woman of twenty-three with the delicate sad beauty of South-East Asia, left her home in Ho Chi Minh City. She carried a small bag containing all her possessions: a pair of trousers, five shirts, a bottle of aspirin, five lemons, a packet of sugar and 1,000 dongs, the equivalent of $50. She had spent $1,000, her lifetime's savings, on a passage out of Vietnam. With her mother, aunt and younger sister she travelled by bus to a small fishing port near Rach Gia on the southern tip of Vietnam.

On the night of 23 December, with sixty-two others, the family boarded a ten metre wooden boat captained by a primary school teacher. The local police had been bribed to stay shut in their office as the boat sailed out into the Gulf.

After ten days at sea they had run out of food and water. They were drifting to conserve what little fuel remained. On the morning of 2 January two fishing boats pulled alongside. The refugees begged for help. The men on the fishing boats drew guns and knives. The captain started the engine and tried to accelerate free, but the pirates swept the deck with rifle fire. Phan heard a scream behind her and turned to find her aunt, shot through the chest, dying on the deck. The captain, terrified, cut the motor and waited for the pirates to come back alongside.

The pirates swarmed onto the deck, striking out at random with clubs and staves. They ordered the refugees to strip, and then brought them forward one by one to the prow. Phan watched in horror as they forced open an old man's mouth and ripped out his gold teeth with pliers. One woman went forward with a baby in her arms. She claimed that her clothes were all she possessed. Her baby was grabbed from her hands and thrown overboard. Two men resisted. They were beaten senseless with rifle-butts.

By ten in the morning the pirates had stripped everything of value from the refugees. They attached tow-lines to the boat and hauled her eight hours to Koh Kra. It was now two years since the Thais had agreed to set up a permanent military base on the island.

In the dying light of the day, the refugees were unloaded onto the beach. Their boat was hauled onto the sand, holed with axes and towed out to sink in the bay. The pirates ordered

The engine room of the *Rainbow Warrior* after the bombing by the French Secret Service. (Associated Press/Topham)

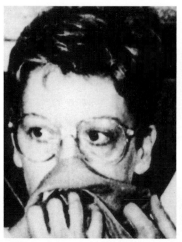

Captain Dominique Prieur (alias Sophie Turenge), part of the French team which sank the *Rainbow Warrior*. (Associated Press/Topham)

Major Alain Mafart (alias Alain Turenge) who posed as Prieur's husband. Their unconvincing act led to the discovery of official French involvement. (Associated Press/Topham)

The *Rainbow Warrior* is finally sent to the bottom in Maturai Bay. (Associated Press/Topham)

The *Achille Lauro*. An unlucky ship. (Associated Press/Topham)

Marilyn Klinghoffer escorted from the *Achille Lauro* at Port Said. She spat in the faces of her husband's killers. (Associated Press/Topham)

Gerardo de Rosa, Captain of the *Achille Lauro* discusses the hijack with a passenger while the ship is held at Port Said. (Associated Press/ Topham)

The three adult hijackers of the *Achille Lauro*. From left to right – Al Molqi Magied, Fataier Abdelatif Ibrahim and Al Assadi Ahmed Marouf. (Associated Press/Topham)

Emilio Changco, the genius of the Phillipine 'Phantom Ship' trade in Manila penitentiary. A few months after the photograph was taken, Changco, despite his bone cancer, was shot trying to escape. (Mike Goldwater/Network)

the women to line up. The captain picked out Phan and then offered his crew the choice of another woman. With a lot of grinning and giggling they selected Lien, a delicate-looking teenager. Still naked, the two women were dragged by their hair on board one of the fishing boats and locked in a hold stinking of decayed fish and diesel.

There is a danger in catalogues of horror and abuse. They begin to sound ordinary. It is impossible to convey what the next three weeks were like for those girls. Every day they were repeatedly and violently raped. Lien simply could not bear it. She huddled in the corner of the hold crying continually. When she fainted the pirates would pour water over her and dunk her head in a bucket until she gagged. Eventually her misery became too much for them. As Phan watched they threw Lien overboard. She did not scream in protest. She sunk without a sound.

When they reached port, Phan was bundled at night into a truck and sold to a village brothel – the 'Paradise Massage Parlour'. The clients were Malays and Singaporeans enjoying a relaxing holiday break; out for a good time. When she became pregnant, the child was aborted by an old woman with a length of bamboo.

After six months she was trusted to go unaccompanied to 'comfort' a geriatric Japanese gentleman in his hotel room. She ran to the police. They locked her up as an illegal immigrant. After four days in a cell she was rescued by the UN. She had relatives in Ohio. In the end she was lucky.

Phan's story was repeated tens of thousands of times – ordinary people escaping to a new life and ending up in hell. The tragedy of the boat people plays a very small part in the revival of interest in security of the sea. It is the loss of tankers and of merchant vessels which has led to the conferences and agreements and task-forces. The Vietnamese were just people. They had no union and were backed by no government.

There are a few isolated cases of boat people fighting back against pirate attacks. In May 1979 a ship-full of refugees scared away a Thai fishing boat by brandishing long-bladed knives and threatening to throw light-bulbs painted to look like hand-grenades. Mostly, though, unarmed and laden with frightened women and children, resistance was impossible. The penalty for fighting could be worse than the pirate attack itself. In 1981, nineteen Vietnamese were sentenced to death after Thai pirates were killed in an attack on their boat.

From 1982 the United Nations funded a programme to monitor and reduce attacks on refugee vessels in the Gulf of Thailand. The Thais mobilised a force of seven anti-pirate boats to control the activities of an estimated 30,000 Thai fishing vessels. Of the seven, the most modern and best-equipped was reserved for use by Admiral Watanapong of the Thai navy for weekend picnics. After 1982 there were a total of five legal proceedings instituted as the result of pirate attacks. The matter was clearly on the top of no one's agenda.

Finally, by the end of the 1980s the exodus had fallen away. Perhaps the Gulf itself was sick of blood.

11.

Columbian Sea-Food

It was the afternoon of 31 July 1980. The day had started hot, close and oppressive, but now the wind was blowing hard from the open Atlantic, threatening a storm.

Harry Yourell and his family were lost and worried. Yourell was a small-time state politician, Democrat Representative for Oak Lawn in Illinois. Like half the population of the snow-belt he had travelled south for some summer fun and sun. Yourell, his wife Milicent and their twenty-year-old son Peter, had gone a little further south than most. In mid-July, in Dania, Florida, they hired a 25 ft power-boat and motored in the warm breeze from island to island through the Bahamas. They had stopped in Bimini and Nassau and were making their way along the Exumas chain of islands to port at Staniel Cay. This was their first hint of bad weather. They wanted to reach harbour before the rain came down.

In the sheltered bay of the tiny island of Pipe Cay, Yourell saw a yacht. He changed course to come alongside and ask directions.

The yacht's name was the *Kalia III*. At first sight, it seemed that she was moored. However, as they approached, they saw that the stern anchor was still on board and that the bow anchor had been cut at the water-line. The yacht was drifting free.

The yacht's dinghy was floating to one side, attached by a line to the rail. The dinghy was listing at a sharp angle, weighed down by the body of a man slumped like a sack over its side. The man was dressed in a T-shirt that had once been white. His lower body, in the dinghy, was trussed in a sail-bag and his torso was arched over the gunwhale, his head and shoulders hidden beneath the water. There was dried blood on the back of his T-shirt.

There was no movement on the deck of the yacht itself. A large suite-cushion hung over the side, half out of the cockpit. The cushion was spattered with reddish stains. There were bullet-holes in the hull and on the deck.

Yourell radioed his gruesome discovery to the Staniel Cay Yacht Club and then to the Bahamian coastguard in Nassau. The owner of the Staniel Cay 'Happy People' Marina sailed out to join Yourell and together they lashed the *Kalia III* to the shore to prevent her drifting out of the bay.

Later that afternoon, a small plane chartered by the Nassau police flew low over Pipe Cay to fix the yacht's position. According to Yourell, they flew low enough to see the body in the dinghy.

However it was not until late on the following day that a police launch arrived to investigate. By then, the man in the dinghy was gone. They towed the *Kalia III* into Staniel Cay. Aboard they found nothing except for a pair of blood-spattered glasses and a peach-coloured bikini top.

The yacht belonged to a Fort Meyers couple – William and Patty Kamerer. William Kamerer was fifty-five, a typical boat-obsessed product of Florida. He financed his love for the sea with odd jobs as an electrical repairman and was a regular contributor to boating and sailing magazines. He had built the 41 ft *Kalia III* himself. In late June, he and Patty left Fort Meyers for a month's cruise in the Bahamas. On 25 July they had been reported missing. Now they had been found.

With the *Kalia III* in Staniel Cay, the Bahamian police issued a missing persons report on the Kamerers, asking for information on their whereabouts. They claimed that there was no evidence of foul play.

Yourell made a fuss. It was clear to him that the Kamerers were dead. The bloodstained glasses belonged to William Kamerer and the bikini top to Patty. Their money was missing, along with a hunting-rifle. He went on board the yacht and inspected the bloodstains and bullet-holes in the cockpit. He confronted Corporal Bradley Pratt, the officer who had flown over the corpse in the dinghy. Pratt claimed to have seen nothing suspicious.

What the Bahamians did not realise was that Yourell had taken photographs of the scene in Pipe Cay. One shot clearly showed a body slumped over the side of a dinghy. Yourell flew back to the States and blazed the photograph over the newspapers and television. He accused the Bahamian Government of a cover-up and the US State Department of complicity. Clearly there was something going on in the Bahamas, and publicity was not welcome.

Even before the *Kalia III* tragedy, boat owners in southern Florida had began to take precautions against armed attack. As Misty Devine, a yacht writer in St Petersburg, Florida, put it: 'You just don't go out there alone and unarmed. It's like walking into the South Bronx at night – asking for trouble.' Some boat-charters were equipping themselves with enough fire-power to launch a small war. They were not exaggerating the risk. By 1980, a war was exactly what was happening in the south-east of the United States – a Cocaine War – a war for the American nose.

Piracy in the Caribbean had first resurfaced in 1960 with the 'Boatwright Case'. At dawn on 24 April, a 30 ft cabin-cruiser, the *Muriel III*, had arrived at Elbow Cay, a remote uninhabited island in the British-owned Cay Sal Group, 120 miles south of Miami and thirty miles north of Varadero Beach in Cuba.

The *Muriel* was a charter boat crewed by a fifty-five-year-old Captain, Angus Boatwright, and his twenty-five-year-old Mate, Kent Hokansun. Aboard were a group of four middle-aged Pennsylvanian tourists – all men on the loose from their wives for a couple of weeks. They were searching for game-fish.

Boatwright's attention was drawn to a mirror flashing on the shore. Three figures signalled to the boat for help. It was an uncertain time in Cuba. In January, the United States had cut off diplomatic relations with Castro and, earlier in April, there had been an attempted invasion by anti-communist exiles. Britain had been forced to land troops on Cay Sal after Cuban complaints that the islands were being used as bases to bomb the mainland. Boatwright was naturally suspicious of anyone marooned so close to Cuba at a time like this. He held the *Muriel III* off from shore and radioed to the Florida Coastguard.

At 9 a.m. a man swam out to the cruiser from the shore. He was in his mid-twenties – a short, wiry, jumpy figure, badly burned from the sun. He said his name was Johnson and that the three of them had been shipwrecked when their yacht *Star* broke up on the reefs. He was angry and impatient. He insisted that Boatwright bring the cruiser in and pick up his companions. One was a woman who could not swim. Boatwright refused. He explained that there were rocks closer to the shore and he was afraid of grounding. Johnson began to twitch with fury. He pulled a revolver. Boatwright turned and ran for the cabin where he kept his shark-rifle. Johnson followed him. As Boatwright fumbled with the clasp on the storage-box, Johnson shot him, grazing his forehead and then shot him again, in the stomach.

Johnson held the revolver on the four Pennsylvanian fishermen while the other man on shore swam out to the cruiser. Boatwright was unconscious on the deck, knocked out by the shot across his forehead, bleeding badly from the wound in his stomach. The new arrival had to struggle in the surf. He was carrying two rifles on his back. The two discussed what they should do with their captives. Johnson wanted to kill them. 'We can't let these fellows stick around here,' he said, 'they know us.' However, eventually they agreed to dump them on Elbow Cay and steal the *Muriel*. The hijackers even allowed Hokansun to radio to the coastguard for help.

They forced the passengers to swim and put Boatwright in a lifebelt and let Hokansun guide him to the beach. The trip was too much for Boatwright. He died before he reached land.

The woman was still standing on the shoreline. She was in her early twenties, dressed only in a blouse and sandals. She looked very much the worse for wear. Johnson's companion called to her to join them, but she refused. She still claimed she couldn't swim. They tired of waiting, started the engine and headed the *Muriel* in the direction of Cuba.

The castaways were rescued towards evening by the Florida Coastguard. The woman was only eighteen, though the past few weeks had aged her somewhat. Her name was Barbara Tables. Johnson's real name was Billy Ray Sees and his companion was Alvin Tables Jr., Barbara's husband. Their story was a classic American tale of rebels on the run without a cause. Tables was twenty-five and Sees twenty-three. The three were wanted for questioning over a trail of bad cheques from Texas through Alabama and Louisiana to Key West, Florida. The previous week in Key West they had posed as buyers of a 30 ft yacht, the *Hiniera*, taken it for a trial and disappeared. The *Hiniera* was a rackety tub fit for gentle runs across the bay, but not for the open sea. It was extraordinary they had come so far. They had sunk off Elbow Cay two days before. Apart from the firearms, they had rescued nothing from the sinking yacht. They had no food and only the clothes on their backs. Billy Ray's desperation had not been an act.

On 25 April, Sees and Tables ran the *Muriel III* aground at a key off Isabela De Sagua, the port of Sagua La Grande, 200 miles east of Havana. It was not the best time for young Americans to land inconspicuously in a provincial Cuban port. They were arrested and the yacht was seized. In November they were extradited to Nassau in the Bahamas for trial. They were found guilty of murder and robbery with violence and sentenced to hang. On 20 April 1961, the Privy Council in London turned down their appeal for clemency and on 9 May they were executed. There is no word on what became of Barbara Tables. If real life has any respect for art, she went back to Bridgeton, New Jersey, married an accountant, and is now a grandmother worried about her pension plan.

* * *

The Boatwright case was an isolated incident – a combination of bad luck and bad timing. It was another ten years before violence against small boats became a habit.

The first of the 'yachtjacks' of the seventies took place thousands of miles to the west.

The *Kamilii* was a higher class of craft than the *Muriel*. She was a 73 ft luxury yacht owned by a wealthy California businessman. She was manned by a highly-experienced professional crew: Bob Washkeit, Frank Power and John Freitas. In August 1971, the boat was moored at the Ala Wai yacht harbour in Honolulu, Hawaii. The crew had orders to prepare to sail to southern California. She was stocked with three months' supply of food and liquor. Everything was the best that money could buy.

The crew were sleeping on board in the early morning, prepared to sail at dawn. They were woken by three men armed with machetes and German-made Walther P-38 automatic pistols. The intruders moved with military precision. They bound and gagged the crew, slipped anchor and sailed out of port before first light. They headed west, but well to the south of the normal shipping-lanes.

Two days out to sea, the hijackers pulled the crew up out of the hold, untied them and ordered them to jump overboard. There was no land for a hundred miles and little chance of a passing ship. The crew begged for a life-raft. They were ignored and forced overboard at gunpoint. A few minutes later, the yacht came about and one of the gunmen threw them an inflatable raft. He smiled down at them from the rail and tossed a dime into the air. 'Here's the coin,' he said, 'that saved your life.' They still had no food and no water and no prospect of survival.

Five hours later, the crew were picked up by an Italian banana freighter, the *Benadir*. The ship had engine trouble and had drifted far out of her normal course. They alerted Honolulu by radio and a long-range coastguard plane found the *Kamilii*. The plane dropped a message ordering the yacht to stop and return to Honolulu. The *Kamilii* continued its course towards Tahiti. She was constantly shadowed from the air. At night she ran without lights and the coastguard planes dropped flares to illuminate her progress. There are times when the entire ocean has not space enough to hide. Finally she was intercepted by the cutter *Point Corwin*. Faced by superior fire-power the three men surrendered.

Their names were Kerry Bryant, Mark Maynard and Michael Melton. They were all in their mid-twenties – all-American kids. They were also veterans of the Vietnam War. They had planned to sail to Thailand and load up with heroin for the West Coast market. The legacy of South-East Asia had begun to come home. There were bored desperate men loose and there was a nation hungry for kicks. The drug decade had arrived.

The mistake the attackers made with both the *Muriel III* and the *Kamilii* was that they let the crew live. Others were to learn from the mistake.

Compared with the excesses that were to come, drug-trafficking in the early seventies was a fairly mellow, low-key business. Marijuana was the major import from the south. Rewards and risks were high, but not exorbitant. The main hard drug was heroin, brought in from Turkey through New York via the French Connection. In 1973, the French Connection was broken. At the same time, cocaine, which had been briefly fashionable in the Roaring Twenties, resurfaced as the cool way to get high.

The remarkable rise of cocaine came about through a combination of circumstances. In the late sixties the world of show-business adopted the drug. Actors and pop stars wrote songs and made films about cocaine and, back in their hotel rooms, they shoved as much white powder up their noses as their nasal septums could stand. To the American public the only apparent side-effects were wealth, fame and the ability to have sex all night with Hollywood starlets. Veterans were returning from Vietnam with a taste for the drug. Marijuana was a little too laid-back now no one believed any more in peace and love.

At the same time as the demand was growing in the United States, a group of sharp-eyed businessmen from Medellin, a recession-hit Columbian textile town, were looking for a ready way to earn foreign exchange. The mountain valleys of Bolivia and Peru had grown coca for centuries. The Indians had chewed the leaf, as they still do, to combat altitude, hunger and fatigue. With the decline in prices of other commodities and official collusion in Bolivia, there was an inexhaustible supply of the raw material. The Medellin businessmen organised the conversion of the leaf into cocaine and transportation to the United States.

The trade grew rapidly through the seventies. In 1978, the Medellin businessmen decided that they could maximise profits by coordinating their infrastructure. They joined together in the Medellin Cartel. By the end of the seventies they were confronting the Government of the United States on equal terms.

The logical entry point for drugs from the south was Florida. The state has almost one and a half thousand miles of coastline and large stretches are sparsely-inhabited swampland. The route from Columbia to Florida passed through the Bahamas – a chain of 730 islands covering 100,000 square miles of ocean. The Bahamian population of 225,000 was spread thinly over only twenty-nine of these islands. The remainder formed a perfect natural staging-post for Columbian 'sea-food'.

Profits from the cocaine trade were almost inconceivable. By 1977, a pound weight of 95% pure powder had a street retail value of $240,000. The drug barons were able to use a small proportion of their income to keep constantly one step ahead of law enforcement. By the mid-seventies a former coastguard buoy-boat, the *Owl And Pussycat*, was patrolling the Florida coast beyond the ten-mile limit. She had been fitted with $5m worth of the most sophisticated electronic bugging and communication equipment then available. Through her, the smugglers were able to monitor all coastguard, police, FBI and drug-enforcement frequencies and alert incoming vessels. The *Owl And Pussycat* itself carried no drugs. She was boarded once, but had broken no laws.

The organised traffickers could afford to buy the best planes and boats on the market. Consignments were flown directly to Florida, brought in on freight ships or shipped to the Bahamas and then taken in from the ten-mile limit aboard speedboats which could outrun the fastest coastguard cutters. The best of these boats were the 'Cigarette' boats, a brand named after a celebrated rum-running cruiser. The Cigarette, with its twin 400 horse-power engines, held the world off-shore racing record at an average speed of 88.9 m.p.h. over 150 miles. Each boat cost $90,000 in 1977. The Customs could only compete with their own fleet of twenty confiscated models. As the firm's designer put it: 'it usually takes a Cigarette to catch a Cigarette.'

At a level beneath this colossal organisation wormed a mass of small-time villains and would-be villains desperate for a slice of the action. In a trade worth by 1980 an estimated $64bn, there was enough room for independents. To enter the business all that was needed was a little capital and some transport. There were as many ways to take the first step as there were ingenious minds in the American South-West. Floyd Cook, a young family man from Daytona Beach, Florida, used his three-year-old daughter as collateral for his first wholesale marijuana purchase. Others perhaps didn't have daughters. As early as 1974, it seemed that a number were taking the same route as the Vietnam veterans who had hijacked the *Kamilii*. They were turning pirate in the waters off the Caribbean. Now, though, they had learned the lesson of the *Muriel* and the *Kamilii*. They were leaving no witnesses.

Between 1971 and May 1974, when the US Coastguard issued its first official warning to boats off the Florida coast, 610 American vessels disappeared in good weather in the south-east Atlantic, the Gulf of Mexico and the Pacific Coast. Two thousand crew-members went missing. The sea is an unpredictable place. Ships will always go down for no apparent reason. Not on this scale.

Most of the lost ships left no trace behind. However, many left an oblique trail pointing to murder.

In the summer of 1973, a $60,000 yacht, the *Imamou*, set sail from Florida for a cruise off the coast of South America. The owner was the 'rich-kid' son of a wealthy family. He was known to be a drug-user, but not a smuggler. He was

199

travelling with a young college friend looking for cheap drugs and lax laws.

The boat was hard work for two men. On the Columbian coast they picked up two young Frenchmen to crew the *Imamou.* They set off north en route for the Panama Canal and the West Coast. The *Imamou* never reached the Canal.

The following year, the US Coastguard received information that the *Imamou* was berthed at the harbour of Pointe-a-Pierre on the French island of Guadeloupe in the Caribbean. The vessel was seized by French police along with two Frenchmen. The Frenchmen claimed that they had been given the yacht by her owner. It was not a particularly likely story.

The rich-kid's uncle employed a private investigator to trace the *Imamou*'s route from Columbia. He uncovered a network of freelance drug-runners along the east coast of Central America. Central America's Caribbean shore is one of the wildest places on earth. South of the Panama Canal is the Darien Gap, a stretch of barely-penetrable disease-ridden jungle that has defied all attempts to build a road link between North and South America. To the north, in the trackless, isolated Atlantic coasts of Nicaragua and Honduras live the wild and unpredictable Miskito Indians. The Miskitos have their own language and their second tongue is a disconcerting eighteenth-century English. Their origin is unknown, but they may be descendants of a mixture of shipwrecked African slaves and local Indians. They have nothing in common with the Latin people of the gentler Pacific coast. Further north is politically-troubled Guatemala, one of the most violent and lawless places on earth. This is natural country for piracy and smuggling. Much of the coast is accessible only by sea, riddled with hidden inlets and lagoons. Central governments have always had a tenuous grip on the area. Coastal patrols are few and ineffective. On the Atlantic Coast it is possible to get away with whatever murder you wish.

The private detective failed to complete his assignment. He was murdered. Something to do with his murder scared the family so badly that they asked the Federal Authorities to close the investigation.

At least they found some answers to the loss of the *Imamou*. Most cases followed the pattern of the *Flying Dutchman* and the *Pirate Lady*.

On Wednesday 27 October 1976, the wife of John Dijt reported her husband missing. Dijt was the owner of the *Flying Dutchman*, a 47 ft pleasure-cruiser. He was on a trip from Panama City Florida to Fort Lauderdale via Cedar Keys with his friend Terry Stone. In many ways John Dijt was a good husband. Every day, without fail, he contacted his wife before 9 p.m. On the 27th, at 11 p.m., she alerted the coastguard.

The last sighting of the *Flying Dutchman* had been at 2.48 p.m. on Tuesday the 26th when she had been logged passing through the John Gorie Memorial Bridge outside the fishing port of Apalachicola, Florida. The weather was good – a perfect balmy Florida autumn afternoon. Visibility was seven miles. Dijt and Stone were both experienced sailors. The cruiser was equipped for any emergency. In case of engine failure she had a spare outboard motor. On board she carried a 16 ft fibreglass dinghy, flares and a powerful radio transmitter.

Coastguard planes and surface vessels carried out an exhaustive search of 107,500 square kilometres of ocean. In the prevailing conditions, they estimated that the probability of sighting was 99%. They found no trace of the *Flying Dutchman*.

Mrs Dijt had been especially anxious on the night of the 27th. The last she had heard from her husband was at midday on the 26th when he had called from Panama City. He had complained of oil-pressure trouble on the trip from Fort Walton and mumbled about 'possible interference from unknown persons'. He had refused to elaborate, giving the impression that someone was listening to his conversation.

It is now that the story turns messy. If one thing is worse than the unexplained disappearance of a husband, it is when the investigation reveals that he may not have been quite the man you knew.

A Dr Westovelt came forward with information. On the night of the 25th, he had been on board the *Flying Dutchman*. There had been quite a party. There were two women on board – 'Ruth' who said she owned a car business outside Montgomery, Alabama and 'Jeannie' . Everyone was very drunk. Westovelt was reticent about what exactly was going on, but it is clear that Ruth and Jeannie were more than just good friends. He was due to carry on to Fort Lauderdale, but cried off, claiming he had bursitis in his arm, but really because he 'didn't feel right about the situation and was tired of lying' to his own wife. It wasn't quite the innocent fishing trip that Mrs Dijt and Mrs Stone had imagined.

Westovelt remembered that John Dijt was nervous through the drink that night. He was uneasy about two other men who for some reason he had promised to take to Fort Lauderdale. The men were never found. Ruth and Jeannie were identified as Ruth Easterly of Mississippi and Jennie

Kelly of Niceville, Florida. They too went the way of the *Flying Dutchman*.

Three weeks after the cruiser disappeared a note was picked up in a bottle on a Gulf Coast beach. The note read: '*Flying Dutchman*, 3 Cubans on board. Heading due East.'

Apalachicola is an inoffensive place. It is best known for its oysters. However, in the mid seventies it began to build a reputation as a vanishing-point for small boats. Before the *Flying Dutchman* there had been inexplicable disappearances in 1969 and 1974. Then, in January 1977, the *Pirate Lady* followed into the great unknown.

The case of the *Pirate Lady* is surrounded by a byzantine web of speculation and suspicion. She was altogether a more professional outfit than the *Flying Dutchman*. The *Pirate Lady* was a fourteen-month-old 75 ft luxury yacht owned by Charles Slater, Managing Director of Pirate International Services, a company servicing oil-rigs in the Gulf of Mexico. She was manned by a professional captain, forty-seven-year-old Anthony Latuso, and David Decidue, a twenty-year-old part-time deck-hand who had lived among boats all his life. The yacht was moored at Apalachicola on the night of 26 January on her way to meet Slater at Clearwater, Florida on the night of the 27th. There is no suggestion of drink or women aboard the *Pirate Lady*. Latuso was an obsessively cautious man. Decidue's parents had driven out to see him on the night of the 26th and noticed nothing unusual.

At 6 a.m. on the 27th, the manager of the Rainbow Inn Motel on the Apalachicola waterfront heard the sound of a boat engine. He looked out of the window and saw the *Pirate Lady* slipping out of harbour in the dark. The lights in the cabin were turned off and he could not identify the figure at the wheel. The last anyone ever saw of her was as she passed beneath the John Gorie Memorial Bridge.

The water that day was rough with a six- to eight-foot swell, but the *Pirate Lady* was built to cope easily with eighteen-foot seas. When she failed to arrive at Clearwater that evening, the coastguard again launched an exhaustive search. Visibility was near-perfect except for a slight haze to the south. No trace was found.

Charles Slater sent one of his supply-vessels, the *Calico Jack* to join the search. In eighteen hours at sea they picked up a lump of charred Formica and an empty tin of condensed milk.

On the day that the yacht disappeared, the coastguard received a report that a 70 ft shrimper, the *Gunsmoke* was unloading bales of marijuana at a beach outside Apalachicola. A cutter gave chase. The *Gunsmoke* evaded pursuit and was sunk, presumably scuttled, seventeen miles off the Florida coast. The incident was later linked to the discovery of the bodies of two young women and two former convicts in Taylor County, Florida – deaths which became known as the 'Sinkhole Murders'. There was wide speculation that the *Pirate Lady* had been somehow caught up in the *Gunsmoke* affair – that Latuso and Decidue had seen something that they shouldn't or their boat had been used in the traffickers' escape.

A more likely theory was that Latuso and Decidue had been overpowered in Apalachicola Harbour, murdered at sea and the yacht sailed to the Columbian coast. Throughout February there were numerous sightings of a yacht that fitted the *Pirate Lady*'s description on or around the Guajira

Peninsula in north-west Columbia, the main departure-point for cocaine shipments to the north.

The last sighting described a vessel of the same dimensions as the *Pirate Lady*, but with spotted red in place of the original green trim and a box-like structure on the bow disguising the recessed lounge. She was registered in Panama. The FBI checked out the registration and found it was false. On 3 March the yacht sent out a distress signal that she was sinking off the coast at Barranquilla. There were no further sightings.

The disappearances continued. The missing yachts and crew joined the mysteries of the sea. A number of incidents were linked to yachts, typically owned by retired couples, picking up crews from the flotsam of southern ports. The authorities advised the careful vetting of all casual deck-hands. However, the scale of the problem was played down. A Florida Coastguard Investigator, Commander Marshall Phillips, the only officer to make a detailed study of the 'yachtjacking' problem, was transferred to the National Highway Traffic Safety Administration and replaced by men who made light of the risk to small boats. Phillips retired, a disillusioned man.

Senior coastguard officials argued that there was no evidence for a plague of piracy. Opponents argued that the secret of success was to leave no evidence behind. It was not in the interests of owners of lost vessels to raise the possibility of piracy. Most insurance policies carried a 'free of capture and seizure' clause which disclaimed liability in the event of loss by other than natural causes. By the late seventies the problems of law enforcement in the waters off Florida were so overwhelming that the hijacking of a few pleasure-craft seemed to pale into insignificance.

By 1979, the Bahamas was overwhelmed. In that year, Lawrence Major, the Assistant Commissioner of Police, revealed the full extent of the problem with two accidental seizures. On Black Rock, a deserted atoll off Grand Bahama, he found a six-foot-high stockpile of marijuana two miles long. On a plane at George Town airport on Exuma Island he found 247 lb of cocaine with a wholesale value of $2bn, eight times the official national income of the islands.

Major was an incorruptible and tireless crusader against the traffickers. However, evidence of corruption was mounting against senior members of the Bahamian Government, up to and including the Prime Minister, Sir Lynden Pindling himself.

However corrupt or otherwise the Bahamian authorities, it is doubtful if they could have withstood the power of the drug barons. They had five patrol craft against a multi-billion dollar industry. The Exuma Chain had become a drug paradise.

In January 1979, Carlos Lehder had arrived at Norman's Cay in the Exumas. Lehder was a major figure in the Medellin Cartel. He had some rather eccentric ideas. Back home in Columbia he kept two caged lions in his car park. His two heroes were Adolf Hitler and John Lennon. In his garden he had a naked statue of Lennon with three bullet holes in the chest and a fig-leaf twined into the word 'LOVE' covering his genitals. He turned Norman's Cay into a tiny cocaine-warehouse republic.

It was in this chain of islands in this atmosphere that the *Kalia III* was found floating, with blood and bullet-holes on the deck and a body in the dinghy. It was never established what happened to William and Patty Kamerer. After first denying that the circumstances were suspicious, the Bahamian Government finally, four months after the tragedy, accepted that there had been a body and that the couple had been murdered after stumbling across a drug-smuggling operation. Pindling tried to use this as a lever to extract money for further patrol boats from the United States. The United States made money conditional on the Bahamas' cooperation in money-laundering investigations. Pindling was not prepared to carry on the conversation.

On 28 January 1994, there was a tragic postscript to the fate of the Kamerers. The $125,000 ocean-racing yacht *Computacenter Challenger* was found at anchor in Codrington Lagoon on the Caribbean island of Barbuda. Aboard were the yacht's British crew – Ian Cridland and Thomas Williams – and a middle-aged American couple, the Clevers, who had been guests aboard the yacht. They had been murdered – horribly tortured and then shot.

At first sight, the *Challenger* seemed another likely victim of drug smugglers. There was speculation that the yacht had stumbled on a transfer or been mistaken for the boat of a rival gang. It now seems they were victims of a far older type of piracy. An investigation by Detective Superintendent Mickey Lawrence of Scotland Yard has led to a small wooden house in the village of Codrington across the lagoon. Two local men are now in custody. The drug war has involved huge movements of money and men, corruption of nations and crises in government. Somewhere beneath all this international turmoil, ordinary men go on living and some will go on stealing and killing.

12.

The End Of The Rainbow

The first explosion blew a hole three metres by two metres in the side of the engine-room on the lower deck. The ship began to list as water flooded through the hull. In the mess-room on the deck above, the crew were thrown to the floor.

Minutes later a second explosion smashed the ship's propulsion system and riddled the adjacent cabins with shrapnel.

Fernando Pereira was the only person on the lower deck when the second bomb exploded. Pereira was a photographer. He didn't want his cameras to sink with the ship. He had found the cameras in the dark cabin when the concussion from the blast knocked him to the floor. He was still stunned when the water flowed in. He drowned there, the straps from his camera-bags twined around his legs. By nature, he was too relaxed and easygoing to choose to die for a cause. At five to midnight on 10 July 1985, in the oily water of Auckland Harbour, the cause found Fernando Pereira.

The story of the sinking of the *Rainbow Warrior* began over thirty years before on a small island 2,000 miles to the north of Auckland, in the middle of the Pacific Ocean.

On 1 March 1954, America exploded the world's first deliverable hydrogen bomb in the sky above Bikini Atoll.

The explosion, the equivalent in destructive power of a thousand of the bombs dropped on Hiroshima, was expected to fry the battered hulk of Bikini. It was not expected that it would make life impossible anywhere within a radius of 200 kilometres.

On the island of Rongelap, 150 kilometres away, those who looked directly at the flash on the horizon were stunned by the enormity and beauty of the explosion. They had been given no warning. It seemed like the end of the world had come. The light was so intense that for several minutes they were blinded.

Over the following day, the island was covered with a five-centimetre-thick layer of ash. The ash burned on contact with the skin and dissolved in the island's streams and springs. When the islanders drank the water they began to vomit uncontrollably.

Three days after the explosion, Rongelap was evacuated. The island had been exposed to 175 rads of radiation, the worst case of human contamination since Nagasaki. In the three years that followed, miscarriages and birth deformities doubled. Babies were born without faces and without bones.

In 1957, US Government inspectors judged that it was safe for the islanders to return. In 1963, the first thyroid tumour was diagnosed. By 1985, three-quarters of those on Rongelap who had been under ten when the bomb exploded had undergone operations for tumours.

Rongelap is part of the Marshall Islands, the chain that also includes Bikini. The United States had taken the islands over from Japan in 1947 under a United Nations trusteeship. In 1985 they offered all the inhabitants a pay-off in compensation for the inconvenience of having been blown out of the water. In return they asked that they waive all rights to sue over the effects of nuclear testing.

Rongelap refused to have anything to do with the deal. The islanders decided to make their own arrangements for evacuation. They approached the environmental group Greenpeace which had taken a special interest in radiation in the Western Pacific. Greenpeace agreed to move the islanders and their possessions 160 kilometres to the uninhabited island of Mejato. The transfer would fit conveniently with Greenpeace's main objective for 1985 – to disrupt the French neutron-bomb programme in French Polynesia.

The French had been quick to appreciate the advantages of the Pacific as a nuclear playground. The greatest attraction of the area was its distance away from anyone with a vote in the French elections.

France had come out of the Second World War with her pride in ruins. Not only had she been defeated by the Germans, but, even worse, she had been rescued by the British and the Americans. De Gaulle set out to re-establish his country as a leading player in world affairs. For this, in the Cold War years, she needed her own bomb.

In 1963, French scientists finally produced the bomb, testing it on Moruroa Atoll in French Polynesia. However, they were now nearly twenty years behind US nuclear technology. De Gaulle rejected all attempts to include France in testing bans and non-proliferation treaties and went ahead with knocking bits off unspoilt pieces of the Pacific.

By 1985 a lot had changed, but not France's obsession with an independent nuclear deterrent. It had become a symbol of national independence and pride. When the Socialist Francois Mitterand became President in 1981, one of his first acts had been to reassure the French military that tests and development would continue. By 1985, it seemed that De Gaulle's dream might at last come true. France led the world in development of the neutron bomb – the weapon of the future which would destroy only animal life and leave buildings and machines in place. However, they needed more tests.

The Greenpeace plan for 1985 had two stages: first to evacuate Rongelap and then to raise a flotilla in New Zealand to disrupt the French testing programme. The plan was to sail up to Moruroa's twelve-mile limit and land groups of volunteers from small boats on the atoll. Each protester would have to be arrested, checked for radiation and then deported. The Greenpeace ships would be packed with journalists and international observers. The whole French programme might be fatally disrupted.

The key to the Greenpeace plan was the *Rainbow Warrior*, a 417 ton converted trawler. The *Warrior* had started life thirty years before at the Hall Russell Shipyard in Aberdeen as the *Sir William Hardy*. After a career as a Ministry of Agriculture research vessel and then a trawler during the Cod Wars between Britain and Iceland, she had been bought by Greenpeace in 1977 for £40,000.

Off the coast of Peru, Spain and Iceland she had faced down whalers. Off North America she had spoilt the dumping of chemical waste. Off Canada she had interfered with the culling of harp seal pups. She had been interned and disabled by the Spanish navy in the harbour of El Ferrol and escaped into a storm in the Eastern Atlantic. She had outrun a flotilla of Russian destroyers in the Bering Sea. For eight years the *Rainbow Warrior* had wandered the seas of the world, like a floating finger in the dyke of environmental disaster.

The *Rainbow Warrior* was vital to the work in the Pacific in 1985. The flotilla needed her communications equipment and her desalination plant to sustain the assault on the Moruroa testing programme.

To half of the world, Greenpeace were quixotic defenders of the future of the planet. To the other half they were a gang of beatniks with more lentils than sense. To the French military they were a serious threat to France as a great power.

On 4 March 1985, Charles Henru, French Minister of Defence, met in Paris with Admiral Henri Fages, Commander of the Nuclear Testing Centre at Moruroa. It was this meeting that was to sink the *Rainbow Warrior* in the slime of Auckland Harbour.

Henru was not a typical Socialist. He drank only champagne with his daily six-course lunches at the best Paris restaurants. He was passionately devoted to the French bomb. He regarded Greenpeace and its Chairman, David McTaggart, with an intense personal hatred.

The hatred went back to 1973. McTaggart, a millionaire and former world badminton champion, was then in the second year of his crusade for a cleaner world. In 1972 he had sailed his yacht *Vega* into France's 260,000 square kilometre exclusion zone around Moruroa. He had been rammed by a French naval corvette and afterwards invited on board for a rather delicious lunch. In 1973 he went back, expecting a similar mixture of charm and violence. This time he got only the violence. A squad of French commandos boarded the *Vega* and beat McTaggart senseless, leaving him in no state for lunch of any kind. The French denied the assault, but it had been photographed by a fellow crew-member. Henru was then already Minister of Defence. The publicity was a severe embarrassment to him and to his Government. Henru neither forgot nor forgave.

During the March meeting, Fages painted a lurid picture of the disruption that Greenpeace could cause to his summer programme. The French had yielded a little to international pressure and moved the testing underground. They claimed this had eliminated any risk to the environment. Greenpeace argued that, if the tests were so safe, there was no reason to conduct them 10,000 miles from France in the middle of the Pacific. The last thing that Fages needed was a procession of hippies with geiger-counters clambering over his island while he was trying to perfect the ultimate deterrent.

Henru left the meeting with Fages and went straight to lunch. Over his champagne he brooded. On returning to his office he summoned Admiral Pierre Lacoste, Head of the DGSE, the Direction Generale Des Services Exterieurs, the French Secret Service.

The DGSE, like all secret services, was intensely conservative and nationalistic. In most countries some effort is made to keep these instincts on a tight political leash, but in France it is hard to see much evidence of restraint. In 1981, Mitterand tried to put his mark on the DGSE by appointing Pierre Marron, a liberal outsider, as controller. Marron lasted less than a year. The organisation closed ranks against him. The final straw came when he was kidnapped from his Paris desk on a Saturday afternoon by masked gunmen, bundled into the boot of a car, driven to the South of France and lifted by helicopter to a trawler off Marseilles. The trip turned out to be a practical joke by DGSE commandos. Marron failed to see the funny side. He suffered a nervous breakdown and was replaced by Lacoste, a safe Services candidate.

Henru instructed Lacoste to increase surveillance on Greenpeace and to prepare contingency plans to disrupt the Pacific campaign. For this he gave him a special allocation of funds direct from the Elysee Palace, authorised by General Saulnier, Chief of the General Staff, and Laurent Fabius, the Prime Minister.

Twelve days after this meeting, the object of this high-level political interest left Mayport, the port of Jacksonville, Florida, headed for the Panama Canal and the Pacific. Aboard *Rainbow Warrior* was a crew of eleven of mixed nationalities, experience and backgrounds. The captain, Peter Willcox, and his key officers were competent seamen with years of merchant marine experience. The deck-hands included a twenty-year-old Swiss cook, a forty-one-year-old New York radio engineer, a twenty-eight-year-old New Zealand sociology graduate and a twenty-three-year-old Irish drifter. The one thing they shared in common was a slightly solemn idealism – a belief that they could save the world. For the first leg of the voyage, to Hawaii, the crew tested the ship's equipment and settled into their operating routine.

Six weeks after the *Rainbow Warrior* had left Mayport, on 23 April, Lacoste put in place his first agent. Christine Huguette Cabon landed at Auckland Airport from Paris. Her job was to infiltrate the Greenpeace Headquarters in Auckland and to report to Paris on the detailed plans for the Moruroa operation.

It is hard to know how to judge Christine Cabon. She comes across, like the entire DGSE operation against the *Rainbow Warrior*, as partly evil, partly tragic, but mostly absurd. The biggest mystery about her is how she had been chosen for the mission in the first place.

In all respects but one, Adolf Hitler would have been a better choice for the job of mixing unobtrusively with a socially-committed pacifist organisation. Christine Cabon spoke hardly a word of English, had no social skills, no knowledge of ecological issues and made no effort to conceal her desire for French domination of the Pacific. Her one asset was that she was a lesbian and this was the single aspect of her character that she had managed to conceal from the French military authorities over thirteen years in the army.

Cabon was thirty-three years old, short and thick-set. She had the appalling manners of the classical French stereotype, but none of the style. She dressed like a Dieppe dock-hand. She had been very good at her chosen career, but her chosen career had not been undercover subversion. In her early twenties she joined the French Army, and by the age of twenty-nine was lieutenant in an elite commando unit. In 1982 her military life was cut short when she damaged her leg in a parachute accident. The DGSE offered her another way to serve her country. She worked underground in Palestine, identifying PLO targets for Israeli bombing. To avoid Palestinian reprisals she had her features rearranged with plastic surgery. Her courage was not in doubt. She was, however, just a little short on tact.

Christine Cabon arrived in New Zealand under a false passport in the name of Frederique Bonlieu. Her cover was as a scientific consultant gathering information for a series of freelance articles on travel and ecology. She arrived at the Greenpeace Auckland office to offer her services as a volunteer dressed in a red sweatshirt, white scarf and blue jeans; a walking, talking French flag.

She made an instant impression. Everyone who met her in the first weeks remembered her as awkward, mean, humourless and boorish. She said she had no money and forced herself into the house of Carol Stewart, Greenpeace national coordinator. She ate all the food in the fridge, contributed nothing to the household bills and refused to do the washing-up. She was cold and sulky. Whenever the subject arose, she argued strongly for the right of France to blow up whatever she liked in the Eastern Pacific.

As an agent, Cabon had some success. She discovered the arrival date of the *Rainbow Warrior* and the itineraries of the other Greenpeace vessels. She also uncovered a plan to land Polynesian islanders on Moruroa from native canoes. The threat of this may have been the deciding factor in the decision to disable *Rainbow Warrior*. In reality, despite her graphic reports, it was never a serious proposition.

Her other work was to prepare the ground for later agents. She made enquiries about hotels and the hire of diving equipment 'for friends', using Stewart as an interpreter because her English was so appalling. She made unobtrusive reconnaissance trips along the coast and was remembered everywhere for her sulkiness, bitterness and hostility. 'It is difficult being French,' she complained to Stewart, 'everybody hates you.'

However, towards the end of Cabon's month in New Zealand, she began to change. The edge went off her bitterness. She moved to a house with three other women peace volunteers and slipped, almost against her will, into a life of easygoing free love. She bought cakes for tea. Now and then she smiled.

Cabon left New Zealand on 24 May. By early June she

217

was back in the Middle East, posing as an archaeologist on an excavation in Israel. From then until the sinking of the *Rainbow Warrior*, she sent a steady stream of letters and postcards to her New Zealand friends and lovers. After the sinking, they never heard from her again. The affection may have been part of an elaborate act. It may have been a sign that her loyalties had become genuinely divided. The latter is perhaps more likely. Whatever she was, Christine Cabon was no Mata Hari.

Meanwhile, the *Rainbow Warrior* had set out for Rongelap. In Hawaii, the crew was joined by a thirty-four-year-old Portuguese photographer. Fernando Pereira had nothing in common with his new shipmates. As a deck-hand, he was a disaster. His main interest was in trying to seduce the women on watch. With his Zapata moustache, tight trousers and love of fast women and flash cars, Pereira dropped into the earnestness of the *Rainbow Warrior* like a glacé cherry onto a mushroom quiche.

All the tensions on board, however, were forgotten in the business of the Rongelap evacuation. In four trips over ten days, 304 islanders and 100 tons of cargo were carried 160 kilometres to the uninhabited island of Mejato. The operation culminated with the draping of a banner on the perimeter fence of the US missile-testing station at Kwajalein Island. The banner read: 'WE CAN'T RELOCATE THE WORLD – STOP STAR WARS.' The landing on Kwajalein was planned like a military operation. The crew expected confrontation with US guards. Instead the landing-party was met on the shoreline by two elderly American ladies who gave them a friendly 'good-morning' and walked on, searching for sea shells.

By 22 June, the *Rainbow Warrior* was heading south towards the Melanesian island group of Vanuatu to collect Charles Rara, a representative of the Vanuatu Government. It was hoped that Rara's presence would give the Greenpeace flotilla a little low-key diplomatic protection when it reached the waters off Moruroa. On the same day two groups of French tourists arrived in New Zealand.

Cabon's information had convinced the DGSE that the Greenpeace programme was a serious threat to the summer's nuclear tests. The operation to sink the *Rainbow Warrior* was now underway. In the world of espionage and subversion there may have been more complex, confusing, amateurish and inefficient operations. If so, they have been sensibly buried in shredded files. 'Sink The *Warrior*' had more in common with Laurel and Hardy than le Carré.

At dusk on the 22nd, the yacht *Ouvea* docked at the tiny North Island Harbour of Parengarenga after a voyage from New Caledonia. The crew were relying for navigation on an eighteenth-century whaling map. It was only by the most extraordinary luck that they avoided grounding and breaking up on the unmarked shallows that ringed the harbour.

There were four Frenchmen on board the *Ouvea*. Three of them – Roland Verge, Gerald Andries and Michel Barcelo – were star graduates of the DGSE 'combat frogman' course at Aspretto, Corsica. The fourth, the only member of the crew using his real name, was a thirty-eight-year-old French doctor, Xavier Christian Jean Manignet, a naval reservist and specialist in diving medicine. In the hold of the yacht were a French-made 'Zodiac' inflatable boat, a Yamaha outboard motor and enough explosives to kill a Portuguese photographer.

219

Parengarenga had been chosen as first land-fall because it had no Customs post. On 24 June, somewhere on the rocky coast between Parengarenga and the Customs post at Whangaroa, the *Ouvea* off-loaded the explosives, the boat and the motor.

The crew of the *Ouvea* remained in New Zealand for a further two and a half weeks. They contributed nothing further to the operation against the *Rainbow Warrior*, but contributed a great deal to French-New Zealand cross-cultural relations.

There was nothing inconspicuous about the *Ouvea* crew. From the moment they landed they embarked on a long and riotous party. Manignet had the looks of an ageing Continental film star. In France he lived on a boat moored on an artificial lake outside Dieppe. The boat was called the *Pussycat Trap*. This was a good indication of Manignet's main interest. He is known to have seduced at least eight women during his short stay in New Zealand. Once he went too far when an opossum-hunter caught him in bed with his wife and he had to run with his trousers round his ankles. Verge, the *Ouvea*'s captain, was a little more constant. He single-mindedly pursued the wife of a local policeman, impressing her in restaurants by cutting the corks off champagne bottles with a bread-knife. The whole crew were regular visitors at the Golden Palace Massage Parlour in Walton Street, Auckland, 'relief massage a speciality'. The sign above the door of the Golden Palace read 'There are no strangers, only friends you haven't yet met.' They are still remembered there with affection.

On the same day that the *Ouvea* crashed into Parengarenga, two rather more subdued tourists arrived at Auckland airport. Their passports described them as a Swiss married couple –

Alain and Sophie Turenge. Madame Turenge spoke very little English. She was a graceless, dumpy woman in her mid-thirties. Her real name was Captain Dominique Prieur. Like Cabon she was a specialist in infiltration and subversion. Also like Cabon, she was awkward, taciturn and unfriendly. She missed her husband and two children back in France. Her companion was Major Alain Mafart, another graduate of the Aspretto frogman course. Mafart was also in his mid-thirties, clean-cut and athletic. He was the only member of the DGSE team who spoke good English and had some knowledge of ecological issues. Mafart had made a close study of the lifecycle of the whale.

The job of Prieur and Mafart was to prepare the ground for the attack on the *Rainbow Warrior* and to clean up afterwards. In contrast to the *Ouvea* crew, the 'Turenges' were regarded as sullen and unfriendly – not only to New Zealanders, but also to each other. They claimed to be on a second honeymoon, but slept in separate beds and acted like total strangers. As one of the detectives who investigated the bombing commented, 'They were remembered wherever they went: typical French – downright bloody rude.'

Over the next two weeks, the other members of the operation arrived: Lieutenant-Colonel Louis-Pierre Dillais, previously in command of the Aspretto Training Centre, who was to be in overall control, an unknown agent travelling as 'Francois Verlet' and finally two further Aspretto graduates – Alain Tornel and Jacques Camurier, travelling as physical education instructors from a girls' school in Tahiti. By 7 July, when the *Rainbow Warrior* finally entered Auckland's Waitamata Harbour there was sufficient French underwater sabotage expertise in New

Zealand to sink a medium-sized battle fleet.

Twenty yachts went out to meet the *Rainbow Warrior* and escort her to her berth at Marsden Wharf, on the city side of the harbour. In 1984, David Lange had been elected New Zealand Prime Minister. One of his first acts had been to ban all vessels carrying nuclear weapons from New Zealand ports. The *Rainbow Warrior* was a welcome guest and on 8 July was visited by five members of Parliament.

On the following day, as half the crew of the *Warrior* left for a week's holiday in the interior, the *Ouvea* finally abandoned the dubious delights of the Golden Palace Massage Parlour and headed back across the Pacific to Norfolk Island. Meanwhile, in the early hours of the morning, Mafart and Prieur drove north from Auckland in a hired camper van to retrieve the Zodiac inflatable, the outboard motor and the explosives from their coastal hiding-place. On a deserted stretch of road, they met Tornel and Camurier and passed over the equipment.

On the night of 10 July there was a party on board the *Rainbow Warrior* to celebrate the birthday of the Greenpeace International campaigns coordinator. The party was not a riotous affair. Groups of committed environmentalists stood around and discussed positive action. The party had one uninvited guest – a Frenchman in his early twenties with short, brushed-back hair, wearing designer jeans. He said he was Francois Verlet, a pacifist in transit from Singapore to Hong Kong. He asked a number of questions about the Greenpeace campaign and left after an hour. His parting words were 'Happy birthday, and good luck with your campaign.'

At 7.50 p.m., Verlet met Camurier, Prieur and Mafart on the darkened slipway of the Sea Bee Air Company Yard on the far side of Auckland Harbour. Verlet had learned, from snatches of conversation aboard the *Rainbow Warrior*, that the party on board the *Warrior* was going to break up for a couple of hours and then carry on into the small hours. At midnight, the cabins on the lower deck should be clear. This assumed that the party did continue, that everyone liked parties and that no one went to bed early. The fact that only one person was killed by the explosions on board the *Warrior* owed nothing to Francois Verlet. They agreed that the attack should be timed for 11.50 p.m. Camurier set off alone in the Zodiac across the dark waters of Waitamata Harbour.

Fernando Pereira had by now settled into the crew of the *Warrior*. He had become especially close to Davey Edward, the Yorkshire Chief Engineer. By the night of 10 July, however, he must have been regretting not having taken the opportunity to explore the interior. In many ways he had more in common with the crew of the *Ouvea* than the earnest company of the *Warrior*. In the early evening he set out with Edward to investigate the Auckland night-life. They missed the massage parlours and the good-time New Zealand women. Instead they found a cold mid-winter town with a series of bars filled with heavy silent men staring at the heads on their beers.

Between 8 and 8.30 p.m., Camurier moored his dinghy to a supporting pile of King's Wharf, adjacent to Marsden. The dinghy contained two 30 lb packs of explosives, two clamps, a length of rope and scuba-diving gear including bubble-less oxygen tanks. The explosives had been primed and set to explode at midnight. They were packed in waterproofed bags with built-in buoyancy tanks. In the shadows of the underside of the wharf, he strapped the oxygen tanks to his back.

Carrying the rope, clamps and explosives he swam beneath the surface towards the *Rainbow Warrior* through water thick with slime, discarded oil, and harbour refuse. He tied the first pack of explosives to the propeller shaft and used the rope to measure along the side of the hull to the wall of the engine-room. Using the clamp, he fixed the second pack of explosives to the protruding ridge on the hull and then swam underwater back to the Zodiac. He paddled out of earshot and then started the motor and headed back across the bay.

Aboard the *Rainbow Warrior*, the party broke up early so that Willcox, the *Warrior*'s captain, could meet with five other captains from the Moruroa flotilla. The meeting finished at eleven. No one felt much like carrying on with the party. Willcox and two other crew-members went down to their cabins to sleep. Pereira and Edward, back from the bleak Auckland bars, sat around and drank a final beer with the five remaining members of the crew.

At 11.50, the bomb against the engine-wall exploded. The explosion relied on the same principle as the RAF 'bouncing bomb' used to destroy the Mohne and the Eder dams in the Second World War. The explosion was cushioned by the water, bouncing all its concussive power back against the side of the ship, blowing a huge hole in the hull.

For a minute after the crash, with the lights blown and the *Rainbow Warrior* listing at a crazy angle, there was confusion on board. Willcox, still groggy from sleep, emerged into the mess-room and ordered the crew to abandon ship. Margaret Mills, the fifty-five-year-old relief cook, was searching frantically for her glasses and had to be carried bodily onto the wharf by Andy Biedeman, the ship's Swiss doctor. Edward, after checking that his engine-room was under water, joined the others on shore. When the second explosion blew apart the propulsion system they found that only Fernando Pereira was missing.

Pereira was found at 4 a.m. by police divers. The bunks in several of the empty cabins were riddled with shrapnel from the engine-room blast. It was only chance that had prevented more deaths.

In the early hours of 11 July, Superintendent Allan Galbraith took over the investigation. Galbraith was a Scotsman in exile. He was a sleuth of the old school. In place of the computers used by most of the developed world's police services he employed the services of a former New Zealand women's shot-putting champion with a photographic memory. The DGSE had shown itself extremely competent at blowing holes in an unguarded trawler in twenty foot of muddy water. If they had been as good at escaping afterwards, Galbraith would have had no suspects and no evidence.

Camurier had arranged to rendezvous with Prieur and Mafart at a container wharf back on the far side of Auckland Harbour. However, they had forgotten to check the tide levels. By the time Camurier reached the wharf, the water was too low to reach the jetty. He was forced to paddle along the line of the shore, while Prieur followed as near as she could in the van and Mafart followed on foot, shouting shrill French advice.

As this circus proceeded, Camurier ditched the Yamaha outboard into the water. He was seen by a passing cyclist who marked the spot. The engine was later recovered by the police and the serial number traced to a member of the *Ouvea*'s crew.

Eventually they hauled the dinghy onto the rocks beside a

marina at Hobson Bay, at the end of Tamahi Drive. A group of members of the marina, sitting outside the clubhouse, watched the operation with interest. Prieur backed up the camper van and Mafart and Camurier loaded the scuba equipment. They drove off, leaving the Zodiac, stripped of identification marks, on the shore.

The watching men were an informal vigilante group, on the lookout for boat thieves. It seemed unusual to them that anyone would be out in the harbour at night without lights dressed in scuba gear in a dinghy without a motor. It seemed even more unusual that they would leave a valuable inflatable unsecured on a dark patch of shoreline. It was almost impossible to obtain a Zodiac in New Zealand. The men took down the registration number of the camper van and phoned it through to the police.

At 9 a.m. on 12 July, Mafart and Prieur arrived at the Auckland Airport office of Newman's self-drive car hire. The staff took an unusually long time to process the return of their hired camper van. The French couple were still waiting for the return of their deposit when the police arrived.

Mafart and Prieur may have been well trained in underwater sabotage, but they were not much good at interrogation. They were questioned separately. They both agreed that they had come across a man in a wet-suit with a dinghy at the end of an unknown dead-end road in a strange town purely by chance and had given him a lift because he was stranded. They had dropped him at an empty featureless street corner. They disagreed on whether he had travelled in the front or in the back of the van. Their passports were a source of some interest to the investigating officers. Although they seemed to have been issued in the same consulate on the same day, their numbers were wildly different. Mafart's passport made no mention of scars or distinguishing marks. He claimed that a long scar across his cheek was the result of a cancerous mole and a scar on his abdomen came from a burst appendix. The mole must have been the size of a cannon-ball. The abdominal scar was several inches away from the appendix.

The passport discrepancies gave Galbraith the excuse to keep Prieur and Mafart in the country while he checked with Interpol. On the morning of the 13th, Interpol confirmed that the passports were forgeries. On the 15th the pair were charged with entering the country illegally. Over the following week, the remainder of their story fell apart. The telephone in their motel room had been bugged and calls monitored to a DGSE safe house in Paris. It became obvious that they were on a trip for business rather than pleasure when they were found not only to have kept receipts for every payment, but also to have altered certain receipts to fiddle their expenses. They were overheard discussing whether the army would carry on paying their salaries if they were sent to prison. Prieur finally admitted that they were not married. The game was up. On 23 July, they were charged with conspiracy to commit arson and murder.

Meanwhile, the original hire of the camper van, along with the ownership of the jettisoned outboard, was traced to the crew of the *Ouvea*. On 13 July, eight detectives flew to Norfolk Island. They took samples from the *Ouvea*'s hold. However, before the samples could be analysed, the Australian authorities released the crew on a technicality and they and the yacht disappeared. Three weeks later they were in hiding in France. Soon after, Manignet was back seducing tourists at the *Pussycat Trap*. It is hard to keep a good man down.

The samples from the hold indicated the recent presence of explosives. However, New Zealand police officers sent to continue the investigation in France met a wall of official obstruction. The French decided it would be safer to look into the matter themselves. In the second week of August, Mitterand ordered an official enquiry under Bernard Tricot, former Secretary-General to the Elysee Palace.

Tricot's report concluded that there was no evidence of DGSE involvement in the sinking of the *Rainbow Warrior*. The report was an obvious whitewash. Tricot's daughter committed suicide out of shame for her father. Further revelations in the French press in September led to the resignations of Henru and Lacoste.

Meanwhile, whatever heads rolled in Paris, the sinking had achieved its objective. The summer test programme at Moruroa went ahead uninterrupted. Mitterand flew to the Pacific from Paris to demonstrate his solidarity with the bomb. The United States and the United Kingdom rallied to France's side. Margaret Thatcher denied that the sinking of the *Rainbow Warrior* could be compared in any way to the state-sponsored terrorism she condemned in the Middle East. 'The two,' she declared, 'are totally different.'

In November, Prieur and Mafart pleaded guilty to charges of manslaughter and wilful damage. There were mutterings in the press that the reduction in the charges from murder and arson were the result of a deal between the New Zealand Solicitor-General and the defence lawyer. Journalists searched for a connection between the two. It was not until later that they found that both had sisters in the same convent of the Sisters of Compassion. Prieur and Mafart were both sentenced to ten years in prison. They were reassured by a message from Paul Quiles, the French Minister of Defence: 'Be of good heart, the French Government and people are proud of you.'

The crew of the *Ouvea* remained safe in France. Christine Cabon left the Middle East on the day that Israel received a request to hold her for questioning. She had received a telegram telling her that her father was ill. Her father had been dead for years. There is no extradition from France for French nationals.

The French, of course, got away with it in the end. Immediately following the convictions of Mafart and Prieur, the Mitterand government began to place obstacles in the way of imports of New Zealand meat and dairy products. In June the two countries asked Perez De Cuellar, Secretary-General of the United Nations, to mediate the dispute. In July, in return for compensation of $7m and agreement to lift the embargo on New Zealand imports, New Zealand agreed to hand Mafart and Prieur over to the French to complete their sentences on an obscure island in French Polynesia. Over the year that followed they were shipped back home for spurious medical treatment. They never returned to their Pacific exile. New Zealand complained, but the complaints were ignored.

The *Rainbow Warrior*, like Fernando Pereira, was beyond reprieve or repair. It was towed out and sunk in Maturai Bay.

13.

Dead In A Box

The piracy of the *Mitzi Ann* and the *Mary C* in July 1985 marked the end of the road for Pedro Martinez and Luis Rodriguez, two small men with big ideas. Martinez finished dead in the water and Rodriguez dead in a box. The trials that followed finally buried the idea of Miami as nothing more than a happy home for bronzed bodies, snow-belt geriatrics and ice-cream cones.

Perhaps more than any other city, Miami is built on greed. In 1819, the Spaniards did not even bother to fight for Florida – they sold the state to the United States. Eighty years later, Miami was still a row of cabins selling seed and hardware to settlers camped in the Everglades. Then, in the 1890s, the railroad arrived, and with it Henry Flager. Flager razed an Indian burial-site on the banks of the Miami River and built the Royal Palm Hotel. To attract visitors, he sold Seminole skulls in the foyer. The Florida tourist industry was born, and with it the 'Sunshine City', blinking into the daylight with dollar-signs in its eyes.

Tourism was, and still is, Miami's main reason for existence. However, her geographical position as the nearest major port to the Caribbean, Central and South America, has given her other commercial advantages. During Prohibition, the rum-runners poured booze down Miami's throat from Cuba and the Bahamas. When the cocaine boom came in the 1970s, Miami was the obvious arrival point.

The city had two big advantages. Firstly, it was less than fifty miles – an hour in a speedboat – from the drugs junction in the Bahamas. Secondly, it was the perfect place for a large number of Latin Americans to blend without attracting obvious attention. Miami's large Cuban population not only provided cover, it also offered an eager reservoir of recruits for the drug war.

When Castro took power from the dictator Batista in 1959, Cuba enjoyed a short honeymoon period. Those most closely associated with Batista's oppression fled for the United States, but among the majority there was optimism for a new era. Many retained this optimism in the years to come. However, as Castro's rule became more dictatorial, more and more Cubans left for America, most of them ending up in Miami. As the Mafia found in Sicily during the rule of Mussolini, dictatorships can affect crime as much as any other personal freedom. The criminals joined the exodus.

Until 1980, the flow of criminals was balanced by honest and hard-working Cubans looking for the American Dream. Then, in April 1980, came the 'Mariel Boatlift'.

During the months leading up to April, relations between Cuba and the USA had turned particularly sour. On 16 February, sixteen armed Cubans had seized a Liberian freighter, the *Lisette* and forced her to sail to Florida. Ten days later three more armed refugees hijacked the fishing boat *Lucero* and followed the example of the *Lisette*. Castro demanded the extradition of those responsible, but they were given parole by the Miami courts.

In April, Castro took his revenge. He opened up the port of Mariel and offered any Cuban who wished the chance to leave the country. The scale of the response stunned him. Eventually the number of arrivals in Miami totalled 118,000. However, Castro found a way to turn this to his advantage. He opened the doors of Cuba's gaols and shepherded down to Mariel the dregs of the Havana underworld. Most of the Mariel criminals remained in Miami. In the cocaine trade, they found their own version of the American Dream.

By 1981, according to sources in the US Drug Enforcement Administration, Florida was the channel for 70% of the USA's supply of cocaine and marijuana and 90% of her quaaludes. In the same year, in the depths of the Reagan recession, the worst since the Great Depression, the Miami branch of the Federal Reserve Bank had a regular surplus of $5bn. Drug income was adding an estimated $7bn to $10bn a year to the South Florida economy. The dope industry was bigger than General Motors, second only in turnover to the oil giant Exxon.

The Medellin Cartel had shown itself remarkably efficient at coordinating production and trafficking. By 1980, Miami was established as the trade's US distribution point. Consignments landing elsewhere in the Gulf of Mexico – on the coasts of Texas and Louisiana – were loaded onto trucks and driven to Miami for logging, sorting and onward shipment, even if the final destination was Houston or New Orleans.

However, for all this efficiency, there were disagreements among the trafficking factions. Everyone wanted more. With so much at stake there were bound to be rip-offs and misunderstandings. From 1979, these misunderstandings led to a level of killing on the streets never before seen in an American city. By 1981, the murder rate was seventy per 100,000 citizens, three times the 1975 level, three and a half times the national average and twice as high as that of New York. An extraordinary 157 out of every 1000 people were victims of violent crime.

It was not so much the level of this violence that horrified America but the staggering brutality. In July 1979, two men walked into a liquor store in a shopping mall in Dade County, the area outside the Miami City limits. They pulled out submachine guns and riddled the bodies of two Columbians who were buying whisky at the counter so comprehensively that a witness later described them as 'a pair of Swiss cheeses'. They then carried on shooting as they made their escape to a delivery truck in the car park, emptying clip after clip into the air and walls. From then on, bodies were regularly discovered around the city. Characteristically, they were bound and gagged with tape and they often showed signs of torture. The killers took no care to hit only their target. Whole families were wiped out. It looked like war.

In April 1981, the *Chicago Tribune* columnist Michael Kilian returned from Miami with a message for the President. 'The Reagan Administration,' he wrote, 'has said that it wants to draw the line in El Salvador, why doesn't it draw the line here in Miami where thousands of Americans are threatened with aggression every day?' Only seven US citizens had, after all, died in El Salvador, and those had been killed by the people Reagan was supporting.

In response to the crisis, in February 1982, Reagan announced a 'War on Drugs'. He set up a task force under Vice-President Bush to coordinate the work of all law-enforcement branches and to flood the drug zone with Federal resources. The task force had some huge successes. By 1986 it had made 15,000 arrests, seized six million pounds of marijuana and 100,000 pounds of cocaine. However, its major impact was measured by the fall in the marijuana trade and the further inexorable rise of cocaine. If the risks were greater, then traffickers naturally gravitated towards low volume and high yield. By 1986, George Heavey, Regional Commissioner of the Customs Service, concluded: 'We're overwhelmed – it's like fighting the Chinese army.'

Luis Rodriguez was a small cog in that Chinese army. Rodriguez was a typical sweeping from the Havana gutter. He was a short, thin man in his mid-forties with receding hair and the face of a ferret. He liked to dress sharp, in white linen suits and gold jewellery. His obituary in the *Miami Herald*, after the discovery of his body packed in a crate on a patch of waste ground next door to the Our Lady Of Mercy Convent, lamented him as 'a small man with big ideas who got shot one day and ended up in a box'. It might not have been the eulogy he would have chosen, but it fitted him as well as any other – as well as the 3 ft by 3 ft packing-case fitted his frail body.

Rodriguez's reputation for unreliability went back to long stretches in prison in Cuba. There he was known as 'El Miador' which literally meant 'The Urinator', but in Cuban slang meant that he was prepared to leak information about anyone or anything for a price. Rodriguez had arrived from Mariel in 1980 without money or contacts. He started out living in a tent city beneath an overpass on Interstate 95, dabbling in minor burglary and small-time drug dealing. By 1985 he had graduated to owner of the Molino Rojo, a bar in

Miami's 'Little Havana'. Aside from bar receipts, the Molino Rojo turned over half a million dollars a month as a wholesale outlet for marijuana and cocaine.

Luis Rodriguez wanted more than money. He wanted respect. His tastes ran beyond gold jewellery to female company below the age of consent. He wanted his fourteen-year-old girlfriends to know they were dealing with a man of importance. He wanted to be a big shot.

In early 1985, Rodriguez began to look around for a major shipment of cocaine. He made contact with a refugee from the Dominican Republic, Pedro Ramos, who ran a radiator repair shop in Little Havana. Ramos was a skilled craftsman. His talents did not stop at radiators. He was occasionally given a commission by Pedro Martinez, another Cuban exile. Ramos was flown to the Bahamas to install concealed compartments in smuggling ships. He was worth the $80,000 he was paid for each job. His handiwork was completely undetectable.

Ramos earned a more than adequate living. However, any business that deals with very large sums of money can distort perspective on wealth. Miami in the 1980s was a money mad-house. Because of regulations aimed at drug proceeds, banks had to declare any deposit of over $10,000 to the Federal authorities. All cash proceeds had to be laundered. This meant there were a lot of notes in circulation. In August 1980, a woman was stopped at Miami Airport bound for Bogota with $1.5m in six Monopoly boxes. In September, at the trial of Isaac Kattan-Kassim, a Cartel banker, it was revealed that he frequently walked around downtown Miami with $1m in a cardboard box. Dealers were buying $60,000 cars for cash and leaving $600 tips for waiters. $200,000 apartments were advertised in the Miami newspapers specifying cash buyers. When police busted a ring of twenty-three baggage handlers at Miami Airport who had diverted consignments past Customs controls, one was found to have accounts in several offshore banks, a $200,000 cashier's cheque, $73,000 in a cheque account, a Porsche, a Ford Bronco 4-wheel drive, two motorcycles, three lots in an industrial park, one in a shopping mall and three residential properties.

In this atmosphere, the odd $80,000 for a trip to the Bahamas seemed like small change to Pedro Ramos. He knew that Martinez, his employer, was making millions. When Luis Rodriguez approached Ramos at the bar of the Molino Rojo, Rodriguez found a receptive audience.

On the morning of 12 July 1985, Ramos told Rodriguez that the *Mitzi Ann*, a converted US coastguard cutter, was expected to moor at Tamiami Marina on a tributary of the Miami River at 9 p.m. that evening. Ramos knew where the drugs were hidden.

Rodriguez was aware of some of his limitations. He was not a strong man and he disliked any sort of violence. His assistant at the Molino Rojo was Armando Un, a fifty-year-old Cuban-Chinese. Un, although a little short in the top storey, was a reliable man in a fight. For the night of the 12th, as extra back-up, Rodriguez recruited a further ten Cuban-Americans. Rodriguez stayed at home, sweating by the telephone.

The *Mitzi Ann* moored on time, but for three hours there was no movement on deck. The raiding party waited and watched by their cars in the shadows beyond the yard's chain-link fence. At midnight they lost patience. They swarmed over the fence and onto the deck of the *Mitzi Ann*. For ten minutes, Ramos searched for the hidden panel in the cutter's fibreglass deck. As he tapped and probed with his screwdriver the watching men fretted. Finally he found what he was looking for. He chipped away the covering of fibreglass, loosened the screws and revealed a compartment packed with black nylon sacks containing 400 kg of pure cocaine. They formed a human chain to ferry the sacks over the fence to the road.

The three-man crew of the *Mitzi Ann* had hidden below when they heard the thump of heavy bodies on the deck. They were found cowering in the hold. They listened with concern while the hijackers considered whether or not to slit their throats. Eventually they were beaten up and thrown overboard into the oily ooze of the Tamiami River.

The crew of the *Mitzi Ann* did not report the theft to the police. One reason is obvious – it would have meant implicating themselves. The other reason was that Un's ten helpers were all dressed in the uniform of the Miami Metro-Dade area police force. The men Rodriguez had recruited were serving members of the city's law-enforcement community.

Corruption in the Miami police force was by no means unknown in the mid-eighties. What was extraordinary about the activities of the Miami River Police was the scale and ambition of that corruption.

Until 1980, the Miami Metro-Dade police force had been a strictly white Anglo-Saxon monopoly. Its officers were completely unsuited to the tensions and aspirations within the black and Hispanic communities. Partly because of colour prejudice and partly because of strict educational requirements, the force entered the eighties badly undermanned.

In May 1980, four white policemen were acquitted by an all-white jury of the murder of Arthur McDuffie, a black insurance agent whom they had beaten to death on the pavement following a high-speed car chase. In the riots that followed, eighteen were killed and $80m worth of property was destroyed. Faced with open hatred of black against white and the growing drug problem in the Hispanic community, the Miami police launched a frantic recruitment campaign. Federal regulations insisted that 80% of the new recruits come from racial minorities. Literacy qualifications were relaxed. By the end of 1982, the new recruits outnumbered pre-1980 officers by two to one.

The toughest of the Cuban recruits were assigned to patrol Little Havana, the ghetto of bars, brothels and drug-dealing where the worst sediment of the *Marielito* immigration had settled. Without proper training, backed only by fellow-novices, they were loosed to keep some sort of order among the pimps, dealers, strong-arm men and hustlers. Not surprisingly, some of them went native.

The new recruits moved day and night among criminals who could treble a policeman's annual salary with a mediocre night's work. The susceptible ones began to look around for a slice of the action.

Some went insane with the unreality of the life they led. When the scandal of police corruption broke in the mid-eighties, the Miami press entertained the public with the testimony of Jacqueline Quintana, a twenty-one-year-old Cuban prostitute who told of affairs with two police officers. Along with mild irregularities such as riding in her lovers' patrol cars dressed only in a police-issue cap and gunbelt, one of her boyfriends had asked her to use her contacts in the underworld to buy a bazooka so that he could blow the doors off the US Customs building and steal the haul of confiscated cocaine.

This proposal did not seem so fanciful in the light of a series of thefts from police secure-storage deposits. In 1986, $150,000 in cash waiting to be used in evidence in a trafficking trial disappeared from a locker in the special investigation squad. Towards the end of the year, a quarter of a ton of marijuana went missing from a safe-storage depot in the Miami police department. The marijuana was in twenty bales, each weighing over 500 lb. The area in which they were kept was under constantly-monitored closed-circuit television surveillance. No one outside the police force had access. It was obvious that, for some officers, the temptation had become irresistible. But by the time the bales disappeared, America knew that something had gone seriously wrong with the Miami law-enforcement. The Miami River Police had seen to that.

Patrolman Armando Estrada and his partner Roman Rodriguez were part of the 1980 intake. At an early stage they began to accept gifts in return for protecting dealers. They moved on to small-scale shake-downs. However, they were ambitious men. When Luis Rodriguez, owner of the Molino Rojo, suggested that there was serious money to be made on the waterfront, they were prepared to listen. They recruited a colleague, Rudy Arias, a former footballer and body-builder who had been nominated as Officer of the Year. Arias had a formidable reputation both for his arrest record and his methods of gentle persuasion. He in turn brought in seven more Little Havana patrolmen.

Through this combination of circumstances, of the twelve

who boarded the *Mitzi Ann* on the night of 12 July, ten were in police uniform, though not strictly on police business.

There was a slight problem with the piracy of the *Mitzi Ann*. Pedro Ramos had not expected to find so much cocaine. None of them, in fact, had ever seen so much white powder gathered together in one place before. They had planned to use one patrol car to carry the drugs to an empty house on NE 30th Avenue. However, they could fit less than half of the black nylon bags into the vehicle. They piled the rest into Armando Un's Ford.

Un set out in search of the safe house with Patrolman Estrada in the passenger seat. They got lost. Every cranny of the inside of the car was stuffed with cocaine. Cocaine filled the back seat to the roof. Un could hardly move his elbows to drive with the sacks sandwiched between him and Estrada on the front bench-seat. Trapped in a bubble of Federal life sentence on deserted streets in the sweaty Florida night, Un panicked. He stopped the car and announced that he intended to dump the cargo in the middle of the road. Estrada kept his head. He directed Un to the house of an elderly woman acquaintance who agreed to store the sacks in her bathroom in exchange for a kilo.

Luis Rodriguez paid Ramos $350,000 and settled with the policemen in cocaine. Each man's share fetched him around $800,000. Rudy Arias was able to pay cash for a $200,000 house for his family, give $60,000 away in gifts and make a down-payment on a condominium flat for his girlfriend. His annual patrolman's salary was $22,754. And forty-five cents.

Gamblers and criminals tend to share an unwillingness to stop while ahead. The history of piracy is one of huge, sometimes unimaginable, wealth. It is also one of skeletons crusted with carbuncles and corpses dangling from gibbets. The Miami river policemen now had enough money to make them comfortable for life. Along with the accumulated proceeds of small-scale graft, most were millionaires. They still wanted more.

Only one of the group felt that the *Mitzi Ann* had been enough. Rudy Arias was happy with the new house and satisfied with one girlfriend. When Pedro Ramos announced that another shipment was due on 27 July, Arias arranged a holiday with his family at Disney World.

Ramos knew from his contacts in the Bahamas that the *Mary C*, a 40 ft fishing boat, was due to dock at the Jones Boatyard on the Miami Canal. He had not worked on the ship and had no idea where to look for the hidden compartment. He knew, however, that the crew planned to unload at midnight.

By 10 p.m. Ramos, Armando Un and twelve members of the Miami River Police were in place at the junction of NW 33rd Avenue and South River Drive. The streets around the river were deserted at that time of night. They had a clear view of the deck of the *Mary C* in the brilliantly-lit boatyard.

In Miami in midsummer, when no breeze blows off the Atlantic, the heat of the day melts into sticky airless night. By 1.30 a.m. the watchers were hot and tired and bored. There had been no movement on the deck of the *Mary C*. They were ready to give up and go home.

Down in the cabin of the fishing boat, Pedro Martinez was being cautious. He insisted on waiting while his crew of three and his two Miami-based unloaders sweated and fumed in the confined space. He wanted to minimise the risk of observation by casual passers-by. He had already lost one shipment that month. His sponsors were becoming impatient.

Pedro Martinez was not a *Marielito*. He was altogether a different class of Cuban. Before the revolution he had been right-hand man to Batista's sadistic Chief of Police, Rafael Salas Canizares. He had left immediately Castro took power. Now, at the age of forty-eight, he was a respected member of Miami's business community. He ran a company which specialised in applying a 'popcorn' finish of stippled paint to people's ceilings. This may have been in questionable taste, but was not in any way criminal. Nor was his ownership of six steel-hulled fishing boats. The use to which he put the boats was another matter.

Finally, at 1.30 a.m., Martinez went up on deck and removed the cover from the hiding-place invisibly moulded into the fibreglass superstructure of the *Mary C*. One of the crew-members jumped down onto the wharf and backed a brown Ford van up to the side of the boat. They began to load 350 kg of cocaine into the back of the brown van. The cocaine was stored in boxes held in black plastic rubbish bags. It is a strange thing about drug smuggling – that something worth so much is usually packed in the cheapest and nastiest containers.

Robert Jones, night-watchman at the Jones Boatyard, was an inoffensive thirty-two-year-old with a finely-tuned sense of self-preservation. When a dozen uniformed police officers, accompanied by two wild-eyed civilians, battered on the gates of the yard at 2 a.m. he did not ask questions. He let them through the office, closed the door after them, and went back to his television set.

As they charged from the office across the wharf towards the *Mary C*, one of the policemen yelled '*Matenlos*!'

'*Matenlos*' is a useful word to know when travelling in the Hispanic world. It means 'Kill them!'

With their hands full of cocaine sacks worth $13m and a dozen large men swarming aboard shouting murder, Pedro Martinez and his five assistants did not hesitate. They dropped the drugs and jumped overboard. The problem was that, of the six, only three could swim. While representatives of the Miami law-enforcement community took their cargo on the last leg of its journey from the mountain valleys of Bolivia, Pedro Martinez and two of the crew of the *Mary C* ended their personal journeys eight foot below the surface of the Miami Canal with their lungs full of oily black water.

By now, Luis Rodriguez had made an estimated $12m. The policemen involved in both raids were all at least double millionaires. If they had stayed quiet, there was no reason to be caught. However, Rodriguez was not built for discretion. He had boasted of his connection with a group of Miami River Police to a fourteen-year-old prostitute. Unfortunately for Luis, the girl had been equipped with a hidden microphone by associates of a Columbian known as 'The Monkey' who had provided finance for the two hijacked consignments. When The Monkey heard rumours of police involvement, Rodriguez became a prime suspect. Three days after the hijack of cocaine from the *Mary C*, Luis Rodriguez was found packed into his 3 ft by 3 ft box with four bullet holes in the back of his head.

The deaths of Martinez and Rodriguez, the one drowned and the other crated, gave the honest Miami police the first leads in their investigation of the mysterious deaths of the three Cubans in the Miami Canal. Pedro Martinez's son turned police informer to revenge his father. The discovery of

Rodriguez's body led investigators to his close contacts with the Miami River Police.

The trials that followed revealed just how deep corruption had gone. Seven of the river police were arrested and charged with a huge list of racketeering and drugs offences. Armando Un and Pedro Ramos turned State's evidence. The first trial began in September 1986 and lasted over three months. The policemen had retained the best lawyers that money could buy. One hundred and fifty witnesses passed through the box, presenting a Byzantine picture of a city gone mad. The evidence against the policemen was overwhelming. The accused, screamed on by a gallery of friends and relatives, smiled, waved and blew imaginary kisses. It was a circus. The defence concentrated on securing one vote from the jury. They sifted through a list of 275 potential jurors to find those most likely to be sympathetic. One juror spoke hardly a word of English, wrote her Christmas cards while hearing evidence, and finally stood up and walked out towards the end of the trial. Another, a seventy-five-year-old retired chef, changed his mind several times in the final deliberations, causing such confusion that eventually, on 5 January 1987, the judge was forced to declare a mistrial.

The law finally caught up with the river cops. In the six months that followed, they made six attempts to assassinate prosecution witnesses. Finally Rudy Arias was persuaded to testify for the prosecution. Four of the policemen were sentenced to long gaol terms and a fifth fled to Costa Rica. In his testimony, Arias implicated seventy members of the Miami Metro-Dade police force in corruption.

Henry Flager would have been proud of what had become of his town.

14.

Death Of A Beach Person

They called themselves the 'Beach People'. They weren't surfers or bikini-babes. They were eleven pensioners from Manhattan and New Jersey, most of them in questionable health. They ganged together at weekends and scooted around the countryside. They took their holidays together. In 1985 they got a little too ambitious. Instead of Cape Cod, they booked onto a Mediterranean cruise. By all accounts they were a nice old crowd. Of all the people who might have emerged as soldiers in the conflict for the Middle East, they were the least likely. Before they boarded the *Achille Lauro*, none of them had ever heard of Abul Abbas and the Palestine Liberation Front. Their highest ambition might have been twenty more years on this earth and a paragraph obituary in the *Secaucus Patriot*. Instead they got a week on the front page of every newspaper on earth and Leon Klinghoffer, wheelchair-bound but still game for a party, got a bullet in the head and a watery grave off the Syrian coast.

The cruise was only scheduled for twelve days. The *Achille Lauro* left its home port of Genoa on 3 October 1985 with 750 passengers and a mostly Italian crew of 331. The sea was calm and the weather was fine. The average age of the passengers may have been over sixty, but they were still set on having a good time. By day they sat in the sun, ate and swam. By night they danced cha-chas and rumbas to the resident Latin dance band.

When first built, the ship had been the last word in liner luxury: 23,629 tons, 643 ft long, 82 ft wide, with a top speed of twenty knots. She had two swimming-pools, a sauna, a gymnasium, a beauty parlour and a disco. By 1985 the facilities were all a little shabby.

The *Achille Lauro*, like most of her passengers, was living a tranquil old age after a troubled life. Her keel had been laid at Flushing in Belgium in 1939 but various circumstances, including five years of Nazi occupation, conspired to hold up completion until 1947. The ship was christened the *William Ruys* and operated peacefully for a while on cruises around the Mediterranean and Near East. In 1953 she collided with her sister ship, the *Oranje* while the two vessels were saluting each other in the Red Sea. In the early sixties the *William Ruys* mysteriously caught fire and sank in Palermo Harbour. She was rebuilt in Palermo and bought by Achille Lauro, the multi-millionaire postwar mayor of Naples who modestly renamed her after himself. In 1972 she caught fire again in Genoa. In 1975 four sailors died when she collided with a Lebanese merchant ship in the Dardanelles. The next year she was sequestered by the Italian police in Genoa after twenty-nine illegal slot-machines were found in the lounge. Finally, in 1981, two passengers were killed when she caught fire yet again off the Canary Islands. Among sailors the superstition still persists that there are 'lucky' and 'unlucky' ships. It is only a superstition.

On the morning of 7 October she arrived in Alexandria. Most of her passengers disembarked to visit the pyramids –

the ancient glories of a new civilisation stopping off to photograph the ancient glories of an old civilisation. The ship left Alexandria at 10 a.m. with the full crew and 210 passengers. She was scheduled to meet the sightseers at Port Said, at the entrance to the Suez Canal.

Most of the passengers who remained on board were either too old or too infirm to wander about in the desert. Among them were six of the 'Beach People', including Leon Klinghoffer, a sixty-nine-year-old semi-retired manager of a small appliance-manufacturing company on Manhattan Island and his fifty-eight-year-old wife Marilyn. Leon Klinghoffer had recently recovered from a stroke. The right-hand side of his body was still semi-paralysed and his speech was badly slurred. He suffered from high blood pressure and could move only with difficulty out of his wheelchair.

The cruise must have been a trial for Klinghoffer. He was a sociable man, but he hated to travel. When they first met, Marilyn lived in New Jersey. Catching the bus across the river to take Marilyn to the cinema had been enough of an ordeal even in his youth. As his daughter Lisa said, 'For him, taking out a girl from New Jersey – that was like climbing the Himalayas.' Other passengers later remembered his lopsided smiling face and the slight embarrassment of trying to hold a conversation with a man who had to make a painful effort to dig each word out of a slack mouth and strangled vocal chords.

Marilyn Klinghoffer, on the other hand, was still active. She worked full-time as personnel manager at a small publishing house. She could have visited the pyramids, but preferred to stay on board and look after her husband.

Four of the passengers who had remained on board were

not infirm at all, at least physically. The four men were travelling on Norwegian passports, but this was their only Scandinavian feature. They were clearly Arabic and, apart from the youngest of the four who possessed a halting and staccato mastery of English, they spoke only Arabic. The leader of the four was Al-Molqi Magied. At twenty-three, he was the oldest. His companions were Fataier Abdelatif Ibrahim, aged twenty, Al Assadi Ahmed Marouf, aged twenty-one, and Al Asker Bassam. Bassam was little more than a child, barely sixteen years old, but childhood is often the briefest of interludes among the Palestinian refugee camps of Southern Lebanon. In their luggage were four Kalashnikov machine-guns, eight pineapple-shaped hand-grenades and nine detonators.

The *Achille Lauro* left Alexandria at mid-morning on Monday 7 October. At 1.15 p.m. almost all the passengers were eating lunch in the main dining-room. They were waiting for their pudding. They heard the sound of shots from the corridor outside the dining-room and then a shout of 'Get down!' Two of the Arabic-speaking 'Norwegian' passengers burst into the room with Kalashnikovs in their hands. The pudding never arrived. The diners were ordered to push back their chairs and lie face-down on the carpet.

The captain of the *Achille Lauro* was a fifty-one-year-old Italian, Gerardo De Rosa, from the tiny fishing village of Casellmarare Di Stabia near Naples. He had something of the poetic Italian soul. Early American press reports gave his name as 'Tristone Benni' after he replied to a radio enquiry about his health that he felt 'sadly well'. De Rosa was up on the bridge when he heard the shots. He ran down to the passenger deck. As he approached the dining-room he was called back up to the bridge on the ship's intercom. On the bridge he was faced by the other two terrorists and the muzzles of their Kalashnikov machine-guns.

De Rosa was ordered to set course for the Syrian port of Tartus. Al-Molqi gave him a message to transmit to the world. The transmission was received at 2 p.m., by a strange quirk of the stratosphere, at a coastal transmitter station in the Swedish port of Goteberg.

The message was directed to the Government of Israel. The hijackers demanded the release of fifty Palestinians held in Israeli gaols. If their demands were not met they threatened to kill the passengers one by one, starting with the Americans.

Among those whose release was demanded were twenty members of the Special Commando Force 17 who had been captured attempting to land behind Israeli lines on beaches in southern Lebanon. Al-Molqi specifically mentioned only one Palestinian prisoner in his demands – 'The Great Man from Nahariya', Samir Al Qantari.

The late seventies and first half of the eighties had been a time of desperate dislocation in the Middle East. In June 1982 the Israelis had launched a full-scale invasion of Lebanon in order to purge once and for all the Palestinian bases on her northern border. The invasion polarised the struggle for Palestine. America failed to act decisively to restrain Israel and from then on was seen by the Palestinians as an ally of Israel. Lebanon was left in seemingly endless civil war. The bitterness of the struggle was fuelled by the Israeli massacres at the refugee camps of Sabra and Chatila in September 1982.

Following the Lebanon invasion, terrorism escalated, particularly against any target associated with the 'Great Satan' across the Atlantic. There were 860 attacks against

251

US targets between 1980 and 1984. However, most of the suffering and most of the violence was shared among the Palestinians, the Israelis and the blasted, shell-shocked population of Lebanon. By the early autumn of 1985 the killings had reached a crescendo. Two massive car-bombs in Beirut in August killed a total of 130. On 1 October, as the Klinghoffers were making their final holiday purchases in downtown Manhattan, the Israelis bombed the headquarters of the Palestine Liberation Organisation south of Tunis, killing sixty-seven, in response to the murder of three Israelis, probably Mossad agents, in Cyprus.

There was a lot of blood and a lot of grief in the Middle East during these years. For the Israelis, however, no single incident had the emotional impact of the pathetic and disastrous assault on the coastal town of Nahariya in April 1979. When the message from the hijacked liner called for the release of Samir Al Qantari, its senders were not appealing to the popular vote in Jerusalem.

In the early morning of 22 April 1979, a party of four guerrillas from the Palestine Liberation Front landed on the beach at Nahariya. They were seen by the Israeli police and in the gun-battle that followed, two of the Palestinians were shot dead. The survivors escaped through the deserted early-morning streets and took refuge in an apartment block. They smashed their way into the Haran family apartment. Semadar Haran grabbed her two-year-old daughter Yael and hid in a closet. The gunmen seized Semadar's husband Danny and their five-year-old daughter, Elnat, and dragged them out of the building onto the sea-front. For a while they considered using them as hostages for safe passage back to Lebanon. Then, in a fit of what must have been madness, Ahmed Abres, the younger of the two terrorists, shot Danny Haran, and Samir Al Qantari dashed Elnat's head against the rocks of the harbour wall.

Both the terrorists were captured alive. The cruellest twist to their story was that when Semadar emerged from hiding she found she had accidentally smothered little Yael to death to prevent the child from crying out. Both Abres and Al Qantari were sentenced to life imprisonment. Abres was released under an amnesty in the spring of 1984, but no amnesty was going to touch Al Qantari, the child-murderer of Nahariya.

While the demands were issued on the radio, the passengers were forced to descend in single file to the main saloon – the Tapestry Room. The procession took three hours. The passengers were dazed and disorientated. They made no attempt at resistance. Once they were all gathered and the stragglers rounded up from the cabins, the Palestinians ringed the room with cans of kerosene and threatened to set the saloon alight at the first sign of trouble.

The gunmen were obviously just as terrified as their captives. They were four lightly-armed men trying to keep control of 547 passengers and crew, only one of them with more than a few words of common language. Their behaviour was a strange mixture of panic, brutality and irrationality. They made clumsy attempts at conciliation. Agatha Zollinger from Switzerland was on the cruise with her two-year-old grandson. They gave the boy bullets to play with. They gave male passengers cigarettes. They acted, according to a passenger from Union City New Jersey, 'like dope-heads or schizophrenics'. They let people get in line for the toilet and then suddenly ordered them to sit down. They made the wife of an American judge and two other women picked at random stand for hours, holding together the contacts of grenades with the pins removed. They pointed to the guns and grenades in their hands. 'Be careful,' they said, 'this is my mother and this is my father.'

Once the message had been sent and the *Achille Lauro* was en route to Tartus, the Palestinians set to work to sort out the passengers. They ordered Captain De Rosa to give them the names of the agents of imperialism – the Jews, the Americans and the British. There were only two Israelis on board and they managed to escape detection. A Portuguese singer who had performed a Jewish ballad in the saloon on the Sunday night persuaded them that it was merely part of his repertoire. Finally they managed to separate nineteen – twelve Americans, including the Klinghoffers, five British – all women from the Ferreres ballet dance troupe – and two Austrian Jews. They herded the chosen ones up to the Arazzi Lounge on the promenade deck.

The ship sailed on through the night. Up on the bridge, De Rosa went half-mad, his every move shadowed by a gunman who insisted on a constant blare from the radio of Arab music at full volume.

In the world outside the ship, there was a frenzy of diplomatic activity. It was an Italian vessel and the crew and most of the passengers were Italian nationals. The Italian Cabinet met in emergency session. Their first instinct was for a diplomatic solution, but they dispatched sixty paratroopers to Akrotiri, the British military base on Cyprus, to prepare for a possible military assault. President Reagan, meanwhile, urged all countries involved to refuse negotiation. He dismissed the hijacking to the visiting Singaporean Prime

Minister, Lee Kwan Yew, as 'a most ridiculous thing'.

At first it was assumed that the Palestine Liberation Organisation was behind the hijack, but the PLO moved quickly to distance itself. Yasser Arafat condemned the attack as 'an act of sabotage against the PLO's own peace efforts'. The terrorists were part of the Palestine Liberation Front, a breakaway group in the complex labyrinth of Palestine politics, veterans of the camps of Sabra and Chatila, who had left the PLO after the Israeli invasion of Lebanon, refusing to consider any negotiation with Israel or her allies.

At 11 a.m. on Tuesday 8 October, the *Achille Lauro* arrived off the Syrian coast. The Palestinians wanted De Rosa to sail to within a mile and a half of the port of Tartus, but De Rosa persuaded them that there was a risk of grounding and the ship held off at seven miles from the port.

The terrorists expected sanctuary and help from the Syrians. Syria more than any other country had reason to hate and fear Israel after the terrible mauling of the Syrian army during the Israeli invasion of Lebanon. Instead they met with a stone wall of indifference.

De Rosa described the strange, eerie feeling as they hove to off Tartus: 'The ships that lay at anchor suddenly sailed away, obviously after receiving an order to that effect from land. In no time at all we were alone: the sea around us was completely empty.'

Al-Molqi established radio contact with land. He demanded that Syria act as intermediary in negotiations with Israel, America and Britain and that the British and American consuls should be brought on board. If their demands were not met, Al-Molqi threatened to kill fifty hostages.

For two hours they waited for the Syrian response. Early

in the morning the terrorists had moved eighteen of the nineteen 'Imperialist' hostages up onto a small round 10 metre diameter platform above the Tapestry Saloon. From there they would be clearly visible to any approaching boats or planes and their bodies would prevent any attempt at a helicopter landing. The hijackers scattered open cans of kerosene across the deck as a warning against any rash move. The group of old people stood there, unprotected from the burning midday sun. The hijackers told them that they would be killed one by one if the negotiations failed. They shuffled the passengers' passports and picked them like playing-cards to settle on the sequence of executions.

Because of his physical state, Leon Klinghoffer could not be hauled up onto the platform. He was kept alone, sat in his wheelchair, out on the open deck below.

The Syrians stalled. They refused to allow the liner to dock in Tartus. They refused to respond to demands for negotiations. Al-Molqi's confidence gave way to impatience and frustration. At 2.42 p.m. he radioed 'What about the negotiators? We will start killing at 15.00 hours.' At 2.58 he radioed: 'We cannot wait any longer. We will start killing.' He put down the handset and left the bridge. At 3.15 he returned with two passports. One of them belonged to Leon Klinghoffer; the other belonged to Mildred Hodes, a sixty-year-old tourist from West Orange, USA. He held up one finger to De Rosa. De Rosa looked down at Al-Molqi's feet. He was wearing cheap imitation American combat boots with a small red, white and blue manufacturer's tag showing the American Eagle. There were bloodstains on the left boot and the left trouser leg.

At 3.23, Al-Molqi radioed to Tartus: 'What are the

developments? We will kill the second. We are losing patience.'

There are various theories as to why the gunmen should have picked Leon Klinghoffer, out of all the passengers. De Rosa believed that they feared a chain reaction of panic if they shot a victim in front of others. Leon Klinghoffer was in some ways an obvious target. Not only American, he was also Jewish. Instead of evoking sympathy, his helplessness seemed to incense the terrorists. The four Palestinian boys had a lifetime's excuse for anger – a life lived in exile from their homeland, shifted from camp to camp, pawns in an international game they barely understood, witnesses to murder, oppression and brutality. Still, it is as hard to understand their actions as it is to sympathise with the madness of 'The Great Man from Nahariya'. Nothing could be more callously bloody futile than to put a bullet in the forehead of a wheelchair-bound sixty-nine-year-old holidaymaker from Greenwich Village.

They turned up the volume of the Arab music station on the ship's PA system, shot Klinghoffer out on the deserted deck and ordered the ship's barber and a ship's officer to dump his body, still in its wheelchair, overboard. Days later, when told the news, all his daughter Lisa could think of to say about her father, with his Jimmy Durante nose and grizzled grey hair, was that he was nice and he was ordinary. 'He was addicted to *Dynasty*,' she said. 'He thought "Joan Collins – wow!" '

After the shooting they herded the remaining seventeen down from the upper deck and told them that Klinghoffer was dead. They told Mildred Hodes that she was next. Perhaps at this stage they realised there was no point. There was no one to witness another pensionable American body thrown over the railings. Al-Molqi announced over the radio that two hostages were dead. At 4.40 p.m. he ordered Captain De Rosa to set course west, back along the North African coast, headed for Libya.

The Italian Government now threw all its energies into a search for a negotiated settlement. The attitude of the US administration was hardening. Reagan instructed Maxwell Rabb, US Ambassador in Rome, to tell the Italian Prime Minister, Bettino Craxi, that if there was no resolution to the crisis by the night of Wednesday the 9th, the Americans would initiate military action. Reagan made it clear that, if necessary, the Americans were prepared to act alone. Craxi persuaded Reagan to hold back while he negotiated with Egypt and the PLO. He argued that there had been no confirmation of any deaths and that the *Achille Lauro*, as an Italian ship, was primarily his responsibility.

At 7.20 p.m. on the evening of the 8th, the four hijackers heard the first intimation that they had friends working on their behalf. They received news that the PLO had sent Abul Abbas as delegate to Egypt to resolve the crisis. They smiled, turned up the music on the bridge and ordered De Rosa to change course for Port Said.

Abul Abbas was in a strange position in the hierarchy of the PLO. The PLO was never a completely unified organisation. In 1982, when most of the Palestine Liberation Front split from the PLO, Abbas headed a faction which remained loyal to Arafat. Abbas was perhaps the most oddly adventurous of the Palestinian leaders. He was in his mid-forties and appeared a carefree, amiable figure – six foot tall, broad-shouldered and well-padded, like an Arab Falstaff.

As a tactician he seemed to be more interested in dramatic gestures than in effective operations. He had organised the stupid doomed assault on Nahariya. In 1981 he launched an equally futile attack on Northern Israel by hang-glider. The next year he sent two gunmen across the border in a hot-air balloon. The Israelis shot down the balloon and the men were killed. In many ways it was a shrewd move by Arafat to send Abbas as his emissary to Egypt. Arafat could continue to distance himself from the affair, and if anyone could resolve the crisis, it was the man who had arranged it in the first place.

At dawn on Wednesday 9 October, the *Achille Lauro* arrived off the Egyptian coast. At 7.30 she anchored out at sea, fifteen miles from Port Said

For the whole of the Tuesday night and through the morning of Wednesday, there was intense diplomatic activity. Italy, Egypt and the PLO were looking for a face-saving solution that would safeguard the lives of the passengers and crew. Abul Abbas had grabbed the world's headlines. Now he wanted his troops safely withdrawn. President Mubarak of Egypt was in a difficult position. Egypt was distrusted enough by the rest of the Arab world after the Camp David accord with Israel. She didn't want to be seen as the pawn of America and Israel. The Abbas solution was the best compromise. Italy had her problems too. By the autumn of 1985 there were disturbing signs that the country was being drawn into the battleground of Middle Eastern politics. In September, a Lebanese-born Palestinian had thrown two hand-grenades into a crowded cafe in the Via Veneto in Rome, wounding thirty-eight. A week later another disaffected Lebanese Palestinian, opposed to Arafat, had wounded fourteen when he threw a bomb at the British Airways check-in desk in Rome airport. The last thing Craxi wanted was further bloodshed. The best thing would be for the whole problem to just melt away.

On Wednesday morning, Arafat proposed a compromise. The terrorists would give themselves up in return for an Egyptian guarantee of safe-conduct to the PLO headquarters in Tunis. There they would face trial for the hijack. By three in the afternoon the agreement had been initialled by Egypt and the Ambassadors of Italy and Germany, which had eleven citizens among the passengers. It was later claimed that the agreement was made on the understanding that there were no casualties on board. It is more likely they felt that any deaths in the past were less important than the need to avoid a massacre in the future. The governments of the United States and Britain refused to sign. They were sticking to the line of no negotiation.

At 3.30 an Egyptian tug drew up alongside the *Achille Lauro* and took off the four gunmen. As the tug lay alongside, a substantial figure in the stern waved up to the passengers crowded on the railing and apologised for the inconvenience. Abul Abbas had come along to welcome his boys.

The Italian Government hailed the end of the crisis as a diplomatic coup. They set up a direct radio link to the bridge of the liner. At twenty past four, the Foreign Minister, Giulio Andreotti, talked to Captain De Rosa. De Rosa informed him that he had regained control of the ship and that all the passengers were well. He forgot to mention Klinghoffer. This was embarrassing for Craxi. At 6.30 he was due to give a news conference to bask in the bloodless conclusion. At 6.10 he too phoned De Rosa.

This time the Captain told him that an American was dead.

There is no doubt that De Rosa was behaving oddly. He has never properly explained his reticence to talk about Klinghoffer's death. He was in a difficult position. He wanted to avoid anything that would exacerbate the crisis. The Egyptians were delaying departure of the vessel. She might still be needed as a bargaining counter. The piracy of the *Achille Lauro* was by no means over yet.

The Egyptians had a problem. Although as late as Wednesday night they announced that 'there have been no killings on board the *Achille Lauro*', they knew, from early afternoon, that this was not true. From ten past six onwards, Craxi was demanding the extradition of the hijackers. Both the Americans and the Israelis were screaming for blood. President Mubarak wanted the whole world to go away until he had a chance to shovel the four gunmen off to Tunis. The agreement to safe passage had been made under false pretences, but if the Egyptians were to breach it, no Egyptian embassy or consulate around the world would be safe from terrorist attack. God knows what the reaction would be on the streets of Cairo.

President Mubarak hid the gunmen away. They were smuggled from the harbour, along with Abul Abbas, to a PLO safe house. From there, on the night of Thursday 10 October, they were transferred, along with a group of Egyptian civil servants and ten armed guards, on board an Egyptian Airlines Boeing 737 bound for Tunis. They took off at 11 p.m.

In the United States, public opinion was sinking into one of its fits of blind xenophobia. In the Cairo Concord Hotel and the Ramases Hilton the passengers who had left the ship to visit the pyramids were reunited with the hostages. Reporters and television cameras recorded their every word. The general feeling, summed up by Thomas Smith, a passenger from Fridonia, New York State, was 'I guess we'll think long and hard before we leave the United States again.'

Back in America, the papers watched with gruesome fascination the progression of emotion in the home of the Klinghoffer family on 70 East 10th Street, Manhattan. First journalists held the glasses as the Klinghoffer daughters uncorked the champagne to celebrate their parents' freedom. Then, two hours later, they watched as the women received the news of Leon's death. America was getting angry. The pathetic image of Marilyn Klinghoffer, desolate and distracted, still dressed in her summer holiday white print cotton dress, walking down the gangplank at Port Said, seemed to epitomise a generous, good-natured nation cruelly abused by deceitful and sadistic foreigners.

US Intelligence sources logged the departure of the Boeing 737. The Americans contacted the Tunisian Government and made it clear that harbouring the terrorists would be seen as a hostile act. Behind the American pressure was the veiled threat of a repeat of the 1 October Israeli bombing raid on Tunis. The Boeing was refused permission to land. The plane turned towards Greece. Again it was turned away. It had no choice but to turn back towards Cairo.

President Reagan was in hospital for the removal of cancerous cells on his nose. He phoned Craxi from his bed and asked for permission to land a plane at the NATO base of Sigarella in Sicily.

At 12.30 a.m. on the morning of Friday 11 October, the Boeing, flying at 450 mph at an altitude of 34,000 feet, was intercepted by four US F-14 jets from the carrier *Saratoga* off the Mediterranean island of Crete. The fighters ordered the Boeing to follow them to Sicily. The plane landed and was surrounded by fifty Italian soldiers. The Italians in turn were surrounded by fifty US 'Delta Force' commandos landed from C141 transport planes under the gung-ho command of General Carl W. Stiner. Stiner had orders to arrest Abbas and the terrorists and transport them back to the United States for trial. The Italians turned to face the Americans. There was stalemate on the landing-strip.

In the United States the reaction to the interception was hysterical relief. Headlines in the tabloids screamed 'WE GOT 'EM' and 'WE BAG THE BUMS'. Reagan emerged from hospital to declare 'my nose is clean' . When asked if the F-14s had been prepared to fire on the Boeing, he replied, in classical cowboy gobbledy-gook: 'That's for them to go to bed every night wondering.' *The New York Times* reported that in the Dewdrop Inn, York, Pennsylvania, Tony Mehassie filled the jukebox with quarters and played the theme tune from *Hang 'Em High* all night long. 'For the American public,' the paper commented, 'from Manhattan subway stops to Los Angeles construction-sites, the capture of Palestinian guerrillas provoked patriotism and euphoria and unleashed a taste for retribution that has been building for years.' The basic feeling was summed up by a factory-hand interviewed on a Chicago street: 'We've had enough of letting those gooks push us around.'

There were very few contrary voices. Alex Odeh, Regional Executive of the Arab–American Anti-Discrimination Committee in Santa Ana, California, appeared on television to defend the role of the PLO in the crisis. On the afternoon of the 11th a bomb demolished the committee's offices, killing Odeh and wounding seven others. No planes were intercepted to catch Odeh's killers.

By 12 October, Marilyn Klinghoffer was back at home in Manhattan. She had stopped off in Sicily formally to identify her husband's murderers. President Reagan phoned to commiserate. 'I spat in their faces,' she said, 'and told them what I thought of them.' 'You did?' said the President, 'Oh! God bless you!'

On the tarmac in Sicily, General Carl W. Stiner had eventually been ordered to back down. President Craxi refused to allow the terrorists to be removed from Italian jurisdiction. In Cairo, President Mubarak was furious. He denounced the interception as 'an act of piracy unheard of under any international law or code'. Nevertheless, finally, at five in the morning, the Egyptians handed the four terrorists to the Italian military.

Through the long hot day the Boeing stood on the landing-strip while the governments of the United States, Italy and Egypt wrangled over the fate of Abul Abbas. The Italians demanded that he too be handed over. The Egyptians refused. They claimed that the plane was on a special Egyptian diplomatic mission and could not be boarded without consent. Abul Abbas was travelling on an Iraqi diplomatic passport and claimed he was immune from arrest.

At 8.15 p.m., the public prosecutor at Syracuse decided to pass the problem on. He gave the plane permission to leave for Rome. At 10.01 the Boeing took off. At this stage the Americans almost went too far. They despatched an F-14 and a T-39 transport with General Carl W. Stiner to repeat Thursday night's interception off Crete. However, the US planes were headed off by four Italian fighters from the military base of Gioila Del Colle near Bari. The T-39 with General Carl W. Stiner, not deterred so easily, landed twelve metres from the Boeing on the runway at Ciampino Airport. The General 'declared an emergency', whatever that might have meant. The emergency was only called off following a sharp diplomatic protest to Washington.

Ambassador Rabb was now galvanised into action. At 5.30 in the morning he arrived on the doorstep of Salvatore Zhara Buda, the Chef de Cabinet of the Italian Minister of Justice with a request for the 'provisional arrest' of Abul Abbas on the basis of a warrant issued by a judge in the District of Columbia. He would have done better to have stayed in bed. Three Italian judges declared the American grounds to be totally insufficient. At 1.30 p.m., the Boeing left for Egypt. At 7.02 p.m. Abul Abbas left on a scheduled flight aboard a Yugoslav airliner bound for Dubrovnik. Only now did the Egyptians allow the *Achille Lauro* to leave Port Said.

In July 1986, three of the terrorists were tried at the Genoa Assizes. Bassam faced a Juvenile Court. They all received life sentences. Abul Abbas was sentenced to life in his absence. The court concluded he had been responsible for the planning and execution of the attack.

In true American fashion, Marilyn Klinghoffer began court proceedings of her own – a suit claiming $1.5 billion against the owners of the *Achille Lauro*, the Italian port officials who had let four Arabic-speaking Norwegians aboard carrying Kalashnikov machine-guns, and the tour operators. It is the saddest of epitaphs for a rather nice old man from Greenwich Village.

15.

Two Gentle People

The Joint Committee on Consolidation Bills is perhaps the dullest of the many dull sub-committees of the British Houses of Parliament. Its job is to clear up the mess of outdated statutes which litter the laws of the United Kingdom. In May 1993, two Opposition peers proposed the removal of an obscure Act of Parliament from the nineteenth century which has not been used since the 1860s. They were strongly opposed by Conservative Members of Parliament on the committee. The measure that caused such concern was the Piracy Act of 1837. Under the terms of the Act, any person committing an offence of any kind, including minor wounding, during a pirate attack, is liable to the sentence of death. The Act also decrees that a convicted pirate should be escorted to the gallows in a procession led by a silver oar and his corpse displayed in a prominent public place.

The Opposition peers argued that the offence and the punishment were somewhat outdated. The Government MPs replied that it was as well to keep a little deterrent on the statute books. If the parliamentarians had listened while they dithered over a dead piece of paper, they might have heard strained laughter from the other side of the world.

On 13 December 1982, an Indonesian naval patrol-boat

intercepted the *Baltimar Zephyr*, a 3,200 ton Bahamian-registered freighter. Aboard the ship were the murdered bodies of the captain and first mate. The patrol-boat escorted the freighter into the Indonesian port of Tanjung Uban and announced that the crew were being held on suspicion of mutiny and murder at sea.

The *Baltimar Zephyr* was one of thousands of medium-size general freight ships – the journeymen of the sea. She was manned by a British captain and an eleven-man Filipino crew. She was loaded with a cargo of mining equipment from the port of Fremantle, Western Australia, bound for Calcutta via Singapore. To reach her destination she had to pass through the Straits of Singapore.

From the 1980s to the start of the 1990s, the South China Seas had once again become the most dangerous waters of the world. The most treacherous areas were the approaches to Singapore. The sea-lanes of the Phillip Channel, the Singapore Strait and the Straits of Malacca form a funnel for trade from the Far East to the Persian Gulf. In parts the straits narrow to a mile. The waters are shallow and the traffic is heavy – up to 200 ships a day, many of them huge oil tankers. Larger vessels have to reduce speed to ten knots to avoid grounding or collision. Tight schedules mean they must often travel at night. With the advances in ship-board technology, crews have been cut to a minimum. Arms are rarely carried on board. Sailors are not trained to use them and are no longer, as they were in the days of the Empire, prepared to risk their lives for the property of the company and the underwriters. Vast stretches of rail and deck are unobserved. The ships are easy targets for the modern pirates of the South China Sea.

Generally the new pirates are small-scale operators. They

use inflatable boats with outboard motors to come up on lumbering cargo vessels. They board the victim, usually at night and usually undetected, using grappling-irons or bamboo ladders. They threaten the crew with firearms and escape with the petty cash from the safe and whatever personal property they can stuff into their pockets. They have more in common with muggers and housebreakers than with the buccaneers of the Spanish Main or the corsairs of Araby.

By the early 1990s the problem was causing panic among the ship owners of the world and the governments of the Far East. Two incidents forced the authorities of the neighbouring states to take action.

In November 1991, the 1,000 ft, Panamanian-registered supertanker *Eastern Power* was boarded by pirates in the Phillip Straits. The ship was carrying 240,000 tons of crude oil. The crew of twenty-four were overcome without resistance and tied up. The pirates looted the safe and left. The crew were still bound hand and foot. The ship was still sailing at a steady fifteen knots. Phillip Straits has the highest concentration of shipping of any stretch of sea. It is riddled with reefs and shoals. The scene was set for a disaster that would, in the words of Michael Farlie, director of the Hong Kong Shipowners' Association, have made 'the Exxon Valdez disaster look like a picnic'. A spillage of oil on the scale of the *Eastern Power* cargo would, according to a US Department of Energy report, completely close the port of Singapore and the Phillip Straits, bring Singapore's economy to its knees, destroy the local fishing industry and cause untold environmental damage. The crisis was averted when, after fifteen minutes, one of the crew managed to cut himself free.

In April of the following year there was another attack on

a tanker, the Cypriot-owned *Valiant Carrier*, off Batam Island in the Phillip Straits. The ship was fully laden with oil, four miles from the Indonesian coast when she was boarded by twelve pirates armed with cutlasses and knives. The pirates distracted the crew by throwing incendiaries onto the deck. While the crew fought the fires, five pirates rushed the bridge and overpowered the officers on watch. They attacked the British third officer, stabbing him in the chest, leg and arm. They slashed the face of the Indian captain's seven-month-old son. They forced the captain to hand over $3,800 from the ship's safe and stole the crew's personal possessions. Before leaving they started fires in the engine-room and cabins.

The fires cut off the ship's electrical supply, leaving it drifting without lights, communications, engine-power and steerage. For $3,800 they left a huge floating bomb adrift in the busiest and most treacherous sea-lane in the world. The fire was eventually brought under control, but it left the shipping world badly shaken.

The three countries most closely concerned were Malaysia, Indonesia and Singapore. In the first half of 1992, international pressure began to grow for them to take effective action against the pirate menace. All the evidence pointed to Indonesia as the main source of the problem. There were even strong suggestions that some of the pirate attacks were carried out by off-duty Indonesian naval officers. Attacks were carried out with military precision using sophisticated weaponry.

Indonesia is a secretive and strange state. She is less a country than an empire – over 3,000 islands ruled from Java. President Suharto has held power since 1967, regularly re-elected every five years in a process that is only nominally democratic. Suharto does not welcome foreign interest in his country's internal affairs. Too much attention might lead to questions about the genocidal policy of Indonesianisation in the colony of East Timor as well as other less savoury aspects of Suharto's regime. When, in early 1992, there were calls from powerful shipping interests for an international force to take over the policing of the approaches to Singapore, Suharto finally took notice and ordered his navy to crack down on pirate bases.

In July 1992, Singapore and Indonesia signed a pact to coordinate naval patrols and allow pursuit of pirates into each others' waters. In a sweep of coastal villages the Indonesian Navy arrested forty-two suspected pirates. The action had an immediate effect. In the second half of 1992, pirate attacks in the Phillip Channel dwindled to a halt. And then came December 1992, and the *Baltimar Zephyr*.

On the night of 11 December, the ship was well south of the normal area of pirate operations. At 8 p.m. the Filipino Chief Officer, Teodolfo Pereja took over the watch from the British captain, John Bashforth. The quartermaster, Charlito De Vera shared the bridge duty with Pereja. Bashforth went below to eat and then returned to the bridge at 8.30 to chat with Pereja and look out onto the velvet Far Eastern night.

Bashforth was in the old tradition of British merchant seamen on the Far Eastern routes. He was forty-five years old, from Hathersage in Derbyshire, and had been at sea since the age of seventeen, rising through the merchant service to the rank of captain by his mid-thirties. His marriage had broken up and his only tie was a daughter living in Chile. He finally tore himself away from the bridge at 10.30 and retired to his cabin to sleep.

At twenty minutes to midnight, Pereja was in the chartroom and De Vera was at the port side of the bridge, gazing at the red flames from the oil rigs off the Indonesian coast. No other vessel was in sight. The ship was moving at a steady eleven knots. Visibility was seven miles. The sky was partly cloudy and the temperature twenty-nine degrees centigrade. A slight westerly breeze cooled the deck. De Vera turned. He saw Pereja with his arms raised and a figure pointing a revolver at his head.

The pirate wore sunglasses and a handkerchief, concealing most of a dark-complexioned face. He carried a rifle on a sling across his back. He pointed the revolver at De Vera and De Vera dropped face-down onto the floor of the bridge. De Vera begged the pirate not to kill them. The pirate ignored him. He demanded that Pereja open the locked door to the radio-room. Pereja claimed that the Captain held the key. The pirate shot out the starboard-side radar screen and cut the VHF radio leading to the radio-room and the wires of the telephone communicating to the engine-room. Pereja remained frozen with his arms in the air. The pirate turned his pistol back to De Vera. 'Officer . . . ? Officer?' he shouted. 'No . . . no!' screamed De Vera. It was one of those moments when promotion is a liability. The pirate turned back to Pereja and led him down the stairway towards 'C' deck and the captain's cabin.

There is fragmentary testimony as to what happened next. The only witnesses to the whole incident are dead or disappeared. The evidence of the surviving members of the crew is panicked and garbled – the evidence of ordinary unheroic men in fear of their lives.

There were three accommodation decks aboard the *Baltimar Zephyr* – 'C' deck with the captain's cabin and adjoining ship's office containing the ship's safe; 'B' deck below, with the cabins of the senior officers; and 'A' deck, the lowest, with the cabins of the ordinary seamen. All doors from the accommodation section to the deck were secure metal apart from a single wooden door on 'A' deck which could not be locked.

At six minutes to midnight, Manolito Guevarra, the Second Officer, was woken in his cabin on 'B' deck by the sound of a gunshot followed by a scream and then a second shot coming from the deck above. The shots also woke his neighbour, Chief Engineer Eduardo Munoz. He described the screaming as in 'a language that sounded like Indonesian'. The shots were followed by the sound of footsteps running down the stairway from 'C' deck to 'A' deck and the sound of a heavy object slamming against the bulkhead directly beneath Guevarra's bunk. Guevarra and Munoz locked themselves in their cabins. Munoz was later quite frank about his train of thought: 'As no alarm was rung, I thought it was a pirate attack and they were shooting to intimidate. I thought to myself: "I have to stay here, because if they are shooting for other reasons, I don't want to be in front of them." '

At midnight, Francis Igano, Acting Third Officer, was woken by the sound of footsteps running past his cabin on 'A' deck. He heard two shots in the corridor outside. He jumped from his bunk, locked the inside of his cabin door and hid behind his locker.

Manuel Agravante, the ship's cook, was woken by the shots. He peered out of his cabin door and saw a body lying at the far end of the corridor by the door to the lavatory. He was not wearing his glasses, so he could not be sure of the identity of the body, but from his clothes he assumed that it was Captain Bashforth. A figure was standing over the Captain – a shortish man, perhaps 5 ft 5 in, wearing dark overalls, his face obscured by a ski-mask. The man was holding a revolver. When he saw Agravante, he turned the pistol towards him. Agravante pulled his head back into the cabin and locked the door. He waited, shaking with terror, hiding behind the door.

Ruben Rosell was in the cabin next to Igano's. He heard a heavy object pushing against his cabin door and then the sound of struggling bodies, a heavy fall and then two shots. He waited ten minutes before he dared look out. He saw the Captain's body in a pool of blood and then heard the sound of the wooden door leading onto the deck being opened and banged shut. He locked himself into his cabin and began to pray. There was a lot of praying going on that night. Jaime Diga, the Second Engineer, heard the shots, locked his door and also consigned himself to his maker.

Up on the bridge, Charlito De Vera had heard the shots from the captain's cabin. Still he had stayed prone on the floor, his hands around his head, terrified that if he moved the pirate would return and kill him. At fifteen minutes past midnight, he inched over to the ship's intercom system and called down to Francis Igano, as next officer on duty, telling him that all was now quiet and asking for help up on the bridge.

Igano put his head outside his cabin door and saw the Captain's body. It may have been his imagination, but he swore that he saw the Captain's leg jerk spasmodically. The sight so unnerved him that he locked himself back into the safety of the cabin. He told De Vera that he would have to find another duty officer.

No one was engaging in unnecessary heroics that night. De Vera next tried the Second Officer, Manolito Guevarra. He too refused to leave his cabin.

Shortly before 1.30 a.m., Igano and Rosell could bear the wait no longer. They were terrified that they would be cornered, trapped in their cabins. The locks would be no use against a man with a gun. Talking through the bulkhead that separated their cabins they agreed to escape to a less conspicuous hiding-place. They climbed out of their portholes and took refuge in the cabin of the No.2 crane. They stayed there for an hour and a half, anxiously watching the bridge and the deck. At 2.15, Igano thought he heard a figure move on deck and so they stayed immobile until 3 a.m. when they returned to their cabins, assuming the danger was past.

At about the same time that Igano and Rosell were running for the crane, De Vera finally got some company on the lonely bridge. He set off the fire-alarm. This finally roused Munoz, the Chief Engineer, who reluctantly made his way up to take control of the vessel which had by now been sailing ahead at eleven knots for nearly two hours with no one at the wheel.

As he made his way up to the bridge, Munoz looked through the open door of the captain's office. He saw a body slumped motionless in a foetal position on the floor beside the desk, and beyond the body, in the adjoining captain's cabin, the open door of the ship's safe. He thought the body was the Captain's but was too afraid to investigate further.

Up on the bridge, De Vera was almost hysterical with relief. Munoz checked on the ship's course and tried to send a distress signal through the AM radio. His signal read 'Mayday. Attacked by pirates. Captain and Chief Officer killed.' The reception was bad. He received several replies, but was unable to make out the words.

Finally Munoz communicated by satellite with the Norwegian Rescue Service, 6,300 miles away in Stavanger. The Norwegians passed the 'Mayday' on to the Indonesian authorities and tried to obtain assistance from one of the fifteen ships at sea in the immediate area. None of them was prepared to approach the *Baltimar Zephyr* for fear that they would themselves be attacked.

The Norwegians transferred Munoz to Stig Anders Jensen, Managing Director of the Baltimar Shipping Line. The nearest port was Jakarta, but the owners had no faith in the Indonesian authorities. Jensen instructed Munoz to continue the thirty hours to Singapore and meanwhile not to touch the scene of the crime.

At 1.45, Munoz was joined on the bridge by Marlon Papio, the ship's Cadet Officer. Papio had slept through the shooting. The Indonesian investigators later expressed some incredulity at this, but to me it sounds perfectly believable. When I was Papio's age I slept through a grenade explosion in the next-door room in a Costa Rican seaside hotel. The innocence of youth.

As the night wore on to dawn, the rest of the crew emerged from hiding and reassembled their shattered nerves. They covered the bodies with white sheets. Pereja had been shot once in the forehead. From the position of his body, it seemed that he had been forced to kneel before the pirate gave the 'coup de grace'. Captain Bashforth had been shot twice – in the leg and the chest.

The owners later pieced together a picture of the deaths from the testimony of the crew, the position of the bodies, bullet-holes and discarded shells. They believed there were two pirates on board – the man with the ski-mask and the man with the handkerchief. The first pirate led Pereja down to the door of the captain's office where his companion was waiting. They woke the Captain and handed him a scrap of paper with a note written in crude block capitals. The note, found on the desk beside Pereja's body, read:

> 'I NEED YOUR ALL MONEY IF YOU DO NOT
> LIKE HURT NO SPEAK FOLLOW ORDER
> ALSO YOU TAKE CREW MONEY NO
> FOLLOW YOU DIE.'

Beside the note was found $US153 and $HK240 in cash. $US1,331 of the money in the safe was missing. It was assumed that Captain Bashforth, under threat from the pirates, had opened the safe. The pirates had not been satisfied with the pathetic pile of notes from the safe. They were not aware, or could not believe, that it was the policy of the Baltimar Line, like most shipping companies in the pirate waters of the South China Sea, to carry no large sums of cash on board. It is likely that the pirates then forced Pereja to kneel and shot him to frighten Bashforth into revealing where the real money was hidden. Bashforth was not the frightening kind. He ran for the lower deck, followed by the pirates. When he reached 'A' deck he tried to hide in the lavatory, but the lock was broken on the door. The pirates caught up, dragged him out and shot him first in the right-hand side of his chest and then in his right leg.

277

While the Captain bled to death, the pirates must have panicked. There was something unearthly about this huge ship with an invisible crew. They must have assumed that by now some alarm had been raised. They did not know there were no guns aboard. They escaped through the faulty wooden door by which they had entered. They had been gone for an hour while the crew were still locked terrified in their cabins.

The *Baltimar Zephyr* was half a day short of Singapore, six and a half miles from Bintan Island at the entrance to the Phillip Straits, at 7 a.m. on 13 December when she was intercepted by the Indonesian Naval Frigate Number 621 *Kri Manbau*. The frigate ordered the ship to proceed to the Indonesian port of Tanjung Uban, on the west side of Bintan Island.

The *Baltimar Zephyr* docked at 1.30 p.m. By 2.00, fourteen Indonesian officials had boarded the vessel – representatives of the Navy, Police, Immigration and Customs. They examined the note and the positions of the bodies. They marked the positions of the bullets and the bullet casings. They interviewed the members of the crew. It was clear from the start that they did not like the piracy story.

It was also clear that they did not welcome outside interference in the investigation. On the afternoon of the 13th, an agent arrived from Baltimar Shipping along with a legal representative from Singapore. They left after twenty-four hours. They were refused access to the ship and were woken from their hotel beds three times during the night for questioning.

On the afternoon of the 14th, a rather more determined man arrived. Captain Suresh Prabhakar was an Indian master mariner working for Jardine Ship Management in Hong Kong.

He had been appointed replacement captain for the *Baltimar Zephyr*. His job was to remove the ship and its crew from Indonesian jurisdiction. He had the inflexible discipline of a lifetime of service. The unstoppable force had met the immovable object. For five days the Indonesian Government insisted that the attack had been mutiny and not piracy. For five days, Prabhakar insisted that they had no evidence to hold his ship.

There can be little doubt that the Indonesians had decided, long before the *Baltimar Zephyr* arrived at Tanjung Uban, and long before they knew a single fact about the incident, that this was a case of mutiny. Piracy was unthinkable because piracy had ceased, by Presidential edict, to exist in Indonesian waters. They seized on what they saw as discrepancies in the crew's account and burrowed for evidence to prove their theory.

The Indonesian claims centred around three circumstantial features of the murders: the weather conditions, the missing money and the unlocked door.

They argued that in Force Two winds it would have been impossible to bring a small boat alongside the ship and to board up a curving hull. Quite apart from the practical difficulties of boarding, the attack took place too far from land for a small boat. Prabhakar countered that it had in fact been proved countless times in the Phillip and Malacca Straits that pirates could come alongside a merchant vessel moving at upwards of eleven knots and board her with grappling-irons. Pirates had often been known to operate small boats from a mother ship to avoid detection.

The Indonesians found it impossible to believe that pirates desperate enough to kill the Captain and the Chief Officer would leave part of the cash from the safe in the captain's cabin. They felt the attack had all the hallmarks of an inside job. Teodolfo Pereja had been overheard by De Vera telling the Captain that he had brought $2,000 in cash to buy a computer in Hong Kong, and boasting that he had hidden the money so cleverly that no pirate would ever find it. Pereja's $2,000 was never found. But why, if the crew had stolen it, was it not found among their effects and why, if they killed Pereja and Bashforth for Pereja's computer money, did they not also take all the cash from the safe?

The third Indonesian contention was that, on the night of 11 December, the accommodation area was securely sealed from the outside deck. On the morning of the eleventh, on the approach to pirate waters, Bashforth issued instructions to the crew. The alarm should be sounded on sighting any suspicious small craft; in the event of armed attack, they should offer no resistance; and all entrance doors to the accommodation area should be locked when there was no work on deck. At five in the afternoon on the eleventh, Rosell, on the orders of the Chief Officer secured all doors. De Vera checked that this had been done at 9 p.m. However, neither had been able to lock the wooden door leading from 'A' deck and it was through here that, from the evidence of the crew, the pirates had left. Prabhakar pointed to evidence that the pirates had searched the outside deck before finding a door that could be opened. A piece of metal stuck beneath the door leading to the main deck indicated that an attempt had been made to force an entrance.

With nothing conclusive to back up their case, the Indonesian authorities searched with mounting desperation for concrete evidence. There was no weapon and no money.

Investigator Rachman of Naval Intelligence thought that he had pinned the crime to De Vera. In De Vera's kitbag he found three ski-masks and under his mattress he found what he believed to be a length of bloodstained rope. However, the ski-masks were common wear for sailors in cold weather and the 'bloodstained rope' proved to be a grease-stained piece of string.

The investigators turned their attention from De Vera's guilt and converted him to chief witness for the prosecution. He was blindfolded and made to lie again on the floor of the bridge. The other crew-members were brought up one by one and made to shout 'Officer? Officer?', the only words De Vera remembered hearing from the pirate. He failed to pick out a suspect.

In a final throw each member of the crew was made to write 'THE QUICK BROWN FOX JUMPS OVER THE LAZY DOG' in capital letters with a black felt-tip pen to compare the writing with the note found in the captain's office.

Any proper examination of forensic evidence was ignored in this farcical homage to the methods of Hercule Poirot and Sherlock Holmes. It is hard not to conclude that the Indonesian investigators were accustomed to more direct methods of obtaining confessions than the tedious business of establishing guilt or innocence from evidence. The actual scenes of crime remained largely untouched. There was no proper examination of the bloodstains on the carpet, the fridge and the panels of the captain's cabin or the floor and lavatory on 'A' deck where Captain Bashforth died.

On the evening of 15 December, on Prabhakar's insistence, the bodies of the dead were finally removed for burial. By now, in the close tropical heat, the smell, permeating the whole accommodation area, was almost unbearable. The bodies were placed in coffins and the crew gathered round while Captain Prabhakar read two prayers before the coffins were lowered into a boat.

The days dragged on. The chief officer in charge of the investigation, Colonel Djamain, thought up test after test to break the crew's resistance. Under pressure from Prabhakar he insisted that he could do nothing towards releasing the ship without the authorisation of Rear Admiral Yussuf Effendi, his commanding officer at Medan. Effendi in turn could do nothing without orders from Admiral Arifin, Chief of the Naval Staff. He presumably was waiting instructions from Suharto. Locked on board, day and night, the crew were pursued by the lingering smell of death.

Before Prabhakar arrived, the crew had signed statements in Indonesian, a language that might as well have been Martian to Filipinos, admitting mutiny and murder. Even Colonel Djamain recognised that these statements would prove nothing without a signed translation. On 18 December, a naval officer finally presented Prabhakar with the real purpose of the investigation. He began by saying that he was convinced that the crew were guilty because the navy believed that the character of Filipinos was generally violent. The real problem, however, was not who had killed the two officers, but the wording of the original distress signal. 'For the goodness of our Government,' the officer explained, 'we do not want to disgrace the Indonesian Government by talking about pirates in the distress message. Is there some way you can change the message?' Unfortunately there was not. The message had been picked up by the radio receivers of the world.

Instead, realising that this was the only way to save Indonesian face, Prabhakar signed a letter on 18 December, saying that 'to the best of my knowledge there is insufficient proof that piracy was the cause of the Master and Chief Officer's killings ... I would like to apologise to the Indonesian Government for any inconvenience caused by any press releases.'

The letter finally secured the ship's release. At 3 p.m. on 19 December Prabhakar and Djamain exchanged farewell letters. The Captain's letter declared that 'the Navy Personnel in this base at all times behaved like perfect gentlemen' and ended 'Wishing you all a Merry Christmas!' Djamain affirmed that 'everything has done well, run well and mutual understanding' and ended 'Thank you and bond voyage.' Perhaps Colonel Djamain had written the note left in the captain's cabin.

There is as yet no postscript to the tragedy of the *Baltimar Zephyr*. For the Indonesians there never can be. No pirates will ever be arrested for the murder, in Stig Anders Jensen's words, of 'two gentle people callously slaughtered'. The blame in the eyes of Jakarta will always rest with a frightened crew far from home.

16.

Ghost Ships

On Christmas Day 1992, a breaker's yard in Shunde in the Guangdong province of Southern China bought a 17,000 ton rusted cargo vessel from a Hong Kong shipping company. The ship was called the *Hai Sin*. She was old and poorly-maintained and was good only for scrap.

When the shipwreckers inspected the hold they found a sealed and long-disused refrigerated compartment. The smell on opening the door was indescribable. Inside was a pile of charred and decomposed human bodies.

There were no personal effects among the bones. The bodies had decayed to such an extent that it was only after detailed forensic examination that the Chinese police could say that they had originally been male, probably Caucasian, probably in their twenties and thirties. Ten skulls were recovered. There were no obvious signs of violence.

In February 1994, there is still no clue as to the identity of the bodies in the hold of the *Hai Sin* or how they died. The bones are still stored in earthenware jars in the Shunde Cemetery. The discovery of the *Hai Sin* solved one mystery, but created ten more.

Hai Sin was only the last of the ship's names. From April 1991 until she ended her life in Shunde, she had been a 'phantom vessel' – a stolen ship passing through a series of different identities, making profit at each stage for a criminal syndicate.

Modern piracy has taken its most visible and dramatic form in armed robbery on the High Seas. Attacks like that on the *Baltimar Zephyr* have made newspaper headlines, but brought only tiny profits to the criminals. The most they can expect is a few thousand dollars from the ship's safe. The serious money is in stealing the ship itself. The people involved are not small-fry moonlighting village fishermen or off-duty coastguards. Where there is serious money, there are serious criminals.

'Phantom ship' fraud at sea is nothing new. As long ago as 1880, Herbert Rennie Smith bought the trading-ship *Ferret,* paying a small deposit with the remainder of the price to fall due in three months. Smith was in his early twenties, a public-school boy who had been brought up to expect a life of idle fun. In 1879, his father lost the family money on a rackety share speculation. Herbert was faced by the prospect of tedious honest work. The prospect lacked charm.

Smith secured a contract with the Highland Railway Company to collect a consignment of sleepers from Marseilles. He recruited a crew and two brainless upper-class friends as partners. Once round Gibraltar, Smith told the captain to put in at a small fishing port on the North African coast. He offered the crew double wages if they would help him disguise the *Ferret* and embark on a new career. The crew agreed. Smith reported that the ship had sunk. He changed the name to the *Benton*. In Marseilles he obtained a contract to carry a cargo of coffee from Brazil. He sailed to Santos, loaded up the beans and then changed the ship's name to the *India* and crossed to Cape Town where he sold the coffee for £11,200. By now, the original owners of the *Ferret* had become suspicious. Lloyds investigated and finally tracked the ship down in Australia living under the name of *Gladys*. Smith and his friends ended up in gaol, but they had started a trend.

There are as many types of ship crime as there are ingenious criminal minds. The 'rust-bucket' fraud dispenses with the messy business of lugging the corpse of the phantom ship around the sea-lanes of the world. In its simplest form a heavily-insured but antiquated boat is loaded with valuable cargo, the cargo is secretly off-loaded and sold before reaching the destination, the ship is scuttled, the owners of the cargo claim insurance on the lost goods and the owners of the vessel claim insurance on the lost ship.

On 17 January 1980, the British Petroleum tanker, *British Trident* came across a lifeboat containing the survivors of another tanker, the *Salem*, sunk off the coast of Senegal in West Africa. The captain of the *British Trident* noticed some strange features about the *Salem* sinking. The *Salem* was a huge ship, as long as three football pitches. Supposedly it was carrying 196,232 tonnes of crude oil, nearly as much as was aboard the *Exxon Valdez* when she polluted a huge swathe of the Alaskan coast. However, there was only a dribble of oil on the surface of the sea. The day was calm. The ship sunk several miles from shore, far from any reefs or rocks. The rescued captain, Dmitrios Georgoulis, claimed that there had been a sudden explosion caused by a build-up of oil vapour in the hold, but such spontaneous explosions happen only when the hold is unladen. Georgoulis himself had had no time to save the ship's log, the first priority after saving

287

life on board. However, he and his crew had enough time to bring their suitcases and sandwiches for the journey.

On investigation, the *Salem* case turned out to be perhaps the biggest single fraud ever perpetrated until the Byzantine financial market scams of the mid-eighties. In November 1979 a Texan had bought the eleven-year-old *Salem* through Oxford Shipping, a Liberian-registered company. The tanker was chartered by an Italian company to carry a load of oil to Genoa. On 10 December the *Salem* filled up with light crude at the Kuwaiti port of Mena Al Ahmadi. Four days out of port, the Italian buyers sold the cargo to Shell for $56 million.

This was the era of South African isolation – of oil sanctions and sanction-busting. During her journey round the foot of Africa, the *Salem* made a small deviation. The crew amended the name on the bow of the ship to the *Lema* and on 27 December put in at Durban, unloaded the oil, changed the name back again to *Salem*, continued the voyage around the Cape of Good Hope and scuttled the ship. Oxford Shipping were paid $45m by Sasol, the South African oil company. They used $12.3m to pay off the purchase price of the *Salem*, leaving them with a profit of $32.7m. Shell were partly reimbursed by Sasol and sued Lloyds for the remainder.

The *Salem* scam went wrong, of course. The Texan was sentenced to thirty-five years in prison. Captain Georgoulis was put on trial in Liberia. Luckily for him, in May 1980, Liberia fell to its first military coup in 120 years, President Tolbert was shot, and his successor, President Doe, released the Captain.

The *Salem* was a maverick. Because of the money involved and the sanction-busting label, it was big news. It was a dirty business, but no one was killed or hurt. It was in the Far East that the 'phantom ship' game became big business and turned seriously messy.

Eric Ellen runs the International Maritime Bureau from an office in the East London suburb of Barking. The IMB was set up in 1981 to monitor crime on the sea and to press for coordinated international action against the criminals. Ellen himself speaks with missionary zeal of his fight to rid the oceans of banditry. IMB representatives investigate major frauds and have infiltrated major organised-crime syndicates in the Far East. In 1991, they set up a regional office at Kuala Lumpur to log all reports of piracy in Eastern waters.

Mr Ellen claims that it is possible to stand at the window of a hotel room overlooking Manila Harbour in the Philippines and select a ship for hijacking. While the major criminal syndicates are based in Singapore, Hong Kong, China, Taiwan, Malaysia, Indonesia and Thailand, it is the Philippines that have been the scene for the worst incidents of the last decade.

As a state, the Philippines are ungovernable. The country covers over 8,000 islands. Corruption is endemic. Huge areas are controlled by guerrilla factions. With money it is possible to buy anything. A ship is a simple matter.

In many parts of the world, pirates try to limit violence as far as possible. Philippine gangs have no such compunction. In September 1981, two stowaways and two members of the crew attacked the *Nuria 767*, a 135 ton motor launch, commuting between two Philippine islands. They robbed the ship and passengers of $380,000 in cash and $126,000 worth of valuables. They then herded the passengers against the deck-rail and opened fire. Out of fifty-five on board, eleven bodies were found on the deck. The rest jumped overboard.

Twenty were later picked out of the water alive, but twenty-four were never found. In August 1984, the *Tawi-Tawi* was pirated near South West Island on a journey between Malaysia and the Philippines. There were fifteen survivors. Three teenage girls were abducted and thirty-three passengers killed.

The string of hijacks in Philippine waters can be traced back to 15 February 1980 with the disappearance of the merchant vessel *Comicon*. Neither the ship nor her crew of twenty-five were ever seen again. Lloyds believe that the crew were either killed or forced overboard in shark-infested waters.

Since then there have been numerous disappearances. Philippine sources put the figure as high as two hundred vessels a year, including small boats and fishing vessels. At least a dozen major cargo ships have been seized.

The *Isla Luzon* experience gave some clues as to the possible fate of the *Comicon*. In June 1989, she left the port of Iligon on the island of Mindanao with a 4,500 metric ton cargo of steel. Soon out of port, three armed men broke into the cabin of the captain, Diosdado Geonanga. The men had stowed away in port. They claimed to be soldiers and they handcuffed Geonanga and led him up to the bridge where they had already handcuffed the officer on duty. They slowed the ship to pick up fifteen more armed men from a waiting boat. They ordered Geonanga to head north at full power.

At midnight on the following day, the pirates lowered an inflatable life-raft designed for fifteen people into the sea, pushed on board the thirty crew-members and cast the boat adrift. They were seventy miles from land. There was warning of a typhoon. The sea was foaming white with mountainous waves.

Early the next morning, the dinghy collapsed and sank. The castaways were left with no food and no water, only life-jackets to keep them afloat, the sea still running high. Five crew members tried to swim towards land. One drowned. The rest were rescued just before nightfall by a passing fishing boat.

The *Isla Luzon*'s $2.5m cargo disappeared. The name of the ship itself was changed to the *Nigel*. A year later she was identified by chance in the South Korean port of Pusan. Her tropical-weather engine had frozen up in the bitter North Korean winter and she had been towed south for repairs. She was now registered to a company named Asia Maritime Express with a fictitious Philippine address. On board was a Burmese crew that knew nothing of the piracy.

The *Isla Luzon* hijack was subsequently traced to Emilio Changco. Changco was originally arrested in early 1989 for his part in the seizure of another freighter, the *Silver Med*, in Manila Bay in September 1988. Changco was reputed to be a seafaring genius. He had gained his master's certificate at the age of twenty-nine. He was also something of a folk-hero in his hometown of Cavite to the south of Manila. When released on bail, he went into hiding among his own people and it was from Cavite that he planned and carried out the *Isla Luzon* piracy. He was sentenced in his absence to eighteen years in prison. After being on the run for three years, he was recaptured in a dawn police raid in March 1992.

Piracy runs in the Changco family. Emilio's brother Cecilio is serving a life sentence in the same maximum-security wing of the Manila Penitentiary. He was recruited by Emilio to take part in the seizure of the tanker *Tabangoa* off the Philippines in March 1991. The *Tabangoa*'s $2m cargo was unloaded and the ship itself, with new documents in the name of the *Galilee,* was sold in Singapore.

Emilio Changco's story ends early in 1993. He was shot trying to escape from Manila Penitentiary. He had climbed over a perimeter wall and was running for the streets of the city when he was spotted by a guard. This is the version of the Philippine authorities. It may or may not be true. There were thirty-eight bullet-holes in Emilio Changco's body. He suffered from bone cancer and could walk only with the help of a cane. There are rumours that he was preparing to reveal details of high-level involvement in his ghost ship operations.

The entire 'phantom ship' business hinges on false documents. The *Silver Med* took on four different identities between its hijack in September 1988 and the end of January 1989, when she was intercepted by Philippine Customs: the *Lambaba*, the *Sea Rex*, the *Stamford* and finally the *Star Ace*. With each change of identity, she was hired out to carry a different cargo – first rubber, then steel bars, then plywood and finally palm-oil. Just like the *Ferret* back in 1880, she disappeared with each cargo and returned under another name.

In most countries of the world it is a difficult business to change the name of a person. In France, it is virtually impossible. However, in other parts of the world, changing the name of a ship the size of Wembley Stadium can take minutes.

According to the IMB, the easiest places to register a ship are the Honduran and Panamanian consulates in Singapore, Hong Kong or Bangkok. The criminal syndicates, operating through a web of intermediaries, deliver forged certificates of ownership to the consulate and receive a 'Certificate of Provisional Registry' valid for three months. Eric Ellen claims that the officials in the registry are often bribed. The going rate is as much as $50,000 per identity. The pirated ship can have as many names as the syndicate is prepared to pay for. To make tracing more difficult, all the specifications and details of the vessel are altered.

After the initial piracy, the crews recruited for phantom ships tend to have no connection to the original crime. However, they, too, often have false identities. Many are Burmese, Thai or Filipino nationals desperate for an opportunity of work abroad. They may pay up to $500 for a place on board. They travel on false passports. The master of one phantom vessel, the *Wing Tai*, had never before set foot on the sea. He was a Malaysian travelling as a Burmese.

This tangle of false trails makes it hard for the genuine owner to prove ownership of a stolen ship. Captain Mukandan of the IMB points out that the *Silver Med* is still marooned in the harbour of San Fernando, 200 miles from Manila with her final cargo of palm oil, her decks patrolled by armed guards. Five years after the ship's capture by Philippine Customs, the genuine owners are threatened with death if they attempt to come aboard their own ship.

Captain Mukandan has seen rather too much of the operation of Philippine justice. Mukandan is himself a former merchant marine master. He joined the IMB at its launch in 1981 'for a bit more excitement'. He was the investigator appointed to look into the labyrinthine case of the *Jasamas II*. The investigation proved more frustrating than exciting. He winces when he recalls the details.

On 10 May 1992 the *Jasamas II* loaded a cargo of 4,200 tons of cashew nuts in Ho Chi Minh City, Vietnam. The ship was owned by Brihop Shipping, a Singapore-based firm registered in Panama. They had a contract to deliver the nuts to the port of Tuticorin in India.

The vessel arrived at Singapore on its way west on 21 May. On 28 May, the owners of the cargo learned that the voyage had run into a little difficulty. The ship had been arrested by the Sheriff of the Singapore Supreme Court because of a dispute over ownership.

There was certainly a good deal of confusion over the ownership of the *Jasamas II*. She had started life as the *Dooyang Jade*. After disappearing in September 1988 with a $7m cargo, she had resurfaced as the *Bona Vista I*. The *Jasamas II* was at least her third phantom ship incarnation.

The next that the cargo owners heard was that, on 1 June, the vessel had sneaked out of Singapore harbour and disappeared yet again. The IMB was called in by the underwriters to track down the vessel and the nuts.

The IMB made discreet enquiries in the Far Eastern markets for any news of a large consignment of cashews. They heard that 4,200 tons were being offered for sale at considerably below the market price by a company in the port of Marivelas in the Bataan Export Processing Zone in the Philippines.

Captain Mukandan flew to the Philippines with photographs of the *Jasamas II* taken in Singapore. In the harbour at Maravelas was a ship of the same specifications called the *Gina III*. It is an easy thing to change the name of a ship, but not so easy to disguise its appearance. The cranes on deck had been repainted, but patches of the old colour still showed through. Most characteristic of all, the rust patterns on the hull precisely matched those of the ship which had slipped from Singapore harbour.

Mukandan discovered that, between 12 and 26 June, the *Gina III* had unloaded its cargo into a warehouse in the free trade zone owned by a company called the Far East General Feeds Corporation. The cargo was described in customs documentation as 'assorted feed grade beans' for animals. Enquiries among the dockers who had handled the cargo confirmed that they had unloaded cashew nuts – unusual beans for very particular livestock. The beans had supposedly been loaded in the port of Kas Kong, Kampuchea on 26 May, on which date the vessel was under arrest in Singapore. Kampuchea has never produced any cashew nuts. Closer examination of the documents supposed to prove loading in Kas Kong revealed that the official stamp used was in fact a stamp from the Inland Revenue of Thailand. Kas Kong itself is a small fishing village with no deep-water harbour.

The IMB tried to have the *Gina III* seized. The coastguard moved quickly, but word had leaked to the owners. Two hours before the coastguard cutter arrived, the ship had once again turned phantom. Nothing further was heard of her until October 1992 when Typhoon Angela struck the southern coast of Thailand. The vessel, still called the *Gina III*, was moored off the port of Songhkla. She was hit with such force by the typhoon that her anchor chain dragged and snapped the town's underwater power cable, plunging the area into darkness. The *Gina III* was swept onto the beach where she stuck solid. She is still there. No one has claimed her. The Thai authorities have tried to find her owners, but no one is keen to meet the compensation payments for destroying Songhkla's power supply.

Back in the Philippines, the IMB and the owners of the cargo began the painful process of trying to repossess the nuts. They were helped by Admiral Jardiniano, administrator of the Free Trade Zone whom Captain Mukandan calls 'a remarkable man – most remarkable because he is utterly incorruptible'. They were hindered by almost everyone else. Captain Mukandan's advice is 'Whatever has happened, whatever the cost, never take legal action in the Philippines.'

Against all the evidence, the judge in the Court of First Instance ruled in favour of the Far East General Feeds Corporation. The case was taken to the Court of Appeal. After three months it was passed down to the Bureau of Customs.

In the meantime, officials of the Free Trade Zone had raided the warehouse to take the cargo into safe-keeping. At night, they forced their way past armed guards with the assistance of local police and began to load the nuts onto carts. Suddenly the lights went out. The guards had cut the power to the warehouse. The officials were forced to withdraw. When they returned the next day, the gates of the warehouse had been padlocked shut and barricaded with a line of fork-lift trucks.

A few weeks later, a column of smoke was seen rising from the warehouse yard. Admiral Jardiniano forced his way inside and found that the guards were burning the jute bags in which the cashews had originally been packed. The bags were marked with the name of the true supplier.

After another five months, the Bureau of Customs held a ten-day hearing. They still declined to come to any decision. The Far East General Feeds Corporation had powerful friends. It seemed as though the saga would continue for ever. The cashews, like the palm oil aboard the *Silver Med*, would grow old in Philippine custody. The owners took the only option left. They came to an arrangement with the Far East General

Feeds Corporation. They bought their own cargo back. Captain Mukandan shrugs his shoulders. 'What can you do?' he says, 'we all have to live in the real world.'

The Far East criminal syndicates are not just involved in stealing cargoes. They trade in another commodity – human beings. On 27 January 1993, US coastguards boarded the *East Wood*, a 310 ft Panamanian-registered 'rust-bucket' in mid-Pacific, 1,500 miles south-west of Hawaii. In the hold were 524 Chinese men, women and children. The stench was unbelievable. They had been locked in the hold for fifty-nine days with no sanitation and a single daily delivery of food and water.

The Chinese were taken to the nearby Marshall Islands and from there shipped back to China on the leaky assurance that they would not be punished. Over a hundred are still in custody. Their crime was to try and emigrate to the USA.

It is estimated that over a hundred thousand Chinese enter the United States illegally each year. Most are smuggled by one of the mainland Chinese or Hong Kong criminal syndicates. The usual price for passage is between $10,000 and $15,000 per person. Very few people in China can afford this sort of money. Usually they put down a deposit of $1,000 and pay the remainder in instalments from their wages once they have arrived in the USA.

This system requires an efficient organisation not only in the Far East, but also in the United States. Chinese Triads are notoriously secretive and impenetrable. News of their activities rarely filters outside the Chinese community. However, New York police believe that two illegal Chinese immigrants found tortured and murdered in New York City on 1 January 1993 were killed because they had failed to keep up payments to the syndicate which had smuggled them into the country.

It is believed that the *Hai Sin*, the ship found with the ten decayed bodies in the shipwreckers yard in Southern China, had been used in the traffic of refugees

The *Hai Sin* was originally called the *Erria Inge*. She was bought in April 1990 by an Australian, Eric Boas. Boas had spent his career in the shipping industry and was looking for an interest for his retirement. The ship was to turn from a hobby into an expensive obsession.

The ship was chartered to a Singapore company which in turn contracted her to a Hong Kong management company. In February 1991, she was seized by the authorities in Bombay for failure to pay wages and charges of $3.5m. Aboard was a cargo of chicken-feed worth $20m. However, just as had happened to the *Jasamas II*, the *Erria Inge* escaped from port.

For seven months, the *Erria Inge* loitered in international waters off Singapore, frustrating Boas's attempts to detain her. Then, in October 1991, Boas heard that a ship answering her description called the *Palu III*, registered in Honduras, was off-loading in Thailand at the deep-water anchorage of Ko Si Chang, two hours south of Bangkok.

Boas travelled to Bangkok and arranged for the vessel to be raided by the Thai police. Aboard they found a new crew who knew nothing about the original flight from Bombay. Boas was assured that, when formalities were completed, the vessel would be returned to his hands. He returned to Australia. Immediately he had left, the *Palu III* shipped anchor and again disappeared. Mr Boas believes that the Thai authorities were bribed to let her escape.

There are rumours that for the next eleven months a Chinese syndicate used the vessel as a floating holding-tank for refugees awaiting transfer to the United States. However, nothing definite is known of her movements until she arrived at Shunde at the mouth of the Pearl River.

Since March 1993, the Chinese authorities have come no nearer to unravelling the mystery of the ten bodies in the hold of the *Hai Sin*. The burning of the bodies was almost certainly caused after death in a clumsy attempt at cremation. With no obvious signs of violence, it is impossible to tell how they met their end. Almost certainly they were the victims of some crime or disaster in the missing eleven months of the ship's life. If the bodies were those of oriental men, it would be easy to deduce they were refugees who had died of disease, hunger or the appalling treatment common to the human traffic of the Far East. However, with all the evidence pointing to Caucasians, the mystery remains impenetrable.

Whatever the train of circumstance that led ten Europeans to end up dead in the hold of a Far Eastern ghost ship in a breaker's yard on the Chinese coast, piracy is as much alive at the end of the twentieth century as in the age of the buccaneers. Piracy has a mystique. To those not directly affected, a mist of romance hangs around events in the closed world of a boat hundreds of miles from a police station. But there is nothing special about a crime purely because it takes place on the sea. There is no natural reason why criminals should stop at the water's edge. Where there is money, there will always be villains. Sometimes money floats.

Bibliography

1. BOOKS

ALLEN, DAVID, ed., *The Cocaine Crisis* (New York 1987)

ARMSTRONG, WARREN, *Last Voyage* (London 1936)

CASSESSE, ANTONIO, *Terrorism, Politics And The Law – The Achille Lauro Affair* (London 1989)

CONNAUGHTAN, R. M., *The War Of The Rising Sun* (London 1988)

CONWAY, BARBARA, *The Piracy Business* (London 1981)

COURSE, CAPTAIN A.G., *Pirates Of The Eastern Seas* (London 1966)

DAVIDSON-HOUSTON, J.V., *The Piracy Of The Nanchang* (London 1961)

DUPONT, PASCAL, *Pirates D'Aujourd Hui* (Paris 1985)

EDDY, PAUL, with SABOGAL, HUGO, and WALDEN, SARA, *The Cocaine Wars* (New York 1988)

ELLEN, ERIC, ed., *Piracy At Sea* (London 1989)

GALLAGHER, THOMAS, *Fire At Sea* (London 1959)

GALVAO, H., *Santa Maria – My Crusade For Portugal* (London 1961)

GOLLOMB, J., *Pirates Old And New* (London 1931)

GRANT, BRUCE, *The Boat People* (London 1979)

HAWTHORNE, LESLEYANNE, ed., *The Vietnamese Experience* (London 1980)

HOUGH, RICHARD, *The Fleet That Had To Die* (London 1988)

HSU, NANCY, *Anguish Of The Innocent* (London 1979)

JOHNSON, CLIFFORD, *Pirate Junk* (London 1934)

JOYNER, NANCY D., *Aerial Hijacking As An International Crime* (New York 1974)

KING, MICHAEL, *Death Of The Rainbow Warrior* (London 1986)

KLINGHOFFER, ARTHUR JAY, *The Salem – Fraud Of The Century* (London 1988)

LILIUS, ALEKO E., *I Sailed With Chinese Pirates* (London 1930)

LOCKHART, J.G., *True Tales Of The Sea* (London 1939)

MACDOUGALL, PHILIP, *Mysteries Of The High Seas* (London 1984)

MILLER, H., *Pirates Of The Far East* (London 1970)

MITCHELL, DAVID, *Pirates* (London 1976)

NEWARK, PETER, *The Crimson Book Of Pirates* (London 1978)

PARRITT, BRIG. BRIAN A.H., ed., *Violence At Sea* (London 1986)

POCATERRA, J.F., *Gomez – The Shame Of America* (Paris 1929)

RABY, D.L., *Fascism And Resistance In Portugal* (Manchester 1988)

RITCHIE, R.C., *Pirates: Myths And Realities* (London 1986)

ROGERS, STANLEY, *Modern Pirates* (London 1939)

RONZITTI, N., *The Achille Lauro And International Law* (London 1990)

ROURKE, THOMAS, *Tyrant Of The Andes* (New York 1937)

SEMENOFF, VALDIMIR, *Rasplata*, (London 1909)

SNOW, EDWARD ROWE, *Women Of The Sea* (London 1963)

SNOW, EDWARD ROWE, *Unsolved Mysteries Of Sea And Shore* (London 1964)

SUNDAY TIMES INSIGHT TEAM, *Rainbow Warrior* (London 1986)

THOMAS, GORDON and MORGAN-WITTS, MAX, *The Strange Fate Of The Morro Castle* (London 1973)

URDANETA, EDMUNDO, *La Revolucion Delgado-Chalbaud* (Caracas 1936)

VILLAR, CAPTAIN ROGER, *Piracy Today* (London 1985)

2. NEWSPAPERS AND PERIODICALS

I have used *Lloyd's List*, *The Times* and the *New York Times* extensively. For the 'Columbian Sea-Food' chapter I consulted reports in the *Miami Herald*. I should mention the following specific articles and reports.

FINER, ALEX, 'Yachtjack!', *Sunday Times Magazine* (27.11.77)

HALL, MALCOLM MACALISTER, 'Pirates, Back In Blood', *Sunday Telegraph Magazine* (24.4.93)

HARRIS, MARGARET and RUSSELL, MATTHEW, 'Skulls And Crossbones', *Sunday Morning Post Magazine* (7.11.93)

INTERNATIONAL MARITIME BUREAU, *Report On Organized Crime In The Far East* (January 1991)

INTERNATIONAL MARITIME BUREAU, *Special Report On Piracy* (June 1992)

INTERNATIONAL MARITIME ORGANIZATION, *Report On The IMO Working Group On The Malacca Strait Area* (1993)

WILKES, PETER, 'Sabotage And Arson', *Nautical Magazine* Vol. 212 (1974)

US DEPARTMENT OF ENERGY, *Piracy: The Threat To Tanker Traffic* (September 1992)

US HOUSE OF REPRESENTATIVES COMMITTEE OF MERCHANT MARINE AND FISHERIES, *Report Of Sub Committee On Coast Guard And Navigation* (August 1974 and November 1977)

VINES, STEVE, 'Troubled Waters', *GQ Magazine* (May 1993)

PUBLIC RECORDS OFFICE, *Depositions In The Trial Of Rau, Smith And Monson* (1903)

Special thanks to Eric Ellen, Captain Mukandan and Captain Abhioankar of the International Maritime Bureau for their time, patience and valuable help on modern piracy in the Far East; to Mrs V. Thomson and Peter Thomson for their loan of papers on the 'Tai On' piracy; to Mr G. Richards for his advice on inter-war piracy in the East; to Karin Sjolin of the International Maritime Organisation; to Peter Godwin and Robert James for their help with Emilio Changco; to Patricia O'Driscoll; to the staff at the National Maritime Museum, Greenwich; to the staff at the Public Records Office, Chancery Lane; to the staff at the British Museum Library; and to the staff of the National Newspaper Library at Colindale.

Index

305

More Fascinating True Crime from Headline

—— JAD ADAMS ——

DOUBLE INDEMNITY

MURDER FOR INSURANCE

Extraordinary true stories of murderers who insured their victims then killed them – or attempted to.

Includes:

- **The solicitor who killed his wife and faked the scene of the crime to make her look like a drug dealer.**
- **The horse dealer who had her former lover tied in a burning car and pushed over a cliff.**
- **The shopkeeper who killed his own son for the insurance.**
- **The doctor who poisoned his mother-in-law, then his wife.**
- **The school teacher who killed a colleague and her two children.**
- **The restaurateur who insured his mother and put a bomb in her luggage.**
- **The insurance company investigator who tried three times to kill his wife.**

NON-FICTION/TRUE CRIME   0 7472 4360 3

A selection of non-fiction from Headline

THE DRACULA SYNDROME	Richard Monaco & William Burt	£5.99	☐
DEADLY JEALOUSY	Martin Fido	£5.99	☐
WHITE COLLAR KILLERS	Frank Jones	£4.99	☐
THE MURDER YEARBOOK 1994	Brian Lane	£5.99	☐
THE PLAYFAIR CRICKET ANNUAL	Bill Frindall	£3.99	☐
ROD STEWART	Stafford Hildred & Tim Ewbank	£5.99	☐
THE JACK THE RIPPER A–Z	Paul Begg, Martin Fido & Keith Skinner	£7.99	☐
THE *DAILY EXPRESS* HOW TO WIN ON THE HORSES	Danny Hall	£4.99	☐
COUPLE SEXUAL AWARENESS	Barry & Emily McCarthy	£5.99	☐
GRAPEVINE: THE COMPLETE WINEBUYERS HANDBOOK	Anthony Rose & Tim Atkins	£5.99	☐
ROBERT LOUIS STEVENSON: DREAMS OF EXILE	Ian Bell	£7.99	☐

All Headline books are available at your local bookshop or newsagent, or can be ordered direct from the publisher. Just tick the titles you want and fill in the form below. Prices and availability subject to change without notice.

Headline Book Publishing, Cash Sales Department, Bookpoint, 39 Milton Park, Abingdon, OXON, OX14 4TD, UK. If you have a credit card you may order by telephone – 0235 400400.

Please enclose a cheque or postal order made payable to Bookpoint Ltd to the value of the cover price and allow the following for postage and packing:
UK & BFPO: £1.00 for the first book, 50p for the second book and 30p for each additional book ordered up to a maximum charge of £3.00.
OVERSEAS & EIRE: £2.00 for the first book, £1.00 for the second book and 50p for each additional book.

Name ....

Address ....

....

....

If you would prefer to pay by credit card, please complete:
Please debit my Visa/Access/Diner's Card/American Express (delete as applicable) card no:

Signature .... Expiry Date ....